Quick & Healthy

This is a Parragon Publishing Book
This edition published in 2004

Parragon Publishing
Queen Street House
4 Queen Street
Bath BA1 1HE, UK

ISBN: 1-40544-386-3

Printed in China

Produced by the Bridgewater Book Company Ltd.

NOTE

This book uses imperial, metric, and US cup measurements. Follow the same
units of measurement throughout; do not mix imperial and metric.
All spoon measurements are level: teaspoons are assumed to be 5 ml,
and tablespoons are assumed to be 15 ml. Unless otherwise stated,
milk is assumed to be whole, eggs and individual vegetables such as potatoes
are medium, and pepper is freshly ground black pepper.

The times given for each recipe are an approximate guide only
because cooking times may vary as a result of the types of oven and
other equipment used.

Recipes using raw or very lightly cooked eggs should be
avoided by infants, the elderly, pregnant women, convalescents, and anyone
suffering from an illness. Pregnant and breastfeeding women are advised to
avoid eating peanuts and peanut products.

Quick & Healthy

p

Contents-Low Carb

Introduction   8

Soups & Appetizers   12

Snacks & Side Dishes   68

Meat & Poultry   102

Fish & Seafood   152

Vegetables   188

Desserts   218

Index   506

Contents-Quick & Easy

Introduction	260
Basic Recipes	262
Soups	264
Appetizers & Snacks	306
Fish & Seafood	344
Meat	384
Chicken & Poultry	408
Pasta & Rice	432
Desserts	490
Index	506

Low Carb

Introduction

What constitutes a healthy diet? In one way, the answer to this question is very straightforward, while in another, it is almost impossible. It is true that a balanced intake of all the various food groups—fats, proteins, and carbohydrates—in their appropriate proportions is the ideal that

nutritionists encourage us to aim for. However, this raises a number of questions: where we are starting from, how old we are, what kind of lives we lead, whether we are men or women, and even how to estimate "a balanced intake" and "appropriate proportions"? For various reasons, many of us have let the extra weight creep on and developed eating patterns that, at best, do our bodies no favors and, at worst, make us sluggish, fat, unhappy, and ill. A low-carbohydrate diet is one very successful way of tackling these sorts of problems, revitalizing and re-energizing the system and trimming off the spare tire around the tummy.

What are carbohydrates?

The name of this food group derives from the chemical elements it contains—carbon, hydrogen, and oxygen—which form compounds such as starch and sugars. When these are eaten, the body breaks them down to release energy. They are found in a wide variety of commonly eaten foods. Grains and cereals, for example, feature in most meals, from the morning's cornflakes, through the lunchtime sandwich, to the evening plate of pasta. Potatoes are a starchy staple and dried peas, beans, and lentils are also high in carbohydrates. Many popular snacks—chocolate bars, cookies, muffins, doughnuts, and soda—are packed with sugars. Carbohydrates are comfort foods, making us feel full and satisfied.

There is a second type of carbohydrate that our bodies cannot digest and this is usually called dietary fiber. This contributes to the feeling of fullness after a meal and helps to regulate the digestive system, but the body cannot break it down to release energy. This kind of carbohydrate is found in wheat bran, fruits, dried peas, beans and lentils, nuts, and leafy green vegetables.

Energy and body weight

The body needs energy to function and it obtains this from the food consumed. Even the process of digestion uses up energy. However, the amount of energy you require depends on a number of factors. It is obvious that an Olympic athlete requires more input than a sedentary office worker, but age is also a consideration because the metabolism begins to slow down from about the age of 30. Body type, including the amount of muscle mass and lean tissue, also affects energy requirements.

Energy is measured as calories, also called kilocalories (kcal), and as kilojoules (kJ). 1 kcal equals about 4 kJ. Many of the calories consumed are used quite quickly for everyday activities, from breathing to walking up the stairs. The energy that is not used is converted by the body to be stored in the muscles or as fat. It is easy to see that if you consume more calories than you use, the body will build up a store of fat.

The following is a guide to the approximate daily calorie intake required by men and women at different life stages.

daily calorie intake

Growing children
Boys and girls—1,800–2,220 calories per day

Adults who exercise/have physical jobs
Men—2,850 calories per day
Women—2,150 calories per day

Adults who do not exercise/have sedentary jobs
Men—2,400 calories per day
Women—2,000 calories per day

Over 50s
Men—2,200 calories per day
Women—1,850 calories per day

How a low-carbohydrate diet can help

Carbohydrates are the main source of energy in our diets, with fats the second most important, so if you want to lose weight, reducing the intake of carbohydrates is a good way to do it. However, cutting them out altogether is neither sensible nor practical, because you will also be cutting out important nutrients. It is also unwise to embark on a drastic reduction of carbohydrates all at once. If you introduce this new eating pattern gradually, you will not encounter the mood swings or hunger pangs that so often go with attempts to diet and usually result in failure.

While it is true that taking in more energy than is expended is the reason why fat accumulates in the body, individual metabolism also plays a part. Some people are simply more intolerant of carbohydrates than others and can almost see their hips growing with every slice of bread. Pay attention to your body and respond to its particular requirements.

Previously, the most difficult aspect of a low-carbohydrate diet was deciding what to eat, not what to leave out. This is because much of the variety and contrast in our "normal" meals is derived from incorporating carbohydrates. Who wants a burger without a bun, steak without French fries, or meatballs without spaghetti? The problem is now solved because this book provides a wealth of recipes for delicious, low-carbohydrate dishes that are easy to make and will also satisfy the appetite. All the thinking, planning, and calorie-counting has been done for you. The recipes, based on meat, poultry, eggs, cheese, and vegetables, offer both variety and enjoyment.

For many people, a low-carbohydrate diet is a lifetime choice, used to maintain their optimum body weight. Others find it a quick way to shed a few pounds before a summer holiday or after an over-indulgent Christmas. The choice is, of course, personal, but do bear in mind that if you return to higher-carbohydrate meals, you are likely to regain the weight.

Choosing low-carbohydrate ingredients

Labels providing nutritional information on packaged foods are not always as clear and helpful as they might be. However, carbohydrate content is normally included and covers both starches and sugars. Dietary fiber, or nondigestible carbohydrates, is usually listed separately. Not all products include a measure of fiber, either because there isn't any or because figures are not available. If you take a calculator shopping with you, you may find it helpful to know that 1 gram of carbohydrate supplies about 3.75 calories or 16 kilojoules of energy.

There is no reason why you shouldn't substitute one ingredient for another in any of the recipes in this book, provided that it does not increase the carbohydrate count. While Brie contains only traces of carbohydrate, some blue cheeses may have 2 grams per 100 grams—a small difference, but it will increase the carbohydrate count. Cauliflower contains almost twice as much carbohydrate as broccoli. Also, bear in mind that some most unexpected foods, including accompaniments and drinks, contain carbohydrates. These will contribute to the overall count. It's no good cooking a low-carbohydrate curry and serving it with a high-carbohydrate chutney. At the same time, there is no point in being obsessive. A strong mustard may contain about 19 grams of carbohydrate per ⅓ cup, but when did you last eat more than about ½ teaspoon at one sitting?

Nowadays, there are some specially manufactured low-carbohydrate products on the market, but they are often quite expensive and their labels require very close scrutiny. Jellies and spreads produced without added sugar will contain some natural fruit sugars but are generally a good buy. Low-carbohydrate baked goods may be lifesavers for the incorrigibly sweet-toothed, but they do vary in quality, while sugarfree candy and chocolates, originally produced for diabetes sufferers, have a good reputation. Other products may boast of a low-carbohydrate count per portion, but you need to check what the manufacturers regard as a portion—sometimes it's risibly small.

11

Soups & Appetizers

Soups are an invaluable part of a healthy low-carbohydrate eating plan, with their comforting and satisfying qualities. They also offer a wide  variety of flavors and textures, as the following recipes show. Choose from a smooth vegetable soup, such as Cream of Artichoke Soup, or a classic Bouillabaisse with chunks of delicious seafood. For something to really tickle the taste buds, try the Mexican inspired Chicken, Avocado & Chipotle Soup.

Tasty and nutritious vegetables also feature highly in the range of appetizers on offer—cool, clean-tasting cucumbers in Tzatziki, succulent mushrooms in a Soufflé Omelet, and sweetly smoky eggplants in the elegant Eggplant Rolls. Or you can major on serious high-protein savories, such as Bang-Bang Chicken.

cream of artichoke soup

serves six

1 lb 10 oz/750 g Jerusalem
   artichokes

1 lemon, thickly sliced

4 tbsp butter or margarine

2 onions, chopped

1 garlic clove, crushed

generous 1 quart vegetable stock

salt and pepper

2 bay leaves

¼ tsp ground mace or
   ground nutmeg

1 tbsp lemon juice

⅔ cup light cream or plain yogurt

TO GARNISH

coarsely grated carrot

chopped fresh parsley or cilantro

NUTRITION

Calories 190	Sugars 0g
Protein 0.4g	Fat 2g
Carbohydrate 0.7g	Saturates 0.7g

1 Peel and slice the artichokes. Place in a bowl of water with the lemon slices.

2 Melt the butter in a large pan. Add the onions and garlic and cook gently for 3–4 minutes, or until soft but not colored.

3 Drain the artichokes, discarding the lemon, and add to the pan. Mix well and cook gently for 2–3 minutes without allowing to color.

4 Add the stock, salt and pepper, bay leaves, mace, and lemon juice. Bring slowly to a boil, then reduce the heat and simmer, covered, for 30 minutes, or until the vegetables are very tender.

5 Remove and discard the bay leaves. Let the soup cool slightly, then press through a strainer into a bowl. Alternatively, process the soup in a food processor or blender until smooth. If liked, a little of the soup may be only partially puréed and added to the rest of the puréed soup, to give extra texture.

6 Pour into a clean pan and bring to a boil. Adjust the seasoning if necessary and stir in the cream. Reheat gently without boiling.

7 Ladle the soup into individual serving bowls and garnish with grated carrot and chopped parsley. Serve immediately.

gazpacho

serves four

½ small cucumber

½ small green bell pepper, seeded
   and very finely chopped

1 lb 2 oz/500 g ripe tomatoes,
   peeled, or 14 oz/400 g canned
   chopped tomatoes

½ onion, coarsely chopped

2–3 garlic cloves, crushed

3 tbsp olive oil

2 tbsp white wine vinegar

1–2 tbsp lemon or lime juice

2 tbsp tomato paste

2 cups tomato juice

salt and pepper

TO SERVE

chopped green bell pepper

thinly sliced onion rings

croutons

NUTRITION

Calories 140	Sugars 12g
Protein 3g	Fat 9g
Carbohydrate 13g	Saturates 1g

1 Coarsely grate the cucumber into a large bowl and add the chopped bell pepper.

2 Place the tomatoes, onion, and garlic in a food processor or blender. Add the oil, vinegar, lemon juice, and tomato paste and process until smooth. Alternatively, finely chop the tomatoes and finely grate the onion, then mix together. Add the garlic, oil, vinegar, lemon juice, and tomato paste and mix well.

3 Add the tomato mixture to the bowl and mix well, then add the tomato juice and mix again.

4 Season to taste with salt and pepper. Cover and let chill in the refrigerator for 6 hours, or preferably longer, to let the flavors meld together.

5 Prepare the side dishes of chopped bell pepper, thinly sliced onion rings, and croutons and arrange them in serving bowls. Ladle the soup into cold bowls, handing round the side dishes separately.

chicken consommé

1½ quarts chicken stock

⅔ cup medium sherry

4 egg whites, plus eggshells

salt and pepper

4 oz/115 g cooked chicken,
    thinly sliced

COOK'S TIP

Consommé is usually garnished with freshly cooked pasta shapes, noodles, rice, or lightly cooked vegetables. For a low-carbohydrate option, you could garnish it with omelet strips, drained first on paper towels.

NUTRITION	
Calories 96	Sugars 1g
Protein 11g	Fat 1g
Carbohydrate 1g	Saturates 0.4g

1 Place the stock and sherry in a large heavy-bottom pan and heat gently for 5 minutes.

2 Add the egg whites and the eggshells to the stock and whisk until the mixture begins to boil.

3 Remove the pan from the heat and let the mixture subside for 10 minutes. Repeat this heating and subsiding process 3 times. This enables the egg white to trap the sediments in the stock to clarify the soup. Let the consommé cool for 5 minutes.

4 Carefully place a piece of fine cheesecloth over a clean pan. Ladle the soup over the cheesecloth and strain into the pan.

5 Repeat this process twice, then gently reheat the consommé.

Season to taste with salt and pepper, then add the cooked chicken slices. Pour the soup into a warmed serving dish or individual serving bowls.

6 Garnish with any of the suggestions in the Cook's Tip and serve.

crab & ginger soup

serves four

1 carrot, chopped

1 leek, chopped

1 bay leaf

3½ cups fish stock

2 medium-size cooked crabs

1-inch/2.5-cm piece fresh
    gingerroot, grated

1 tsp light soy sauce

½ tsp ground star anise

salt and pepper

NUTRITION

Calories 145	Sugars 2.4g
Protein 40g	Fat 5.7g
Carbohydrate 2.7g	Saturates 2.6g

1 Place the carrot, leek, bay leaf, and stock in a large pan and bring to a boil over medium heat. Reduce the heat, then cover and let simmer for 10 minutes, or until the vegetables are nearly tender.

2 Meanwhile, remove the meat from the cooked crabs. Break off the claws and break the joints, then remove the meat (you may need a fork or skewer for this). Add the crabmeat to the stock in the pan.

3 Add the ginger, soy sauce, and star anise to the stock and bring to a boil. Reduce the heat and let simmer for 10 minutes, or until the vegetables are tender and the crab is heated through. Season to taste with salt and pepper.

4 Ladle the soup into 4 warmed serving bowls and garnish with crab claws. Serve immediately.

COOK'S TIP

To prepare cooked crab, loosen the meat from the shell by banging the back of the underside with a clenched fist. Stand the crab on its edge with the shell toward you. Force the shell from the body with your thumbs. Twist off the legs and claws and remove the meat. Twist off the tail and discard. Remove and discard the gills from each side of the body. Cut the body in half along the center and remove the meat. Scoop the brown meat from the shell.

COOK'S TIP

If fresh crabmeat is unavailable, use drained canned crabmeat or thawed frozen crabmeat instead.

fish soup with won tons

serves four

4½ oz/125 g cooked,
    shelled shrimp

1 tsp snipped fresh chives, plus
    extra to garnish

1 small garlic clove, finely chopped

1 tbsp vegetable oil

12 won ton skins

1 small egg, beaten

3½ cups fish stock

6 oz/175 g white fish fillet, diced

dash of chili sauce

1 fresh red chili, sliced, to garnish

NUTRITION

Calories 115	Sugars 0g	
Protein 16g	Fat 5g	
Carbohydrate 1g	Saturates 1g	

VARIATION

You can replace the shrimp with
cooked crabmeat for an
alternative flavor.

1 Coarsely chop a fourth of the shrimp and mix together with the chives and garlic.

2 Heat the oil in a preheated wok or large heavy-bottom skillet until it is really hot.

3 Stir-fry the shrimp mixture for 1–2 minutes. Remove from the heat and let cool completely.

4 Spread out the won ton skins on a counter. Spoon a little of the shrimp filling into the center of each skin. Brush the edges of the skins with beaten egg and press the edges together, scrunching them to form a "moneybag" shape. Reserve while you are preparing the soup.

5 Pour the stock into a large pan and bring to a boil. Add the fish and the remaining shrimp and cook for 5 minutes.

6 Add chili sauce to taste, then add the won tons and cook for an additional 5 minutes.

7 Spoon into warmed bowls and garnish with the sliced chili and extra snipped chives, then serve.

hot & sour soup

serves four

12 oz/350 g whole raw or cooked
   shrimp in shells
1 tbsp vegetable oil
1 lemongrass stem,
   coarsely chopped
2 fresh kaffir lime leaves, shredded
1 fresh green chili, seeded
   and chopped
1 quart chicken or fish stock
1 lime
1 tbsp Thai fish sauce
salt and pepper
1 fresh red Thai chili, seeded and
   thinly sliced
1 scallion, thinly sliced
1 tbsp finely chopped cilantro,
   to garnish

NUTRITION

Calories 71	Sugars 0g
Protein 8g	Fat 4g
Carbohydrate 1g	Saturates 0g

1 Shell the shrimp and reserve the shells. Cut a slit along the back of each shrimp and remove the black vein. Place in a bowl, cover, and chill.

2 Heat the oil in a large heavy-bottom pan. Add the shrimp shells and stir-fry for 3–4 minutes, or until they turn pink. Add the lemongrass, lime leaves, green chili, and stock. Pare a thin strip of rind from the lime and grate the rest. Add the grated rind to the pan.

3 Bring to a boil, then reduce the heat, and let simmer, covered, for 20 minutes.

4 Strain the liquid and pour it back into the pan. Squeeze the juice from the lime and add to the pan with the fish sauce and salt and pepper to taste.

5 Bring to a boil, then reduce the heat and add the shrimp. Simmer for 2–3 minutes.

6 Add the red chili and scallion. Sprinkle with the chopped cilantro and lime rind strip and serve.

spinach & tofu soup

serves four

8 oz/225 g firm tofu
  (drained weight)
4½ oz/125 g fresh spinach leaves
3 cups water or
  vegetable stock
1 tbsp light soy sauce
salt and pepper

COOK'S TIP

Soup is an integral part of a Chinese meal; it is usually presented in a large bowl placed in the center of the table, and consumed as the meal progresses. It serves as a refresher between different dishes and as a beverage throughout the meal.

NUTRITION

Calories 33	Sugar 1g
Protein 4g	Fat 2g
Carbohydrate 1g	Saturates 0.2g

1 Using a sharp knife to avoid squashing it, cut the tofu into small cubes about ¼ inch/5 mm thick.

2 Rinse the spinach leaves thoroughly under cold running water and drain well.

3 Cut the spinach leaves into small pieces or shreds, discarding any discolored leaves and tough stems. (If possible, use fresh young spinach leaves, which have not yet developed tough ribs. Otherwise, it is important to cut out all the ribs and stems for this soup.) Reserve the spinach until required.

4 Bring the water to a rolling boil in a preheated wok or large heavy-bottom skillet.

5 Add the tofu and soy sauce, then return to a boil and simmer for 2 minutes over medium heat.

6 Add the spinach and simmer for an additional 1 minute, stirring gently. Skim the surface of the soup to make it clear and season to taste with salt and pepper.

7 Transfer the soup to a warmed soup tureen or warmed individual serving bowls and serve with chopsticks and a broad, shallow spoon.

chicken soup with almonds

serves four

1 large or 2 small skinless, boneless
   chicken breasts

1 tbsp corn oil

4 scallions, thinly sliced
   diagonally

1 carrot, cut into julienne strips

3 cups chicken stock

finely grated rind of ½ lemon

½ cup ground almonds

1 tbsp light soy sauce

1 tbsp lemon juice

salt and pepper

¼ cup slivered almonds,
   toasted

NUTRITION

Calories 219	Sugars 2g
Protein 18g	Fat 15g
Carbohydrate 2g	Saturates 2g

1 Cut each chicken breast into 4 strips lengthwise, then slice very thinly across the grain to give shreds of meat.

2 Heat the oil in a preheated wok, swirling it around until really hot.

3 Add the scallions and cook for 2 minutes, then add the chicken and toss it for 3–4 minutes, or until sealed and almost cooked through, stirring constantly. Add the carrot strips and stir well.

4 Add the stock to the wok and bring to a boil. Add the lemon rind, ground almonds, soy sauce, lemon juice, and plenty of salt and pepper. Return to a boil and let simmer, uncovered, for 5 minutes, stirring occasionally.

5 Adjust the seasoning if necessary, then add most of the toasted almonds and continue to cook for an additional 1–2 minutes.

6 Serve the soup hot, in individual serving bowls, sprinkled with the remaining toasted almonds.

COOK'S TIP

To toast slivered almonds, place them in a dry skillet over medium heat and stir until lightly browned. Keep a close eye on them because they burn very easily.

chicken, avocado & chipotle soup

serves four

1¼ quarts chicken stock

2–3 garlic cloves, finely chopped

1–2 dried chipotle chilies, cut into
   very thin strips (see Cook's Tip)

1 avocado

lime or lemon juice, for tossing

3–5 scallions, thinly sliced

12–14 oz/350–400 g cooked
   chicken breast meat, torn or cut
   into shreds or thin strips

2 tbsp chopped cilantro

1 lime, cut into wedges,
   to serve

NUTRITION

Calories 216	Sugars 1g
Protein 28g	Fat 11g
Carbohydrate 2g	Saturates 2g

VARIATION

Add 14 oz/400 g canned, drained
chickpeas to the bowls with the
scallions, chicken, avocado,
and cilantro.

1 Place the stock in a large heavy-
bottom pan with the garlic and
chilies and bring to a boil.

2 Meanwhile, cut the avocado in
half around the pit. Twist apart,
then remove the pit with a knife.
Carefully peel off the skin and dice the
flesh, then toss in lime juice to prevent
discoloration.

3 Arrange the scallions, chicken,
avocado, and cilantro in the
bottom of 4 soup bowls or in a large
serving bowl.

4 Ladle hot stock over and serve
with lime wedges.

COOK'S TIP

Chipotle chilies are smoked and
dried jalapeño chilies. They are
available canned or dried from
specialty stores. They add a
distinctive smoky flavor to dishes
and are very hot. Use chipotles
canned in adobo marinade for
this recipe, if possible. Drain the
canned version before using.
Dried chipotles need to be
reconstituted before using by
soaking in hot water until soft.

chili & watercress soup

serves four

1 tbsp corn oil

9 oz/250 g smoked tofu (drained weight), sliced

3 oz/85 g shiitake mushrooms, sliced

2 tbsp chopped cilantro

4½ oz/125 g watercress

1 fresh red chili, seeded and finely sliced, to garnish

STOCK

1 tbsp tamarind pulp

2 dried red chilies, chopped

2 fresh kaffir lime leaves, torn in half

1-inch/2.5-cm piece fresh gingerroot, chopped

2-inch/5-cm piece fresh galangal, chopped

1 lemongrass stem, chopped

1 onion, cut into fourths

4 cups cold water

NUTRITION	
Calories 90	Sugars 1g
Protein 7g	Fat 6g
Carbohydrate 2g	Saturates 1g

1 Place all the ingredients for the stock in a pan and bring to a boil.

2 Simmer the stock for 5 minutes. Remove the pan from the heat and strain, reserving the stock.

3 Heat the oil in a preheated wok or large heavy-bottomed skillet. Add the tofu and cook over high heat for 2 minutes, stirring constantly so that the tofu cooks evenly on both sides. Add the strained stock to the skillet.

4 Add the mushrooms and cilantro and boil for 3 minutes.

5 Add the watercress and boil for an additional 1 minute. Serve, garnished with red chili slices.

VARIATION

You might like to try a mixture of different types of mushroom. Oyster, white, and straw mushrooms are all suitable.

spinach & ginger soup

serves four

2 tbsp corn oil

1 onion, chopped

2 garlic cloves, finely chopped

1-inch piece/2.5-cm piece fresh
  gingerroot, finely chopped

9 oz/250 g fresh young
  spinach leaves

1 small lemongrass stem,
  finely chopped

4 cups chicken or
  vegetable stock

1 small potato, chopped

1 tbsp rice wine or dry sherry

salt and pepper

1 tsp sesame oil

NUTRITION

Calories 38	Sugars 0.8g
Protein 3.2g	Fat 1.8g
Carbohydrate 2.4g	Saturates 0.2g

1 Heat the corn oil in a large pan. Add the onion, garlic, and ginger and stir-fry gently for 3–4 minutes, or until softened but not browned.

2 Reserve 2–3 small spinach leaves. Add the remaining leaves and lemongrass to the pan, stirring until the spinach is wilted. Add the stock and potato to the pan and bring to a boil. Reduce the heat, then cover and simmer for 10 minutes.

3 Transfer the soup to a food processor or blender and process until completely smooth.

4 Return the soup to the pan and add the rice wine, then season to taste with salt and pepper. Heat until just about to boil.

VARIATION

To make a creamy-textured spinach and coconut soup, stir in 4 tablespoons creamed coconut, or replace 1¼ cups of the stock with coconut milk. Serve the soup with fresh coconut shavings sprinkled on the top.

5 Finely shred the reserved spinach leaves and sprinkle some over the top. Drizzle with a few drops of sesame oil and serve hot, garnished with the remaining finely shredded spinach leaves.

bouillabaisse

serves six–eight

1 lb/450 g raw jumbo shrimp

1 lb 10 oz/750 g firm white fish
   fillets, such as sea bass, snapper,
   or angler fish

4 tbsp olive oil

grated rind of 1 orange

1 large garlic clove, finely chopped

½ tsp chili paste or harissa

1 fennel bulb, finely chopped

1 large onion, finely chopped

8 oz/225 g potatoes, halved and
   thinly sliced

9 oz/250 g raw scallops, shelled

salt and pepper

STOCK

1 large leek, sliced

1 onion, halved and sliced

1 red bell pepper, seeded and sliced

3–4 tomatoes, cored and cut
   into 8 wedges

4 garlic cloves, sliced

1 bay leaf

pinch of saffron threads

½ tsp fennel seeds

2½ cups water

1 quart fish stock

1 Shell the shrimp and reserve the shells. Cut the fish fillets into pieces about 2 inches/5 cm square. Trim off any ragged edges and reserve. Place the fish in a bowl with 2 tablespoons of the oil, the orange rind, chopped garlic, and chili paste. Turn to coat well, then cover and chill the shrimp and fish separately in the refrigerator.

2 For the stock, heat 1 tablespoon of the remaining oil in a large pan over medium heat. Add the leek, sliced onion, and bell pepper. Cover and cook for 5 minutes, stirring, until the onion softens. Stir in the tomatoes, sliced garlic, bay leaf, saffron, fennel seeds, shrimp shells, fish trimmings, water, and stock. Bring to a boil, then reduce the heat and simmer, covered, for 30 minutes. Strain the stock.

3 Heat the remaining oil in a separate large pan. Add the fennel and chopped onion and cook for 5 minutes, or until softened. Add the stock and potatoes and bring to a boil. Reduce the heat and cover, then cook for 12–15 minutes, or until tender.

4 Reduce the heat and add the fish, thick pieces first and thinner ones after 2–3 minutes. Add the shrimp and scallops and let simmer until all the seafood is cooked and opaque throughout.

5 Taste and adjust the seasoning if necessary. Ladle into warmed bowls and serve.

NUTRITION	
Calories 273	Sugars 4g
Protein 36g	Fat 9g
Carbohydrate 13g	Saturates 2g

celery root, leek & potato soup

serves four–six

- 1 tbsp butter
- 1 onion, chopped
- 2 large leeks, halved lengthwise and sliced
- 1 celery root (about 1 lb 10 oz/ 750 g), peeled and diced
- 1 potato, diced
- 1 carrot, cut into fourths and thinly sliced
- 1 quart water
- ⅛ tsp dried marjoram
- 1 bay leaf
- salt and pepper
- freshly grated nutmeg
- celery leaves, to garnish

NUTRITION

Calories 81		Sugars 5g	
Protein 3g		Fat 3g	
Carbohydrate 11g		Saturates 2g	

1. Melt the butter in a large pan over medium heat. Add the onion and leeks and cook for 4 minutes, stirring frequently, until just softened but not colored.

2. Add the celery root, potato, carrot, water, marjoram, bay leaf, and a large pinch of salt. Bring to a boil, then reduce the heat and let simmer, covered, for 25 minutes, or until the vegetables are tender. Remove and discard the bay leaf.

3. Let the soup cool slightly. Transfer to a food processor or blender and process until smooth. (If using a food processor, strain off the cooking liquid and reserve. Process the soup solids, moistened with a little cooking liquid, then combine with the remaining liquid.)

4. Return the soup to a clean pan and stir to blend. Season to taste with salt, pepper, and nutmeg. Stir constantly until reheated.

5. Ladle the soup into warmed soup bowls and garnish with celery leaves, then serve.

leek, potato & bacon soup

serves four–six

2 tbsp butter

1 cup diced potatoes

4 leeks, shredded

2 garlic cloves, crushed

¼ cup diced smoked bacon

3½ cups vegetable stock

1 cup heavy cream

2 tbsp chopped fresh parsley

salt and pepper

TO GARNISH

vegetable oil

1 leek, shredded

NUTRITION	
Calories 316	Sugars 3g
Protein 11g	Fat 27g
Carbohydrate 9g	Saturates 15g

1 Melt the butter in a large pan. Add the potatoes, leeks, garlic, and bacon and cook gently for 5 minutes, stirring constantly.

2 Add the stock and bring to a boil. Reduce the heat, then cover and let simmer for 20 minutes, or until the potatoes are cooked. Stir in the cream and mix well.

3 Meanwhile, make the garnish. Half fill a pan with oil and heat to 350–375°F/180–190°C, or until a cube of bread browns in 30 seconds. Add the shredded leek and deep-fry for 1 minute, or until browned and crisp, taking care because it contains water. Drain the shredded leek thoroughly on paper towels and reserve.

4 Reserve a few pieces of potato, leek, and bacon. Transfer the rest of the soup, in batches, to a food processor or blender and process each batch for 30 seconds. Return the soup to a clean pan and heat through.

5 Stir in the reserved vegetables, bacon, and chopped parsley, then season to taste with salt and pepper. Pour into warmed soup bowls and garnish with the fried leeks.

VARIATION

For a lighter soup, omit the cream and stir plain yogurt into the soup at the end of the cooking time.

exotic mushroom soup

serves four

1 oz/25 g dried porcini mushrooms

1½ cups boiling water

4½ oz/125 g fresh porcini or other
exotic mushrooms

2 tsp olive oil

1 celery stalk, chopped

1 carrot, chopped

1 onion, chopped

3 garlic cloves, crushed

1 quart vegetable stock
or water

leaves from 2 fresh thyme sprigs

salt and pepper

1 tbsp butter

3 tbsp dry or medium sherry

2–3 tbsp sour cream

chopped fresh parsley, to garnish

NUTRITION

Calories 130	Sugars 5g
Protein 3g	Fat 9g
Carbohydrate 6g	Saturates 5g

1 Place the dried mushrooms in a heatproof bowl and pour the boiling water over them. Let soak for 10–15 minutes.

2 Brush or wipe the fresh mushrooms. Trim and reserve the stems. Slice any large mushroom caps.

3 Heat the oil in a large pan. Add the celery, carrot, onion, and mushroom stems and cook, stirring frequently, for 8 minutes, or until the onion begins to color. Stir in the garlic and cook for an additional 1 minute.

4 Add the stock, thyme leaves, and a pinch of salt. Using a slotted spoon, transfer the soaked dried mushrooms to the pan. Strain the soaking liquid through a cheesecloth-lined strainer into the pan. Bring to a boil, then reduce the heat and simmer gently, partially covered, for 30–40 minutes, or until the carrots are tender.

5 Remove the pan from the heat and let cool slightly, then transfer the soup solids with enough of the cooking liquid to moisten to a food processor or blender and process until smooth. Return the soup to the pan and combine with the remaining cooking liquid, then cover and simmer gently.

6 Meanwhile, melt the butter in a skillet. Add the fresh mushroom caps and season to taste with salt and pepper. Cook, stirring occasionally, for 8 minutes, or until the mushrooms begin to color, stirring more frequently as the liquid evaporates. When the skillet becomes dry, add the sherry and cook briefly.

7 Add the mushrooms and sherry to the soup. Taste and adjust the seasoning, if necessary. Ladle into warmed soup bowls, place a spoonful of sour cream in each, and garnish with parsley. Serve immediately.

chicken & corn soup

serves four

2 tsp corn oil

1 tbsp butter or margarine

1 small onion, finely chopped

1 chicken leg quarter or
    2–3 drumsticks

1 tbsp all-purpose flour

2½ cups chicken stock

½ small red, yellow, or orange bell
    pepper, seeded and
    finely chopped

2 large tomatoes, peeled
    and chopped

2 tsp tomato paste

scant 1¼ cups corn kernels, drained

generous pinch of dried oregano

¼ tsp ground coriander

salt and pepper

chopped fresh parsley, to garnish

NUTRITION

Calories 200	Sugars 6g
Protein 10g	Fat 12g
Carbohydrate 13g	Saturates 5g

1 Heat the oil and butter in a pan. Add the onion and cook until beginning to soften. Cut the chicken quarter, if using, into 2 pieces. Add the chicken and cook until golden brown.

2 Add the flour and cook for 1–2 minutes. Add the stock and bring to a boil, then reduce the heat and simmer for 5 minutes.

3 Add the bell pepper, tomatoes, tomato paste, corn, oregano, coriander, and salt and pepper to taste. Cover and let simmer gently for 20 minutes, or until the chicken is very tender.

4 Remove the chicken from the soup, then strip off the flesh and chop finely. Return the chopped meat to the soup.

5 Taste and adjust the seasoning if necessary and simmer for an additional 2–3 minutes. Sprinkle with parsley and serve very hot.

provençal fish soup

serves four–six

1 tbsp olive oil

2 onions, finely chopped

1 small leek, thinly sliced

1 small carrot, finely chopped

1 celery stalk, finely chopped

1 small fennel bulb, finely
   chopped (optional)

3 garlic cloves, finely chopped

1 cup dry white wine

14 oz/400 g canned tomatoes

1 bay leaf

pinch of fennel seeds

2 strips of orange rind

¼ tsp saffron threads

1 quart water

12 oz/350 g white fish
   fillets, skinned

salt and pepper

celery leaves, to garnish (optional)

NUTRITION

Calories 122	Sugars 6g
Protein 12g	Fat 3g
Carbohydrate 7g	Saturates 0g

1 Heat the oil in a large pan. Add the onions and cook, stirring occasionally, for 5 minutes, or until softened. Add the leek, carrot, celery, fennel, if using, and garlic and cook for an additional 4–5 minutes, or until the leek is wilted.

2 Add the wine and simmer for 1 minute. Add the tomatoes, bay leaf, fennel seeds, orange rind, saffron, and water. Bring just to a boil. Reduce the heat and simmer gently, covered, stirring occasionally, for 30 minutes.

3 Add the fish and cook for an additional 20–30 minutes, or until it flakes easily. Remove and discard the bay leaf and orange rind.

4 Remove the pan from the heat and let cool slightly, then transfer to a food processor or blender and process to a smooth purée, working in batches if necessary. (If using a food processor, strain the cooking liquid and reserve. Process the soup solids with enough cooking liquid to moisten them, then combine with the remaining liquid.)

5 Return the soup to the pan. Season to taste with salt and pepper, if necessary, then simmer for 5–10 minutes, or until heated through. Ladle into warmed bowls and garnish with celery leaves, if desired. Serve.

beef broth

serves four

7 oz/200 g celery root, finely diced

2 large carrots, finely diced

2 tsp chopped fresh marjoram

2 tsp chopped fresh parsley

2 plum tomatoes, peeled, seeded,
  and diced

salt and pepper

BEEF STOCK

1 lb 4 oz/550 g beef stewing steak,
  cut into large cubes

1 lb 10 oz/750 g veal, beef, or
  pork bones

2 onions, cut into fourths

2¼ quarts water

4 garlic cloves, sliced

2 carrots, sliced

1 large leek, sliced

1 celery stalk, cut into 2-inch/
  5-cm pieces

1 bay leaf

4–5 fresh thyme sprigs or
  ¼ tsp dried thyme

salt

NUTRITION

Calories 21	Sugars 3g
Protein 1g	Fat 1g
Carbohydrate 4g	Saturates 0g

1 Preheat the oven to 375°F/190°C. To make the stock, trim the fat from the beef and place the beef and fat in a large roasting pan with the bones and onions. Roast in the oven for 30–40 minutes, or until browned, turning once or twice. Transfer to a large flameproof casserole and drain off the beef fat.

2 Add the water (it should cover by at least 2 inches/5 cm) and bring to a boil. Skim off any foam, then reduce the heat and add the garlic, carrots, leek, celery, bay leaf, thyme, and a pinch of salt. Simmer for 4 hours, skimming occasionally. If the ingredients emerge from the liquid, top up with water. Strain the stock through a cheesecloth-lined strainer into a container and remove as much fat as possible. Use the meat in another recipe and discard the bones and vegetables.

3 Gently boil the stock until reduced to 1¼ quarts. Taste and adjust the seasoning if necessary.

4 Bring a pan of salted water to the boil. Add the celery root and carrots, then reduce the heat and simmer, covered, for 15 minutes, or until tender. Drain. Add the herbs to the beef stock. Divide the vegetables and tomatoes between warmed soup bowls and ladle over the stock. Serve.

aïoli

serves four

4 large garlic cloves, or to taste
  (see Cook's Tip)
sea salt and pepper
2 large egg yolks
1¼ cups extra virgin olive oil
1–2 tbsp lemon juice
1 tbsp fresh white bread crumbs
TO SERVE
selection of raw vegetables, such as
  sliced red bell peppers, zucchini
  slices, whole scallions, and
  tomato wedges
selection of blanched and cooled
  vegetables, such as baby
  artichoke hearts, cauliflower or
  broccoli florets, or green beans

NUTRITION

Calories 239	Sugars 0g
Protein 1g	Fat 26g
Carbohydrate 1g	Saturates 4g

1 Finely chop the garlic on a cutting board. Add a pinch of sea salt to the garlic and use the tip and broad side of a knife to work the garlic and salt into a smooth paste.

2 Transfer the garlic paste to a food processor or blender. Add the egg yolks and process until well blended, scraping down the side of the bowl with a rubber spatula, if necessary.

3 With the motor running, slowly pour in the oil in a steady stream through the feeder tube, processing until a thick mayonnaise forms.

4 Add 1 tablespoon of the lemon juice and all the bread crumbs and process again. Taste and add more lemon juice if necessary. Season to taste with sea salt and pepper.

COOK'S TIP

The amount of garlic in a traditional Provençal aïoli is a matter of personal taste. Local cooks use 2 cloves per person as a rule of thumb, but this version is slightly milder, although still bursting with flavor.

5 Place the aïoli in a bowl, then cover, and let chill until ready to serve. To serve, place the bowl of aïoli on a large platter and surround with a selection of raw and lightly blanched vegetables.

tzatziki

serves twelve

2 large cucumbers

2½ cups thick plain yogurt

3 garlic cloves, crushed

1 tbsp finely chopped fresh dill

1 tbsp extra virgin olive oil

salt and pepper

TO GARNISH

1 tbsp sesame seeds

cayenne pepper

fresh dill sprigs (optional)

NUTRITION

Calories 75	Sugars 2g
Protein 4g	Fat 6g
Carbohydrate 2g	Saturates 3g

1 Using the coarse side of a grater, grate the cucumbers into a bowl lined with an absorbent, perforated kitchen cloth. Pull up the corners of the cloth to make a tight bundle and squeeze very hard to extract all the moisture (see Cook's Tip).

1

2 Place the cucumber in a bowl and stir in the yogurt, garlic, dill, and oil. Season to taste with salt and pepper. Cover with plastic wrap and let chill for at least 3 hours so that the flavors blend.

2

3 When ready to serve, remove the dip from the refrigerator and stir. Taste and adjust the seasoning if necessary.

4 Place the sesame seeds in a small, ungreased skillet and dry-fry them over medium heat until they turn golden and begin to give off their aroma. Immediately pour them out of the skillet onto the tzatziki—they will sizzle.

4

5 Sprinkle some cayenne onto a plate. Lightly dip the tip of a dry pastry brush into the cayenne, then tap a light sprinkling of cayenne over the tzatziki. Garnish with dill sprigs, if using. Ungarnished tzatziki will keep for up to 3 days in the refrigerator.

COOK'S TIP

It is essential to squeeze all the moisture out of the cucumbers in Step 1, or the dip will be unpleasantly watery and will separate.

authentic guacamole

serves four

1 ripe tomato

2 limes

2–3 ripe small–medium avocados
or 1–2 large ones

¼–½ onion, finely chopped

pinch of ground cumin

pinch of mild chili powder

½–1 fresh green chili, such as
jalapeño or serrano, seeded and
finely chopped

1 tbsp finely chopped cilantro
leaves, plus extra to garnish

salt (optional)

vegetable sticks, to serve
(optional)

NUTRITION

Calories 212	Sugars 1g
Protein 2g	Fat 21g
Carbohydrate 3g	Saturates 4g

1 Place the tomato in a heatproof bowl, then cover with boiling water and let stand for 30 seconds. Drain and plunge into cold water. Peel off the skin. Cut the tomato in half, then seed and chop the flesh.

2 Squeeze the juice from the limes into a small bowl. Cut 1 avocado in half around the pit. Twist the 2 halves apart in opposite directions, then remove the pit with a knife. Peel off the skin, then dice the flesh and toss in the lime juice to prevent the flesh discoloring. Repeat with the remaining avocados. Mash the avocado flesh coarsely with a fork.

3 Add the onion, tomato, cumin, chili powder, fresh chili, and cilantro to the avocados. If using as a dip for tortilla chips, do not add salt. If using as a dip for vegetable sticks, add salt to taste.

4 To serve the guacamole, transfer to a serving dish and garnish with cilantro, then serve with vegetable sticks.

VARIATION

Try spooning guacamole into soups, especially chicken or seafood. Spoon guacamole over refried beans and melted cheese, then eat it with a salsa of your choice.

hummus

serves eight

1 cup dried chickpeas

2 large garlic cloves

scant ½ cup extra virgin olive oil,
    plus extra for drizzling

2½ tbsp tahini

1 tbsp lemon juice

salt and pepper

paprika

cilantro sprigs, to garnish

vegetable crudités, to serve

NUTRITION

Calories 204		Sugars 1g
Protein 7g		Fat 14g
Carbohydrate 13g		Saturates 2g

1 Place the chickpeas in a bowl. Pour in at least twice their volume of water and soak for 12 hours, or until they double in size.

2 Drain the chickpeas. Place them in a large flameproof casserole or pan and add twice their volume of water. Bring to a boil and boil vigorously for 10 minutes, skimming the surface.

3 Reduce the heat and let simmer, skimming the surface occasionally, for 1–2 hours, or until the chickpeas are tender.

4 Meanwhile, cut the garlic in half, then remove and discard the green or white cores and coarsely chop the cloves. Reserve.

5 Drain the chickpeas, reserving 4 tablespoons of the cooking liquid. Place the oil, garlic, tahini, and lemon juice in a food processor and process to a smooth paste.

6 Add the chickpeas and pulse until they are finely ground but the hummus is still lightly textured. Add a little of the reserved cooking liquid if the mixture is too thick. Season to taste with salt and pepper.

7 Scrape the hummus into a bowl, then cover and chill in the refrigerator until ready to serve. Drizzle with some oil and sprinkle a little paprika over. Garnish with cilantro and serve with vegetable crudités.

parsley, chicken & ham pâté

serves four

8 oz/225 g skinless, boneless lean
    chicken, cooked

3½ oz/100 g lean cooked ham

small bunch of fresh parsley

1 tsp grated lime rind, plus extra
    to garnish

2 tbsp lime juice

1 garlic clove, peeled

½ cup lowfat cream cheese

salt and pepper

TO SERVE

lime wedges

crispbread

NUTRITION

Calories 119	Sugars 2g
Protein 20g	Fat 3g
Carbohydrate 2g	Saturates 1g

1 Coarsely dice the chicken. Trim off and discard any fat from the ham and dice the meat. Place the chicken and ham in a food processor.

2 Add the parsley, lime rind and juice, and garlic and process until finely ground. Alternatively, finely chop the chicken, ham, parsley, and garlic and place in a bowl. Gently stir in the lime rind and juice.

COOK'S TIP

Most types of crispbreads contain around ⅛ oz/6 g of carbohydrate per slice.

3 Transfer the mixture to a bowl and stir in the cream cheese. Season to taste with salt and pepper, then cover with plastic wrap and chill in the refrigerator for 30 minutes.

4 Spoon the pâté into individual serving dishes and garnish with extra grated lime rind. Serve the pâté with lime wedges and crispbread.

fat horses

serves four

2 tbsp creamed coconut

4 oz/115 g lean pork

4 oz/115 g skinless, boneless
  chicken breast

4 oz/115 g canned crabmeat,
  drained

2 eggs

2 garlic cloves, crushed

4 scallions, chopped

1 tbsp Thai fish sauce

1 tbsp chopped cilantro leaves
  and stems

1 tbsp raw brown sugar

salt and pepper

butter, for greasing

TO GARNISH

finely sliced daikon or turnip

fresh chive lengths

fresh chili flowers (see page 158)

cilantro sprigs

NUTRITION

Calories 195	Sugars 1g
Protein 23g	Fat 11g
Carbohydrate 1g	Saturates 6g

1 Mix the coconut with 3 tablespoons of hot water. Stir to dissolve the coconut.

2 Place the pork, chicken, and crabmeat in a food processor and process briefly for 10–15 seconds, or until ground. Alternatively, chop them finely by hand and place in a large bowl.

3 Add the coconut mixture to the food processor with the eggs, garlic, scallions, fish sauce, cilantro, and sugar. Season to taste with salt and pepper and process for an additional few seconds. Alternatively, mix these ingredients into the chopped pork, chicken, and crabmeat.

4 Grease 6 ramekin dishes with a little butter. Spoon in the ground mixture, smoothing the surface. Place them in a steamer, then set the steamer over a pan of gently simmering water. Cook for 30 minutes, or until set.

5 Lift out the dishes and let cool for a few minutes. Run a knife around the edge of each dish, then invert onto warmed plates. Serve immediately, garnished with finely sliced daikon, chive lengths, a red chili flower, and cilantro sprigs.

eggplant dip

serves six–eight

2 large eggplants

1 tomato

1 garlic clove, chopped

4 tbsp extra virgin olive oil

2 tbsp lemon juice

2 tbsp pine nuts, lightly toasted

salt and pepper

2 scallions, finely chopped

fresh vegetables, to serve

TO GARNISH

ground cumin

2 tbsp finely chopped fresh
   flatleaf parsley

NUTRITION

Calories 90	Sugars 2g
Protein 1g	Fat 8g
Carbohydrate 2g	Saturates 1g

1 Preheat the oven to 450°F/230°C. Using a fork or metal skewer, pierce the eggplants all over. Place them on a large cookie sheet and roast in the preheated oven for 20–25 minutes, or until they are very soft.

2 Use a folded dish towel to remove the eggplants from the cookie sheet and let cool.

3 Place the tomato in a heatproof bowl and pour boiling water over to cover. Let stand for 30 seconds. Drain, then plunge into cold water to prevent it cooking. Peel the tomato, then cut in half and scoop out the seeds with a teaspoon. Finely dice the flesh and reserve.

4 Cut the cooled eggplants in half lengthwise. Scoop out the flesh with a spoon and transfer to a food processor. Add the garlic, oil, lemon juice, and pine nuts and season to taste with salt and pepper. Process until smooth. Alternatively, mash by hand.

5 Scrape the mixture into a bowl and stir in the scallions and diced tomato. Cover and let chill for 30 minutes before serving.

6 Garnish the spread with a pinch of cumin and chopped parsley, then serve with fresh vegetables.

eggplant rolls

serves four

2 eggplants, thinly sliced
  lengthwise
salt and pepper
5 tbsp olive oil, plus extra
  for oiling
1 garlic clove, crushed
4 tbsp pesto
6 oz/175 g mozzarella cheese,
  grated
fresh basil leaves, torn into pieces,
  plus extra leaves to garnish

NUTRITION

Calories 278	Sugars 2g
Protein 4g	Fat 28g
Carbohydrate 2g	Saturates 7g

COOK'S TIP

Most eggplants produced
commercially these days do
not have bitter juices that must
be removed before cooking.
Nevertheless, salting is a good
idea if the eggplants are to be
fried, because it prevents them
absorbing too much oil.

1 Preheat the oven to 350°F/180°C. Sprinkle the eggplant slices liberally with salt and let stand for 10–15 minutes. Turn the slices over and repeat. Rinse well with cold water and drain on paper towels.

2 Heat the oil in a large skillet. Add the garlic and eggplant slices, a few at a time, and fry the eggplant lightly on both sides. Remove with a slotted spoon and drain on paper towels.

3 Spread a little pesto onto one side of each of the eggplant slices. Top with the grated mozzarella cheese and sprinkle with the torn basil leaves. Season with a little salt and pepper. Roll up the slices and secure them with wooden toothpicks.

4 Arrange the eggplant rolls in an oiled ovenproof baking dish and bake in the preheated oven for 8–10 minutes.

5 Transfer the eggplant rolls to a warmed serving plate. Sprinkle with basil leaves and serve.

soufflé omelet

serves four

6 oz/175 g cherry tomatoes

8 oz/225 g mixed mushrooms, such
   as white, cremini or portabello,
   shiitake, and oyster

4 tbsp vegetable stock

small bunch of fresh thyme, tied
   with string

4 eggs, separated

½ cup water

4 egg whites

4 tsp olive oil

1 oz/25 g arugula leaves

fresh thyme sprigs, to garnish

NUTRITION

Calories 146	Sugars 2g
Protein 10g	Fat 11g
Carbohydrate 2g	Saturates 2g

1 Halve the tomatoes and place them in a pan. Wipe the mushrooms with paper towels, then trim if necessary, and slice if large. Place the mushrooms in the pan with the tomatoes.

2 Add the stock and the bunch of thyme to the pan. Bring to a boil, then reduce the heat and simmer, covered, for 5–6 minutes, or until tender. Drain, remove the thyme, and discard. Keep the mixture warm.

3 Meanwhile, whisk the egg yolks with the water until frothy. Whisk the 8 egg whites in a clean, greasefree bowl until stiff and dry.

4 Spoon the egg yolk mixture into the egg whites and, using a metal spoon, fold together until well mixed. Take care not to knock out too much of the air.

5 Preheat the broiler to medium. For each omelet, brush a small omelet pan with 1 teaspoon of the oil and heat until hot. Pour in a fourth of the egg mixture and cook for 4–5 minutes, or until the mixture has set.

6 Finish cooking the omelet under the hot broiler for 2–3 minutes.

7 Transfer the omelet to a warmed serving plate. Fill the omelet with a few arugula leaves and a fourth of the mushroom and tomato mixture. Flip over the top of the omelet, then garnish with thyme sprigs and serve.

spinach cheese molds

serves four

3½ oz/100 g fresh spinach leaves
1⅓ cups skim milk soft cheese
2 garlic cloves, crushed
fresh parsley, tarragon, and chive
    sprigs, finely chopped
salt and pepper
mixed salad greens and fresh herbs,
    to serve

NUTRITION	
Calories 119	Sugars 2g
Protein 6g	Fat 9g
Carbohydrate 2g	Saturates 6g

1 Trim the stems from the spinach leaves and rinse the leaves under cold running water. Pack the leaves into a pan while they are still wet, then cover and cook over medium heat for 3–4 minutes, or until wilted—they will cook in the steam from the wet leaves (do not overcook). Drain well and pat dry with paper towels.

2 Line the bottoms of 4 small ovenproof bowls or individual ramekin dishes with parchment paper. Line the dishes with the spinach leaves so that the leaves overhang the edges.

3 Place the cheese in a bowl and add the garlic and herbs. Mix together thoroughly and season to taste with salt and pepper.

4 Spoon the cheese and herb mixture into the dishes and pull over the overlapping spinach to cover the cheese, or lay extra leaves to cover the top. Place a waxed paper circle on top of each dish and weigh down with a 3½ oz/100 g weight. Let chill in the refrigerator for 1 hour.

5 Remove the weights and peel off the paper. Loosen the molds gently by running a small spatula around the edges of each dish and turn them out onto individual serving plates. Serve immediately with a mixture of salad greens and fresh herbs.

figs & prosciutto

serves four

1½ oz/40 g arugula leaves

4 fresh figs

4 slices prosciutto

4 tbsp olive oil

1 tbsp fresh orange juice

1 tbsp clear honey

1 small fresh red chili

1 Tear the arugula leaves into manageable pieces and arrange on 4 individual serving plates.

2 Using a sharp knife, cut each of the figs into fourths and place them on top of the arugula.

COOK'S TIP

Fresh chilies can burn the skin for several hours after chopping, so it is advisable to wear gloves when you are handling any very hot varieties and to wash your hands afterward.

NUTRITION

Calories 121	Sugars 6g
Protein 1g	Fat 11g
Carbohydrate 6g	Saturates 2g

3 Using a sharp knife, cut the prosciutto into strips and sprinkle over the arugula and figs.

4 Place the oil, orange juice, and honey in a screw-top jar. Shake the jar vigorously until the mixture emulsifies and forms a thick dressing. Transfer the dressing to a bowl.

5 Using a sharp knife, dice the chili. (You can remove the seeds first if you prefer a milder flavor.) Add the diced chili to the dressing and mix well.

6 Drizzle the dressing over the prosciutto, arugula, and figs, tossing to mix well. Serve immediately.

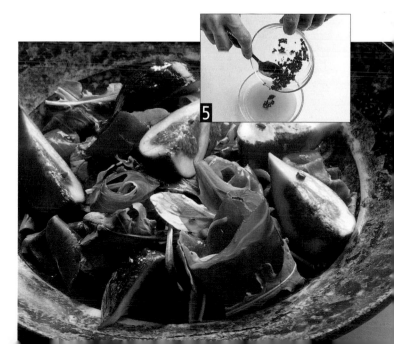

eggplant & rice rolls

serves four

3 eggplants (about 1 lb 10 oz/
   750 g in total)

generous ¼ cup mixed long-grain
   and wild rice

4 scallions, thinly sliced

3 tbsp chopped cashew nuts or
   toasted chopped hazelnuts

2 tbsp capers, drained and rinsed

1 garlic clove, crushed

2 tbsp freshly grated
   Parmesan cheese

1 egg, beaten

salt and pepper

1 tbsp olive oil, plus extra
   for oiling

1 tbsp balsamic vinegar

2 tbsp tomato paste

⅔ cup water

⅔ cup dry white wine

cilantro sprigs, to garnish

NUTRITION

Calories 142	Sugars 3g
Protein 6g	Fat 9g
Carbohydrate 9g	Saturates 3g

1 Preheat the oven to 350°F/180°C. Cut off the stem end of each eggplant, then cut off and discard a strip of skin from alternate sides of each eggplant. Cut each eggplant into thin slices to give a total of 16 slices.

2 Blanch the eggplant slices in boiling water for 5 minutes, then drain on paper towels.

3 Cook the rice in boiling salted water for 12 minutes, or until just tender. Drain and place in a bowl. Add the scallions, nuts, capers, garlic, cheese, egg, and salt and pepper to taste and stir well.

4 Spread a thin layer of rice mixture over each slice of eggplant and roll up, securing with a wooden toothpick. Place the rolls in an oiled flameproof dish and brush each one with oil.

5 Mix the vinegar, tomato paste, and water together. Pour over the rolls. Cook in the oven for 40 minutes, or until tender and most of the liquid has been absorbed. Transfer to a dish.

6 Add the wine to the pan juices and heat until the sediment loosens, then simmer for 2–3 minutes. Taste and adjust the seasoning if necessary and strain the sauce over the eggplant rolls. Let stand until cold, then chill thoroughly.

7 Garnish the eggplant rolls with cilantro sprigs and serve.

crispy pork & peanut baskets

serves four

2 sheets phyllo pastry, each about
16½ x 11 inches/42 x 28 cm

2 tbsp vegetable oil

1 garlic clove, crushed

generous 1 cup ground pork

1 tsp Thai red curry paste

2 scallions, finely chopped

3 tbsp chunky peanut butter

1 tbsp light soy sauce

1 tbsp chopped cilantro

salt and pepper

cilantro sprigs, to garnish

COOK'S TIP

When using phyllo pastry,
remember that it dries out very
quickly and becomes brittle and
difficult to handle. Work quickly
and keep any sheets you're not
using covered with plastic wrap
and a dampened dish towel.

NUTRITION

Calories 243		Sugars 1g	
Protein 12g		Fat 16g	
Carbohydrate 12g		Saturates 3g	

1 Preheat the oven to 400°F/
200°C. Cut each sheet of phyllo
pastry into 24 squares, 2¾ inches/7 cm
across, to make a total of 48 squares.
Brush each square lightly with oil, and
arrange the squares in stacks of 4 in
12 small tartlet pans, pointing
outward. Press the pastry down into
the pans.

2 Bake the pastry shells in the
preheated oven for 6–8 minutes,
or until golden brown.

3 Meanwhile, heat the remaining
oil in a preheated wok. Add the
garlic and fry for 30 seconds, then stir
in the pork and stir-fry over high heat
for 4–5 minutes, or until the meat is
golden brown.

4 Add the curry paste and scallions
and stir-fry for an additional
1 minute, then stir in the peanut butter,
soy sauce, and chopped cilantro.
Season to taste with salt and pepper.

5 Spoon the pork mixture into the
phyllo baskets and serve hot,
garnished with cilantro sprigs.

crispy golden seafood

serves four

7 oz/200 g prepared squid

7 oz/200 g raw jumbo shrimp,
    shelled and deveined

5½ oz/150 g whitebait

1¼ cups oil, for deep-frying

⅓ cup all-purpose flour

salt and pepper

1 tsp dried basil

Garlic Mayonnaise, to serve
    (see Cook's Tip)

COOK'S TIP

To make the Garlic Mayonnaise, crush 2 garlic cloves and stir into 8 tablespoons of mayonnaise, then season to taste with salt and pepper and 1 tablespoon of chopped fresh parsley. Cover and chill in the refrigerator until ready to serve.

NUTRITION

Calories 393	Sugars 0.2g
Protein 27g	Fat 26g
Carbohydrate 12g	Saturates 3g

1 Carefully rinse the squid, shrimp, and whitebait under cold running water, completely removing any accumulated dirt or grit.

2 Using a sharp knife, slice the squid into thick rings, but leave all the tentacles whole.

3 Heat the oil in a large pan to 350–375°F/180–190°C, or until a cube of bread browns in 30 seconds.

4 Place the flour in a large bowl and season to taste with salt, pepper, and the dried basil.

5 Toss the squid, shrimp, and whitebait in the seasoned flour until coated thoroughly all over. Carefully shake off any excess flour.

6 Cook the seafood, in batches, in the hot oil for 2–3 minutes, or until crispy and golden all over. Remove each batch of seafood with a slotted spoon and let drain thoroughly on paper towels.

7 Transfer the deep-fried seafood to 4 large serving plates and serve immediately with the Garlic Mayonnaise (see Cook's Tip).

steamed crab cakes

serves four

1–2 banana leaves
2 garlic cloves, crushed
1 tsp finely chopped lemongrass
½ tsp pepper
2 tbsp chopped cilantro
3 tbsp creamed coconut
1 tbsp lime juice
7 oz/200 g cooked crabmeat, flaked
1 tbsp Thai fish sauce
2 egg whites
1 egg yolk, lightly beaten
8 cilantro leaves
corn oil, for deep-frying
chili sauce, to serve

NUTRITION

Calories 156	Sugars 1g
Protein 13g	Fat 11g
Carbohydrate 2g	Saturates 4g

1 Line 8 ½-cup ramekin dishes or foil containers with the banana leaves, cutting them to shape.

2 Mix the garlic, lemongrass, pepper, and cilantro together in a bowl. Mash the creamed coconut with the lime juice in a separate bowl until smooth. Stir the 2 mixtures together and add the crabmeat and fish sauce.

3 Whisk the egg whites in a clean, greasefree bowl until stiff, then lightly and evenly fold them into the crab mixture.

4 Spoon the mixture into the prepared ramekin dishes and press down lightly. Brush the tops with egg yolk and top each with a cilantro leaf.

5 Place in a steamer half-filled with boiling water, then cover with a close-fitting lid and steam for 15 minutes, or until firm to the touch. Pour off the excess liquid and remove from the ramekin dishes.

6 Heat the oil in a large pan to 350°–375°F/180–190°C, or until a cube of bread browns in 30 seconds. Add the crab cakes and deep-fry for 1 minute, turning them over once, until golden brown. Serve hot with chili sauce.

sardines with pesto

serves four

16 large sardines, cleaned and scaled

scant 1 cup fresh basil leaves

2 garlic cloves, crushed

2 tbsp pine nuts, toasted

½ cup freshly grated
Parmesan cheese

⅔ cup olive oil

salt and pepper

lemon wedges, to garnish

NUTRITION	
Calories 617	Sugars 0g
Protein 27g	Fat 56g
Carbohydrate 1g	Saturates 11g

1 Preheat the broiler. Wash the sardines and pat dry with paper towels. Arrange them on a broiler pan.

2 Place the basil leaves, garlic, and pine nuts in a food processor and process until finely chopped. Transfer to a small bowl and stir in the Parmesan cheese and oil. Season to taste with salt and pepper.

3 Spread a little of the pesto over one side of the sardines and place under the hot broiler for 3 minutes. Turn the fish and spread with more pesto. Broil for an additional 3 minutes, or until the fish are cooked through.

4 Serve the sardines immediately with extra pesto and garnished with lemon wedges.

VARIATION

This treatment will also work well with other small oily fish, such as herrings and sprats.

wild rice blinis

serves four–six

butter or vegetable oil, for frying

4 scallions, thinly sliced diagonally

4 oz/115 g smoked salmon,
   thinly sliced into strips
   or shredded

½ cup sour cream

snipped fresh chives, for sprinkling

BLINIS

5 tbsp lukewarm water

1½ tsp active dry yeast

generous ⅓ cup all-purpose flour

scant ½ cup buckwheat flour

2 tbsp sugar

½ tsp salt

1 cup milk

2 eggs, separated

2 tbsp butter, melted

generous 1 cup cooked wild rice

TO GARNISH

orange twist

fresh mint sprig

1 To make the blinis, pour the water into a small bowl and sprinkle the yeast over it. Let stand until the yeast has dissolved and the mixture is beginning to froth.

2 Sift the flours into a bowl and stir in the sugar and salt. Make a well in the center. Warm ¾ cup of the milk and add to the well with the yeast mixture. Gradually whisk the flour into the liquid to form a smooth batter. Cover and let stand in a warm place until light and bubbly.

3 Beat the remaining milk with the egg yolks and the melted butter, then beat into the batter.

4 Using an electric mixer, whisk the egg whites until soft peaks form. Fold a spoonful into the batter, then fold in the remaining egg whites and the rice alternately. Do not overmix.

5 Heat just enough butter in a large skillet to coat lightly. Drop tablespoonfuls of the batter into the pan and cook for 1–2 minutes, or until tiny bubbles form on the surface. Turn and cook for 30 seconds. Remove and keep warm in a low oven while cooking the remaining batter. Add a little more butter if necessary.

6 Top with the scallions, smoked salmon, sour cream, and a sprinkling of snipped chives. Garnish with an orange twist and mint sprig and serve.

NUTRITION	
Calories 37	Sugars 1g
Protein 1g	Fat 2g
Carbohydrate 4g	Saturates 1g

61

bang-bang chicken

serves four

4 cups water

2 chicken quarters

1 cucumber, cut into
    short thin sticks

SAUCE

2 tbsp light soy sauce

1 tsp sugar

1 tbsp finely chopped scallions, plus
    extra to garnish

1 tsp red chili oil

¼ tsp pepper

1 tsp white sesame seeds, plus
    extra to garnish

2 tbsp peanut butter, creamed with
    a little sesame oil

NUTRITION

Calories 82	Sugars 1g
Protein 13g	Fat 3g
Carbohydrate 2g	Saturates 1g

1 Bring the water to a rolling boil in a large pan. Add the chicken pieces, then reduce the heat and cook, covered, for 30–35 minutes.

2 Remove the chicken from the pan and immerse in a bowl of cold water for at least 1 hour, to cool it ready for shredding.

3 Remove the chicken pieces and drain, then dry on paper towels. Take the meat off the bone.

4 Pound the chicken with a rolling pin on a flat surface, then tear the meat into shreds with 2 forks. Mix the chicken with the cucumber and arrange in a serving dish.

5 To serve, mix all the sauce ingredients together until thoroughly combined and pour over the chicken and cucumber in the serving dish. Sprinkle some sesame seeds and chopped scallions over the sauce and serve.

COOK'S TIP

Take the time to tear the chicken meat into similar-size shreds, to make an elegant-looking dish. You can do this quite efficiently with 2 forks, although Chinese cooks would do it with their fingers.

turkey & vegetable loaf

serves six

1 onion, finely chopped

1 garlic clove, crushed

2 lb/900 g ground lean turkey

1 tbsp chopped fresh parsley

1 tbsp snipped fresh chives

1 tbsp chopped fresh tarragon

salt and pepper

1 egg white, lightly beaten

2 zucchini, 1 medium and 1 large

2 tomatoes

tomato and herb sauce, to serve
   (optional)

NUTRITION

Calories 165	Sugars 1g
Protein 36g	Fat 2g
Carbohydrate 1g	Saturates 0.5g

COOK'S TIP

To test if the loaf is cooked, insert a skewer into the center—the juices should run clear. The loaf will also shrink away from the sides of the pan.

1 Preheat the oven to 375°F/190°C. Line a nonstick loaf pan with parchment paper. Place the onion, garlic, and turkey in a bowl, then add the herbs and season to taste with salt and pepper. Mix together with your hands, then add the egg white to bind the mixture together.

2 Press half the turkey mixture into the bottom of the pan. Thinly slice the medium zucchini and the tomatoes and arrange the slices over the meat. Top with the rest of the turkey mixture and press down firmly. Cover with a layer of foil and place in a roasting pan. Pour in enough boiling water to come halfway up the sides of the loaf pan. Bake in the oven for 1–1¼ hours, removing the foil for the last 20 minutes of cooking.

3 Cut the large zucchini lengthwise into thin slices with a vegetable peeler. Bring a pan of water to a boil and blanch the zucchini for 1–2 minutes, or until just tender. Drain and keep warm.

4 Remove the loaf from the pan and transfer to a warmed serving platter. Drape the zucchini ribbons over the turkey loaf and serve with a tomato and herb sauce, if desired.

asian pork balls in broth

serves six

1¾ quarts chicken stock

3 oz/85 g shiitake mushrooms, thinly sliced

6 oz/175 g bok choy or other Chinese greens, sliced into thin ribbons

6 scallions, finely sliced

salt and pepper

PORK BALLS

8 oz/225 g ground lean pork

1 oz/25 g fresh spinach leaves, finely chopped

2 scallions, finely chopped

1 garlic clove, very finely chopped

pinch of Chinese five-spice powder

1 tsp soy sauce

NUTRITION

Calories 67	Sugars 1g
Protein 9g	Fat 2g
Carbohydrate 3g	Saturates 1g

1 To make the pork balls, place the pork, spinach, scallions, and garlic in a bowl. Add the five-spice powder and soy sauce and mix until thoroughly combined.

2 Shape the pork mixture into 24 balls. Place them in a single layer in a steamer that will fit over the top of a large pan.

3 Bring the stock just to a boil in a pan that will accommodate the steamer. Reduce the heat so that the liquid just bubbles gently. Add the mushrooms to the stock and place the steamer, covered, on top of the pan. Steam for 10 minutes. Remove the steamer and let stand on a plate.

4 Add the bok choy and scallions to the pan and cook gently in the stock for 3–4 minutes, or until the leaves are wilted. Season the broth to taste with salt and pepper.

5 Divide the pork balls evenly between 6 warmed serving bowls and ladle the soup over them. Serve immediately.

spare ribs

serves four

2 lb/900 g pork spare ribs

2 tbsp dark soy sauce

3 tbsp hoisin sauce

1 tbsp rice wine or dry sherry

pinch of Chinese five-spice
     powder

2 tsp brown sugar

¼ tsp chili sauce

2 garlic cloves, crushed

cilantro sprigs, to garnish
     (optional)

NUTRITION

Calories 436	Sugars 3g
Protein 21g	Fat 37g
Carbohydrate 3g	Saturates 14g

1 Cut the spare ribs into separate pieces if they are joined together. If desired, you can chop them into 2-inch/5-cm lengths using a cleaver.

2 Mix the soy sauce, hoisin sauce, rice wine, five-spice powder, sugar, chili sauce, and garlic together in a large bowl.

3 Place the ribs in a shallow dish and pour the mixture over them, turning to coat the ribs thoroughly. Cover with plastic wrap and let marinate in the refrigerator, turning the ribs occasionally, for at least 1 hour.

4 Preheat the oven to 350°F/180°C. Remove the ribs from the marinade and arrange them in a single layer on a wire rack placed over a roasting pan half-filled with warm water. Using a pastry brush, coat the ribs with the marinade, reserving the remaining marinade.

5 Cook the ribs in the preheated oven for 30 minutes. Remove the roasting pan from the oven and turn the ribs over. Brush with the remaining marinade and return to the oven for an additional 30 minutes, or until cooked through. Add more hot water to the roasting pan during cooking, if required. Do not let it dry out, because the water steams the ribs and aids in their cooking.

6 Transfer the ribs to a warmed serving dish. Garnish with cilantro sprigs, if using, and serve immediately.

Snacks & Side Dishes

Vegetables in their wealth of different forms are rich in essential nutrients, and the more varieties you eat, the greater the range of these health-promoting vitamins and minerals you can benefit from. The following recipes take the pick of the crop and, using a range of cooking methods and seasonings, turn them into truly exciting and tempting dishes—perfect for serving with broiled or grilled meat, poultry, or fish, or to enjoy on their own as a low-carb filler at any time of day. Try the speedy stir-fried Bok Choy with Crabmeat or the grilled Roast Leeks. Alternatively, opt for the slower-paced yet easy Braised Fennel.

Salads are another low-carbohydrate mainstay, and offer a feast of fresh flavor and color—like the Grapefruit & Cheese Salad, with pink grapefruit and avocado.

sesame seed chutney

serves four

8 tbsp sesame seeds

2 tbsp water

½ bunch of cilantro

3 fresh green chilies, seeded
  and chopped

1 tsp salt

2 tsp lemon juice

chopped fresh red chili,
  to garnish

NUTRITION	
Calories 120	Sugars 0g
Protein 4g	Fat 12g
Carbohydrate 0.2g	Saturates 2g

COOK'S TIP

Dry roasting brings out the flavor
of spices and takes just a
few minutes. You will be able to
tell when the spices are ready
because of the wonderful
fragrance that develops. Stir the
spices constantly to ensure that
they do not burn.

1 Place the sesame seeds in a large
heavy-bottom pan and dry roast
them, stirring constantly. Remove from
the heat and let cool.

2 Place the sesame seeds in a
mortar and, using a pestle, grind
to a fine powder, or process in a food
processor.

3 Add the water to the ground
sesame seeds and mix thoroughly
to form a smooth paste.

4 Finely chop the cilantro. Add the
green chilies and cilantro to the
sesame seed paste and grind again.

5 Add the salt and the lemon
juice to the mixture and grind
once again.

6 Transfer the mixture to a small
serving dish. Garnish with
chopped red chili and serve.

okra bhaji

serves four

1 tbsp corn oil

1 tsp black mustard seeds

1 tsp cumin seeds

1 tsp ground coriander

½ tsp ground turmeric

1 fresh green chili, seeded and
   finely chopped

1 red onion, finely sliced

2 garlic cloves, crushed

1 orange bell pepper, seeded and
   thinly sliced

1 lb 2 oz/500 g okra, blanched

generous 1 cup vegetable juice

salt

⅔ cup light cream

1 tbsp lemon juice

NUTRITION

Calories 173	Sugars 11g
Protein 6g	Fat 11g
Carbohydrate 13g	Saturates 5g

1 Heat the oil in a preheated wok or large heavy-bottom skillet. Add the mustard seeds and cover the wok until they begin to pop.

2 Stir in the cumin seeds, coriander, turmeric, and chili. Stir constantly for 1 minute, or until the spices give off their aroma.

3 Add the onion, garlic, and bell pepper and cook, stirring frequently, for 5 minutes, or until soft.

4 Add the blanched okra to the wok and stir well.

5 Pour in the vegetable juice, then bring to a boil and cook over high heat, stirring occasionally, for 5 minutes.

6 When most of the liquid has evaporated, taste and adjust the seasoning, adding salt if necessary.

7 Add the cream and return to a boil, then continue to cook the mixture over high heat for 12 minutes, or until it is almost dry.

8 Sprinkle the lemon juice over the okra bhaji. Transfer to a warmed serving dish and serve immediately.

vegetables à la grecque

serves four–six

9 oz/250 g small pickling onions

9 oz/250 g mushrooms

9 oz/250 g zucchini

2 cups water

5 tbsp olive oil

2 tbsp lemon juice

2 strips of lemon rind

2 large garlic cloves, thinly sliced

½ Spanish onion, finely chopped

1 bay leaf

15 black peppercorns,
   lightly crushed

10 coriander seeds, lightly crushed

pinch of dried oregano

finely chopped fresh flatleaf parsley
   or cilantro, to garnish

NUTRITION

Calories 67	Sugars 4g
Protein 2g	Fat 4g
Carbohydrate 6g	Saturates 1g

1 Place the pickling onions in a heatproof bowl and cover with boiling water. Let stand for 2 minutes, then drain. Peel and reserve.

2 Trim the mushroom stems. Cut the mushrooms into halves or fourths, or leave whole if small. Cut thin strips of peel from the zucchini for a decorative finish, then cut into ¼-inch/5-mm slices. Reserve the mushrooms and zucchini.

3 Place the water, oil, lemon juice and rind, garlic, Spanish onion, bay leaf, peppercorns, coriander seeds, and oregano in a pan over high heat and bring to a boil. Reduce the heat and simmer for 15 minutes.

4 Add the small onions and simmer for an additional 5 minutes. Add the mushrooms and zucchini and simmer for an additional 2 minutes.

5 Using a slotted spoon, transfer all the vegetables to a large heatproof dish.

6 Return the liquid to a boil and boil until reduced to 6 tablespoons. Pour the liquid over the vegetables and let cool completely.

7 Cover with plastic wrap and let chill for at least 12 hours.

8 To serve, place the vegetables and cooking liquid in a serving dish and sprinkle the fresh herbs over them.

bok choy with crabmeat

serves four

2 heads bok choy, about 9 oz/
    250 g in total

2 tbsp vegetable oil

1 garlic clove, thinly sliced

2 tbsp oyster sauce

3½ oz/100 g cherry tomatoes,
    halved

6 oz/175 g canned white
    crabmeat, drained

salt and pepper

VARIATION

If bok choy is not available,
Napa cabbage makes a good
alternative for this dish.

1 Trim the bok choy and cut into
1-inch/2.5-cm thick slices.

2 Heat the oil in a large skillet or
wok. Add the garlic and stir-fry
over high heat for 1 minute.

3 Add the bok choy and stir-fry for
2–3 minutes, or until the leaves
wilt but the stems are still crisp.

4 Add the oyster sauce and
tomatoes and stir-fry for an
additional 1 minute.

5 Add the crabmeat and season to
taste with salt and pepper. Stir to
heat thoroughly and break up the
distribution of crabmeat before serving.

NUTRITION	
Calories 101	Sugars 2g
Protein 9g	Fat 6g
Carbohydrate 3g	Saturates 1g

stir-fried ginger mushrooms

serves four

2 tbsp vegetable oil

3 garlic cloves, crushed

1 tbsp Thai red curry paste

½ tsp ground turmeric

15 oz/425 g canned straw
mushrooms, drained and halved

¾-inch/2-cm piece fresh gingerroot,
finely shredded

generous ⅓ cup coconut milk

1½ oz/40 g dried shiitake
mushrooms, soaked, drained,
and sliced

1 tbsp lemon juice

1 tbsp light soy sauce

2 tsp sugar

½ tsp salt

8 cherry tomatoes, halved

7 oz/200 g firm tofu (drained
weight), diced

cilantro leaves, to garnish

1 Heat the oil in a skillet. Add the garlic and stir-fry for 1 minute. Stir in the curry paste and turmeric and cook for an additional 30 seconds.

2 Stir in the straw mushrooms and ginger and stir-fry for 2 minutes. Stir in the coconut milk and bring to a boil.

3 Stir in the dried shiitake mushrooms, lemon juice, soy sauce, sugar, and salt and heat thoroughly. Add the tomatoes and tofu and toss gently to heat through.

4 Sprinkle the cilantro leaves over the mushroom mixture and serve immediately.

NUTRITION	
Calories 174	Sugars 7g
Protein 8g	Fat 9g
Carbohydrate 15g	Saturates 1g

brindil bhaji

serves four

1 lb 2 oz/500 g eggplants, sliced

2 tbsp vegetable oil or ghee

1 onion, thinly sliced

2 garlic cloves, sliced

1-inch/2.5-cm piece fresh
    gingerroot, grated

½ tsp ground turmeric

1 dried red chili, finely chopped

½ tsp salt

14 oz/400 g canned tomatoes

1 tsp garam masala

cilantro sprigs, to garnish

NUTRITION

Calories 117	Sugars 8g
Protein 3g	Fat 8g
Carbohydrate 9g	Saturates 5g

VARIATION

Other vegetables can be used
instead of the eggplants. Try
zucchini, potatoes, or bell
peppers, or any combination of
these vegetables, using the
same sauce.

1 Cut the eggplant slices into finger-width strips.

2 Heat the oil in a heavy-bottom pan. Add the onion and cook over medium heat, stirring constantly, for 7–8 minutes, or until very soft and just beginning to color.

3 Add the garlic and eggplant strips, then increase the heat and cook, stirring constantly, for 2 minutes. Stir in the ginger, turmeric, chili, salt, and tomatoes with their can juices. Use the back of a wooden spoon to break up the tomatoes. Reduce the heat and let simmer, uncovered, for 15–20 minutes, or until the eggplants are very soft.

4 Stir in the garam masala and simmer for an additional 4–5 minutes.

5 Transfer the brindil bhaji to a warmed serving plate and garnish with cilantro sprigs, then serve immediately.

roasted vegetables

serves six

1 small red cabbage

1 fennel bulb

1 orange bell pepper, cut into
   1½-inch/4-cm dice

1 eggplant, halved and sliced into
   ½-inch/1-cm pieces

2 zucchini, thickly sliced
   diagonally

6 fresh rosemary twigs, about
   6 inches/15 cm long, soaked in
   cold water

olive oil, for brushing

salt and pepper

NUTRITION

Calories 16	Sugars 3g
Protein 1g	Fat 0.3g
Carbohydrate 3g	Saturates 0g

1 Preheat the broiler or grill. Cut the red cabbage through the middle of its stem and heart. Divide each piece into fourths, each time including a section of the stem in the slice to hold it together.

2 Prepare the fennel in the same way as the red cabbage.

3 Blanch the red cabbage and fennel in boiling water for 3 minutes, then drain well.

4 With a wooden skewer, carefully pierce a hole through the middle of each piece of vegetable.

VARIATION

If you are using a grill, fruit skewers make a quick and easy dessert. Thread pieces of banana, mango, peach, strawberry, apple, and pear onto soaked wooden skewers and cook over the dying embers. Brush with sugar syrup toward the end of cooking.

5 Thread a piece of bell pepper, fennel, red cabbage, eggplant, and zucchini onto each rosemary twig, gently pushing the rosemary through the skewer holes.

6 Brush liberally with oil and season with plenty of salt and pepper.

7 Cook under the hot broiler or over hot coals for 8–10 minutes, turning occasionally. Serve.

tomato sauce

serves four

1 tbsp olive oil

1 small onion, chopped

1 garlic clove, crushed

7 oz/200 g canned chopped
    tomatoes

2 tsp tomato paste

½ tsp sugar

½ tsp dried oregano

1 bay leaf

salt and pepper

NUTRITION

Calories 41	Sugars 3g
Protein 1g	Fat 3g
Carbohydrate 3g	Saturates 0.4g

1 Heat the oil in a pan. Add the onion and garlic and cook for 5 minutes until soft but not browned.

2 Add the tomatoes, tomato paste, sugar, oregano, bay leaf, and salt and pepper to taste. Stir well.

3 Bring the sauce to a boil, then cover and let simmer gently for 20 minutes, stirring occasionally, until you have a thickish sauce.

4 Remove the bay leaf and season to taste with salt and pepper. Let cool completely before using. This sauce keeps well in a screw-top jar in the refrigerator for up to 1 week.

roast leeks

serves four

4 leeks

3 tbsp olive oil

2 tsp balsamic vinegar

sea salt and pepper

NUTRITION

Calories 71	Sugars 2g
Protein 2g	Fat 6g
Carbohydrate 3g	Saturates 1g

COOK'S TIP

Use a good quality French or Italian olive oil for this deliciously simple yet sophisticated vegetable accompaniment.

1 Preheat the grill. Cut the leeks in half lengthwise, making sure that you hold the knife straight, so that the leek is held together by the root. Brush each leek liberally with oil.

2 Cook the leeks over hot coals for 6–7 minutes, turning once.

3 Remove the leeks from the grill and brush them lightly with the vinegar.

4 Season to taste with salt and pepper and serve hot or warm.

sweet & sour zucchini

serves four–six

1 lb 2 oz/500 g zucchini

3 tbsp olive oil

1 large garlic clove, finely chopped

3 tbsp white wine vinegar

3 tbsp water

6–8 anchovy fillets, canned
   or salted

3 tbsp pine nuts

3 tbsp raisins

salt and pepper

fresh flatleaf parsley sprigs,
   to garnish

VARIATION

Replace the raisins with golden raisins. Add a little grated lemon or orange rind for added zing.

---

1 Cut the zucchini into long thin strips. Heat the oil in a large heavy-bottom skillet over medium heat. Add the garlic and cook, stirring constantly, for 2 minutes.

2 Add the zucchini and cook, stirring frequently, until they just begin to turn brown. Add the vinegar and water. Reduce the heat and simmer for 10 minutes.

3 Meanwhile, drain the anchovies, if canned, or rinse if they are salted. Coarsely chop, then use the back of a wooden spoon to mash them to a paste.

4 Stir the anchovies, pine nuts, and raisins into the skillet. Increase the heat and stir until the zucchini are coated in a thin sauce and are tender. Taste and adjust the seasoning, remembering that the anchovies are very salty.

5 Either serve immediately or let cool completely, then serve at room temperature. To serve, garnish with parsley sprigs.

NUTRITION	
Calories 90	Sugars 5g
Protein 3g	Fat 4g
Carbohydrate 5g	Saturates 1g

braised fennel

serves four–six

2 lemon slices

3 fennel bulbs

4½ tsp olive oil

3 tbsp butter

4 fresh thyme sprigs or ½ tbsp
   dried thyme

pepper

¾ cup chicken or vegetable stock

¾ cup freshly grated
   Parmesan cheese

NUTRITION	
Calories 149	Sugars 2g
Protein 6g	Fat 13g
Carbohydrate 2g	Saturates 7g

1 Preheat the oven to 400°F/200°C. Bring a pan of water to a boil and add the lemon slices. Slice the fennel lengthwise and add to the pan. Return the water to a boil, then reduce the heat and simmer for 8 minutes, or until just tender. Drain.

2 Place the oil and butter in a flameproof casserole over medium heat. Swirl the melted mixture around so the bottom and sides of the casserole are well coated.

COOK'S TIP

This is an ideal way to serve older fennel bulbs, but will not improve any that have been stored too long and dried out.

3 Add the fennel slices and stir until coated. Add the thyme and season to taste with pepper. Pour in the stock and sprinkle the Parmesan cheese over the top.

4 Bake in the preheated oven for 25–30 minutes, or until the fennel has absorbed the stock and is tender and the cheese has melted and become golden brown. Serve immediately.

steamed lotus rice

serves four

2 lotus leaves

4 dried shiitake mushrooms

generous ¾ cup long-grain rice

1 cinnamon stick

6 cardamom pods

4 cloves

1 tsp salt

2 eggs

1 tbsp vegetable oil

2 scallions, chopped

1 tbsp soy sauce

2 tbsp sherry

1 tsp sugar

1 tsp sesame oil

NUTRITION

Calories 163	Sugars 0.1g
Protein 5g	Fat 6g
Carbohydrate 2.1g	Saturates 1g

1 Unfold the lotus leaves and cut along the fold to divide each leaf in half. Lay on a cookie sheet and pour over enough hot water to cover. Let soak for 30 minutes, or until softened.

2 Meanwhile, place the mushrooms in a bowl, then cover with warm water and let soak for 20–25 minutes.

3 Bring a pan of water to a boil. Add the rice, cinnamon stick, cardamoms, cloves, and salt and return to a boil, then cook for 10 minutes—the rice should be partially cooked. Drain well and remove the cinnamon stick. Place the rice in a bowl.

4 Beat the eggs lightly in a separate bowl. Heat the vegetable oil in a preheated wok and cook the eggs quickly, stirring until set. Remove and reserve.

5 Drain the mushrooms, squeezing out the excess water. Remove the tough stems and chop the mushrooms. Stir into the rice with the egg, scallions, soy sauce, sherry, sugar, and sesame oil.

6 Drain the lotus leaves and divide the rice into 4 portions. Place a portion in the center of each leaf and fold up to form a package. Place in a steamer, then cover and steam over simmering water for 20 minutes. To serve, cut the tops of the lotus leaves open to expose the rice inside.

bamboo with spinach

serves four

3 tbsp peanut oil

8 oz/225 g fresh spinach, chopped

6 oz/175 g canned bamboo shoots,
    drained and rinsed

1 garlic clove, crushed

2 fresh red chilies, sliced

pinch of ground cinnamon

1¼ cups vegetable stock

pinch of sugar

pinch of salt

1 tbsp light soy sauce

NUTRITION

Calories 105	Sugars 1g
Protein 3g	Fat 9g
Carbohydrate 3g	Saturates 2g

COOK'S TIP

Fresh bamboo shoots are rarely
available in the West. Canned
bamboo shoots are quite
satisfactory, because they are
used to provide a crunchy
texture, rather than for their
flavor, which is quite bland.

1 Heat the oil in a preheated wok
or large heavy-bottom skillet,
swirling the oil around the bottom of
the wok until it is very hot.

2 Add the spinach and bamboo
shoots to the wok and stir-fry for
1 minute.

3 Add the garlic, chilies, and
cinnamon to the wok and stir-fry
for an additional 30 seconds.

4 Stir in the stock, sugar, salt, and
soy sauce, then cover and cook
over medium heat for 5 minutes, or
until the vegetables are cooked
through and the sauce has reduced.
(If there is too much cooking liquid,
blend a little cornstarch with double
the quantity of cold water and stir it
into the sauce.) Transfer the bamboo
shoots and spinach to a serving dish
and serve.

easy cauliflower & broccoli

serves four

2 baby cauliflowers

8 oz/225 g broccoli

salt and pepper

SAUCE

8 tbsp olive oil

4 tbsp butter or margarine

2 tsp grated fresh gingerroot

juice and rind of 2 lemons

5 tbsp chopped cilantro

5 tbsp grated Cheddar cheese

COOK'S TIP

Lime or orange could be used instead of the lemon for a fruity and refreshing sauce.

1 Preheat the broiler. Cut the cauliflowers in half and the broccoli into very large florets.

2 Cook the cauliflower and broccoli in a pan of boiling salted water for 10 minutes. Drain well, then transfer to a shallow ovenproof dish and keep warm until required.

3 To make the sauce, place the oil and butter in a skillet and heat gently until the butter melts.

NUTRITION

Calories 433	Sugars 2g
Protein 8g	Fat 44g
Carbohydrate 3g	Saturates 9g

4 Add the ginger, lemon juice and rind, and chopped cilantro and simmer for 2–3 minutes, stirring occasionally.

5 Season the sauce to taste with salt and pepper, then pour over the vegetables in the dish and sprinkle the cheese on top.

6 Cook under the hot broiler for 2–3 minutes, or until the cheese is bubbling and golden brown. Let cool for 1–2 minutes, then serve.

mushroom salad

serves four

5½ oz/150 g firm white mushrooms

4 tbsp virgin olive oil

1 tbsp lemon juice

5 canned anchovy fillets, drained
    and chopped

salt and pepper

1 tbsp fresh marjoram, to garnish

NUTRITION

Calories 121	Sugars 0.1g
Protein 13g	Fat 13g
Carbohydrate 0.1g	Saturates 2g

COOK'S TIP

Do not season the mushroom salad with salt until the very last minute, because it will cause the mushrooms to blacken and the juices to leak. The result will not be so tasty, because the full flavors won't be absorbed, and it will also look very unattractive.

1 Gently wipe each mushroom with a damp cloth or damp paper towels in order to remove any dirt.

2 Using a sharp knife, thinly slice the mushrooms and place in a bowl.

3 To make the dressing, whisk the oil and lemon juice together in a small bowl.

4 Pour the dressing mixture over the mushrooms. Toss together so that the mushrooms are completely coated with the lemon juice and oil.

5 Stir the anchovy fillets into the mushrooms. Season the mixture to taste with pepper and garnish with the marjoram.

6 Let the mushroom salad stand at room temperature for 5 minutes before serving to let all the flavors be absorbed.

7 Season the mushroom salad with a little salt (see Cook's Tip), then serve immediately.

mixed leaf salad

serves four

½ head frisée
½ head oak leaf lettuce
few leaves of radicchio
1 head Belgian endive
1 oz/25 g arugula leaves
few fresh basil or flatleaf
    parsley sprigs
edible flowers, to garnish
    (optional)

FRENCH DRESSING
1 tbsp white wine vinegar
pinch of sugar
½ tsp Dijon mustard
3 tbsp extra virgin olive oil
salt and pepper

COOK'S TIP
Violets, hardy geraniums, nasturtiums, chive flowers, and pot marigolds add vibrant colors and a sweet flavor to this salad. Use it as a centerpiece at a dinner party, or to liven up a simple everyday meal.

1 Tear the frisée, oak leaf lettuce, and radicchio into pieces. Place the salad greens in a large serving bowl or individual bowls, if you prefer.

2 Cut the Belgian endive into diagonal slices and add to the bowl with the arugula and basil.

3 To make the dressing, beat the vinegar, sugar, and mustard together in a small bowl until the sugar has dissolved. Gradually beat in the oil until the dressing is creamy and thoroughly mixed. Season to taste with salt and pepper.

4 Pour the dressing over the salad and toss thoroughly. Sprinkle a mixture of edible flowers over the top and serve.

NUTRITION	
Calories 51	Sugars 0.1g
Protein 0.1g	Fat 6g
Carbohydrate 1g	Saturates 0.4g

sesame seed salad

serves four

1 large eggplant

salt and pepper

3 tbsp sesame seed paste

juice and rind of 1 lemon

1 garlic clove, crushed

pinch of paprika

1 tbsp chopped cilantro

Boston lettuce leaves

TO GARNISH

pimiento strips

lemon wedges

toasted sesame seeds

NUTRITION

Calories 89	Sugars 1g
Protein 3g	Fat 8g
Carbohydrate 1g	Saturates 1g

1 Cut the eggplant in half, then place in a colander and sprinkle with salt. Let stand for 30 minutes so that the juices drain. Rinse thoroughly under cold running water and drain well. Pat dry with paper towels.

2 Preheat the oven to 450°F/ 230°C. Place the eggplant halves, skin-side uppermost, on an oiled cookie sheet. Cook in the preheated oven for 10–15 minutes. Let cool.

3 When the eggplant halves are cool enough to handle, cut them into cubes and reserve until required.

4 Mix the sesame seed paste, lemon juice and rind, garlic, paprika, and cilantro together in a medium-size bowl. Season to taste with salt and pepper and stir in the eggplant cubes.

5 Line a serving dish with lettuce leaves and spoon the eggplant cubes into the center. Garnish the salad with pimiento slices, lemon wedges, and toasted sesame seeds and serve immediately.

cool cucumber salad

serves four

8 oz/225 g cucumber

1 fresh green chili, finely chopped
  (optional)

DRESSING

cilantro leaves, finely chopped

2 tbsp lemon juice

½ tsp salt

1 tsp sugar

TO GARNISH

fresh mint sprigs

red bell pepper strips

COOK'S TIP

For the best results, you can use
a vegetable peeler to thinly slice
the cucumber.

NUTRITION

Calories 11	Sugars 2g
Protein 0.4g	Fat 0g
Carbohydrate 2g	Saturates 0g

1 Slice the cucumber thinly. Arrange the cucumber slices on a round serving plate.

2 Sprinkle the chili, if using, over the cucumber.

3 To make the dressing, mix the cilantro, lemon juice, salt, and sugar together in a bowl.

4 Cover the cucumber and let chill in the refrigerator for at least 1 hour, or until required. When ready to serve, transfer the cucumber to a serving dish. Pour the salad dressing over the cucumber just before serving and garnish with mint sprigs and red bell pepper strips.

italian mozzarella salad

serves six

7 oz/200 g fresh baby spinach leaves

4½ oz/125 g watercress

4½ oz/125 g mozzarella cheese

8 oz/225 g cherry tomatoes

2 tsp balsamic vinegar

4½ tsp extra virgin olive oil

salt and pepper

NUTRITION

Calories 79	Sugars 2g
Protein 4g	Fat 6g
Carbohydrate 2g	Saturates 2g

1 Rinse the spinach and watercress under cold running water and drain thoroughly on paper towels. Remove any tough stems. Place the spinach and watercress leaves in a large serving dish.

2 Cut the mozzarella into small pieces and sprinkle them over the spinach and watercress leaves.

3 Cut the tomatoes in half and sprinkle them over the salad.

4 Sprinkle over the vinegar and oil and season to taste with salt and pepper. Toss the mixture together to coat the leaves. Serve immediately or let chill in the refrigerator until required.

lobster salad

serves two

2 raw lobster tails

radicchio leaves

LEMON-DILL MAYONNAISE

1 large lemon

1 large egg yolk

½ tsp Dijon mustard

⅔ cup olive oil

salt and pepper

1 tbsp chopped fresh dill

TO GARNISH

lemon wedges

fresh dill sprigs

NUTRITION	
Calories 487	Sugars 2g
Protein 24g	Fat 42g
Carbohydrate 2g	Saturates 6g

1 To make the lemon-dill mayonnaise, finely grate the lemon rind and squeeze the juice. Beat the egg yolk in a small bowl and beat in the mustard and 1 teaspoon of the lemon juice.

2 Using a balloon whisk or electric mixer, beat in the oil, drop by drop, until a thick mayonnaise forms. Stir in half the lemon rind and 1 tablespoon of the juice.

3 Season to taste with salt and pepper and add more lemon juice if desired. Stir in the dill and cover with plastic wrap. Chill in the refrigerator until required.

4 Bring a large pan of lightly salted water to a boil. Add the lobster tails, then return to a boil and cook for 6 minutes, or until the flesh is opaque and the shells are red. Drain immediately and let cool.

5 Remove the lobster flesh from the shells and cut into bite-size pieces. Arrange the radicchio leaves on individual serving plates and top with the lobster flesh. Place a spoonful of the lemon-dill mayonnaise on the side. Garnish with lemon wedges and dill sprigs and serve.

smoked trout & apple salad

serves four

2 orange-red dessert apples

2 tbsp French Dressing
  (see page 89)

½ bunch of watercress

1 smoked trout, about 6 oz/175 g

HORSERADISH DRESSING

½ cup lowfat plain yogurt

½–1 tsp lemon juice

1 tbsp horseradish sauce

milk (optional)

salt and pepper

TO GARNISH

1 tbsp snipped fresh chives

fresh chive flowers (optional)

NUTRITION

Calories 133	Sugars 11g
Protein 12g	Fat 5g
Carbohydrate 11g	Saturates 1g

1 Leaving the skin on, cut the apples into fourths and remove the cores. Slice the apples into a bowl and toss in the French Dressing to prevent them turning brown.

2 Break the watercress into sprigs and arrange on 4 serving plates.

3 Skin the trout and take out the bones. Carefully remove any fine bones that remain, using your fingers or tweezers. Flake the trout into fairly large pieces and arrange with the apple between the watercress.

4 To make the Horseradish Dressing, whisk all the ingredients together, adding a little milk if too thick, then drizzle over the trout. Sprinkle the snipped chives and flowers, if using, over the trout and serve.

mozzarella & tomato salad

serves four–six

1 lb/450 g cherry tomatoes

4 scallions

½ cup extra virgin olive oil

2 tbsp balsamic vinegar

salt and pepper

7 oz/200 g buffalo mozzarella (see
   Cook's Tip), cut into cubes

scant ¼ cup fresh flatleaf parsley

generous ⅓ cup fresh basil leaves

NUTRITION		
Calories 295	Sugars 3g	
Protein 9g	Fat 27g	
Carbohydrate 3g	Saturates 7g	

1 Using a sharp knife, cut the tomatoes in half and place them in a large bowl. Trim the scallions and finely chop both the green and white parts, then add to the bowl.

2 Pour in the oil and vinegar and use your hands to toss together. Season to taste with salt and pepper, then add the mozzarella and toss again. Cover with plastic wrap and let chill in the refrigerator for 4 hours.

3 Remove the salad from the refrigerator 10 minutes before serving. Finely chop the parsley and add to the salad. Tear the basil leaves and sprinkle them over the salad. Toss all the ingredients together again. Adjust the seasoning and serve.

COOK'S TIP

For the best flavor, buy buffalo mozzarella—*mozzarella di bufala*—rather than the factory-made cow's milk version. This salad would also look good made with bocconcini, which are small balls of mozzarella. Find them in Italian delis.

capri salad

serves four

2 beefsteak tomatoes

4½ oz/125 g mozzarella cheese

12 black olives

8 fresh basil leaves

1 tbsp balsamic vinegar

1 tbsp extra virgin olive oil

salt and pepper

fresh basil leaves, to garnish

NUTRITION

Calories 95	Sugars 3g
Protein 3g	Fat 8g
Carbohydrate 3g	Saturates 3g

COOK'S TIP

Beefsteak tomatoes are excellent both cooked and raw, because they have a good flavor. When buying tomatoes, always look for ones that are firm to the touch and have a bright red color.

1 Preheat the broiler. Cut the tomatoes into thin slices.

2 Drain the mozzarella, if necessary, and cut into slices.

3 Pit the olives and slice them into rings.

4 Layer the tomatoes, mozzarella slices, olives, and basil leaves in a stack, finishing with a layer of cheese on top.

5 Place each stack under the hot broiler for 2–3 minutes, or just long enough to melt the mozzarella.

6 Drizzle over the vinegar and oil and season to taste with salt and pepper.

7 Transfer to individual serving plates and garnish with basil leaves. Serve immediately.

grapefruit & cheese salad

serves four

½ romaine lettuce

½ oak leaf lettuce

2 pink grapefruit

2 ripe avocados

6 oz/175 g Gorgonzola cheese,
   thinly sliced

fresh basil sprigs, to garnish

DRESSING

4 tbsp olive oil

1 tbsp white wine vinegar

salt and pepper

NUTRITION	
Calories 390	Sugars 3g
Protein 13g	Fat 36g
Carbohydrate 4g	Saturates 13g

1 Arrange the lettuce leaves on 4 individual serving plates.

2 Remove the peel and pith from the grapefruit with a sharp serrated knife, catching the grapefruit juice in a bowl.

3 Segment the grapefruit by cutting down each side of the membrane. Remove all the membrane. Arrange the segments on the serving plates.

COOK'S TIP

Pink grapefruit segments make a very attractive color combination with the avocados, but ordinary grapefruit will work just as well. To help avocados to ripen, keep them at room temperature in a brown paper bag.

4 Peel, pit, and slice the avocados, dipping them in the grapefruit juice to prevent them turning brown. Arrange the slices on the salad with the cheese.

5 To make the dressing, mix any remaining grapefruit juice, oil, and vinegar together in a bowl. Season to taste with salt and pepper and mix thoroughly to combine.

6 Drizzle the dressing over the salads. Garnish with basil sprigs and serve immediately.

Meat & Poultry

Meat and poultry dishes minus our beloved high-carbohydrate components need not be uninspiring or unsatisfying, as these recipes will soon reveal. Here, plain broils and grills are transformed by first marinating in spices, herbs, and citrus juices, vinegars, or wine, which not only boosts the flavor but also tenderizes the flesh. All that is required is a little advance preparation—the cooking takes just a few minutes.

Other recipes make clever use of stuffings and wrappings, for added flavor interest, such as lean pork stuffed with a Parmesan and basil filling, wrapped in prosciutto, and pieces of tender turkey breast stuffed with soft cheese and sage, wrapped in bacon.

Fruits are also put to creative use in this chapter—ham is paired with spiced apple, duck with piquant raspberries, and chicken with sweet-scented mango.

beef in barolo

serves four

4 tbsp corn oil

2 lb 4 oz/1 kg rolled rib or
  rib-eye roast

2 garlic cloves, crushed

4 shallots, sliced

1 tsp chopped fresh rosemary

1 tsp chopped fresh oregano

2 celery stalks, sliced

1 large carrot, diced

2 whole cloves

1 bottle Barolo wine

freshly grated nutmeg

salt and pepper

cooked vegetables, such as broccoli
  and carrots, to serve

NUTRITION

Calories 744	Sugars 1g
Protein 66g	Fat 43g
Carbohydrate 1g	Saturates 16g

1 Heat the oil in a flameproof casserole and brown the meat all over. Remove the meat from the casserole and reserve.

2 Add the garlic, shallots, herbs, celery, carrot, and cloves to the casserole and cook for 5 minutes.

3 Replace the meat on top of the vegetables. Pour in the wine, then cover and simmer gently for 2 hours, or until tender. Remove the meat from the casserole and let rest before slicing, then keep warm.

4 Press the remaining contents of the casserole through a strainer or process in a food processor, adding a little hot beef stock if necessary. Season to taste with nutmeg, salt, and pepper.

5 Serve the meat with the sauce and accompanied by cooked vegetables, such as broccoli and carrots.

COOK'S TIP

Barolo is a famous wine from the Piedmont area of Italy. If it is unavailable, choose another full-bodied red wine instead.

beef with exotic mushrooms

serves four

4 tenderloin or sirloin steaks

2 tbsp butter

1–2 garlic cloves, crushed

5½ oz/150 g mixed exotic
   mushrooms

2 tbsp chopped fresh parsley

TO SERVE

salad greens

cherry tomatoes, halved

NUTRITION

Calories 414	Sugars 0g
Protein 49g	Fat 24g
Carbohydrate 1g	Saturates 13g

COOK'S TIP

Exotic mushrooms, such as shiitake, oyster, and chanterelle, are now readily available in supermarkets. Look for boxes of mixed exotic mushrooms, which are usually cheaper than buying the different types individually.

1 Preheat the grill. Place the steaks on a cutting board and, using a sharp knife, cut a slit in the side of each steak.

2 To make the stuffing, heat the butter in a skillet, then add the garlic and cook gently for 1 minute.

3 Add the mushrooms to the pan and cook for 4–6 minutes, or until tender. Stir in the parsley.

4 Divide the mushroom mixture into fourths and insert a portion into the slit of each steak. Seal the slit closed with a wooden toothpick. If preparing ahead, let the mixture cool before stuffing the steaks.

5 Cook the steaks over hot coals, searing the meat over the hottest part of the grill for 2 minutes on each side. Move the steaks to an area with slightly less intense heat (usually the sides) and cook for an additional 4–10 minutes on each side, depending on how well done you like your steaks.

6 Transfer the steaks to serving plates and remove the toothpicks. Serve the steaks with salad greens and cherry tomatoes.

beef, tomato & olive kabobs

makes eight

1 lb/450 g tenderloin or sirloin steak

16 cherry tomatoes

16 large pitted green olives

salt and pepper

BASTE

4 tbsp olive oil, plus extra for oiling

1 tbsp sherry vinegar

1 garlic clove, crushed

FRESH TOMATO RELISH

1 tbsp olive oil

½ red onion, finely chopped

1 garlic clove, chopped

6 plum tomatoes, peeled, seeded,
   and chopped

2 pitted green olives, sliced

1 tbsp chopped fresh parsley

1 tbsp lemon juice

1 Preheat the grill. Trim any fat from the beef and cut into 24 pieces.

2 Thread the meat onto 8 presoaked wooden skewers, alternating the pieces with cherry tomatoes and olives.

3 To make the baste, combine the oil, vinegar, garlic, and salt and pepper to taste in a bowl.

4 To make the relish, heat the oil in a small pan. Add the onion and garlic and cook for 3–4 minutes, or until softened. Add the plum tomatoes and olives and cook for 2–3 minutes, or until the tomatoes are softened slightly. Stir in the parsley, lemon juice, and salt and pepper to taste. Reserve.

5 Cook the skewers on an oiled rack over hot coals for 5–10 minutes, basting and turning frequently. Serve with the relish.

NUTRITION	
Calories 166	Sugars 1g
Protein 12g	Fat 12g
Carbohydrate 1g	Saturates 3g

scallops & italian sausage

serves four

1 tbsp olive oil

6 canned anchovy fillets, drained

1 tbsp capers, drained

1 tbsp chopped fresh
    rosemary leaves

finely grated rind and juice of
    1 orange

2¾ oz/75 g Italian sausage,
    diced

3 tomatoes, peeled and chopped

4 turkey or veal scallops, about
    4½ oz/125 g each

salt and pepper

NUTRITION

Calories 233	Sugars 1g
Protein 28g	Fat 13g
Carbohydrate 1g	Saturates 1g

1 Heat the oil in a large skillet. Add the anchovies, capers, rosemary, orange rind and juice, Italian sausage, and tomatoes and cook for 5–6 minutes, stirring occasionally.

2 Meanwhile, place the turkey scallops between sheets of waxed paper. Pound the meat with a meat mallet or the end of a rolling pin to flatten it.

3 Add the meat to the mixture in the skillet. Season to taste with salt and pepper, then cover and cook for 3–5 minutes on each side, slightly longer if the meat is thicker.

4 Transfer to serving plates and serve immediately.

COOK'S TIP

Try using 4-minute steaks, slightly flattened, instead of the turkey or veal. Cook them for 4–5 minutes on top of the sauce in the skillet.

meatball brochettes

serves four

2½ tbsp bulgur wheat

12 oz/350 g ground lean beef

1 onion, finely chopped (optional)

1 tbsp tomato ketchup

1 tbsp brown fruity sauce

1 tbsp chopped fresh parsley

beaten egg, to bind (optional)

8 cherry tomatoes

8 white mushrooms

vegetable oil, for basting

assorted cooked vegetables,
    to serve

NUTRITION

Calories 120		Sugars 2g	
Protein 17g		Fat 5g	
Carbohydrate 2g		Saturates 2g	

1 Preheat the grill. Place the bulgur wheat in a heatproof bowl and cover with boiling water. Let soak for 20 minutes, or until softened. Drain well and let cool.

2 Place the soaked wheat, beef, onion, if using, ketchup, brown sauce, and parsley together in a large bowl and mix well until all the ingredients are well combined. Add a little beaten egg if necessary to bind the mixture together.

3 Using your hands, shape the meat mixture into 18 even-size balls. Cover and let chill in the refrigerator for 30 minutes.

4 Thread the meatballs onto 8 presoaked wooden skewers, alternating them with the tomatoes and mushrooms.

5 Brush the brochettes with a little oil and cook over hot coals, turning occasionally and brushing with a little more oil if the meat begins to dry out, for 10 minutes, or until cooked through.

6 Transfer to warmed serving plates and serve with vegetables.

ground lamb with peas

serves four

6 tbsp corn oil

1 onion, sliced

2 fresh red chilies, chopped

1 bunch of cilantro, chopped

2 tomatoes, chopped

1 tsp salt

1 tsp finely chopped fresh
   gingerroot

1 garlic clove, crushed

1 tsp chili powder

1 lb/450 g ground lean lamb

scant 1 cup peas

2 fresh green chilies, to garnish

COOK'S TIP

The flavor of garlic varies
in strength depending on how
it is prepared. For instance,
a whole garlic clove added
to a dish will give it the
flavor but not the pungency
of garlic; a halved clove will
add a little "bite"; a finely
chopped garlic clove will
release most of its flavor;
and a crushed clove will
release all of the flavor.

1 Heat the oil in a medium-size pan. Add the onion slices and cook until golden brown, stirring.

2 Add the red chilies, half the chopped cilantro, and the tomatoes to the pan, then reduce the heat to a simmer.

3 Add the salt, ginger, garlic, and chili powder to the mixture in the pan and stir well.

4 Add the ground lamb to the pan and stir-fry the mixture for 7–10 minutes.

5 Add the peas to the mixture in the pan and cook for an additional 3–4 minutes, stirring occasionally.

6 Transfer to serving plates and garnish with green chilies and the remaining cilantro.

NUTRITION	
Calories 357	Sugars 3g
Protein 25g	Fat 26g
Carbohydrate 6g	Saturates 6g

moroccan lamb kabobs

serves four

1 lb/450 g lean lamb

1 lemon

1 red onion

4 small zucchini

couscous, to serve (see Cook's Tip)

MARINADE

grated rind and juice of 1 lemon

2 tbsp olive oil

1 garlic clove, crushed

1 fresh red chili, sliced (optional)

1 tsp ground cinnamon

1 tsp ground ginger

½ tsp ground cumin

½ tsp ground coriander

COOK'S TIP

Serve these kabobs with couscous. Allowing ⅓ cup couscous per person, soak the couscous in cold water for 20 minutes, or until softened. Drain and steam for 10 minutes, or until piping hot.

1 Cut the lamb into even, bite-size chunks and place in a large nonmetallic dish.

2 To make the marinade, mix the lemon rind and juice, oil, garlic, chili, if using, cinnamon, ginger, cumin, and coriander together.

3 Pour the marinade over the lamb and toss to coat. Cover and let marinate in the refrigerator for at least 2 hours, or preferably overnight.

4 Preheat the grill. Cut the lemon into 8 pieces. Cut the onion into wedges, then separate each wedge into 2 pieces.

5 Using a canelle knife or potato peeler, cut thin strips of peel from the zucchini, then cut the zucchini into even-size chunks.

NUTRITION	
Calories 348	Sugars 2g
Protein 30g	Fat 24g
Carbohydrate 2g	Saturates 10g

6 Remove the meat from the marinade, reserving the liquid for basting. Thread the meat onto metal skewers, alternating with the onion, lemon, and zucchini.

7 Cook over hot coals for 8–10 minutes, turning and basting with the marinade. Serve on a bed of couscous (see Cook's Tip).

lamb with bay & lemon

serves four

4 lamb chops

1 tbsp corn oil

1 tbsp butter

⅔ cup white wine

⅔ cup lamb or vegetable stock

2 bay leaves

pared rind of 1 lemon

salt and pepper

NUTRITION

Calories 268	Sugars 0.2g
Protein 24g	Fat 16g
Carbohydrate 0.2g	Saturates 7g

COOK'S TIP

Your local butcher will offer you good advice on how to prepare the lamb noisettes, if you are wary of preparing them yourself.

1 Using a sharp knife, carefully remove the bone from each lamb chop, keeping the meat intact. Alternatively, ask the butcher to prepare the lamb noisettes for you.

2 Shape the meat into rounds and secure with a length of string.

3 Heat the oil and butter together in a large skillet until the mixture begins to froth.

4 Add the lamb noisettes to the skillet and cook for 2–3 minutes on each side, or until browned all over.

5 Remove the pan from the heat. Remove the meat, then drain off all of the excess fat and discard. Place the noisettes back in the pan.

6 Return the pan to the heat. Add the wine, stock, bay leaves, and lemon rind and cook for 20–25 minutes, or until the lamb is tender. Season the lamb and sauce to taste with a little salt and pepper.

7 Transfer to serving plates. Remove the string from each noisette and serve with the sauce.

114

red wine lamb skewers

serves four

1 lb/450 g lean lamb

12 pearl onions or shallots, unpeeled

12 white mushrooms

MARINADE

⅔ cup red wine

4 tbsp olive oil

2 tbsp brandy (optional)

1 onion, sliced

1 bay leaf

fresh thyme sprig

2 fresh parsley sprigs

TO SERVE

salad greens

cherry tomatoes

1 Carefully trim away any excess fat from the lamb. Cut the lamb into large pieces.

2 To make the marinade, mix the wine, oil, brandy, if using, onion, bay leaf, thyme, and parsley together in a nonmetallic dish.

NUTRITION

Calories 353	Sugars 5g
Protein 24g	Fat 21g
Carbohydrate 7g	Saturates 6g

3 Add the meat and toss to coat. Cover and let marinate in the refrigerator for at least 2 hours, or preferably overnight.

4 Preheat the grill. Bring a pan of water to a rolling boil, then drop in the pearl onions and blanch them for 3 minutes. Drain and refresh under cold water, and then drain again. Trim the onions and remove their skins.

5 Remove the meat from the marinade, reserving the liquid for basting. Thread the meat onto metal skewers, alternating with the pearl onions and mushrooms.

6 Cook the kabobs over hot coals for 8–10 minutes, turning and basting the meat and vegetables with the reserved marinade a few times.

7 Transfer the kabobs to warmed serving plates and serve with salad greens and cherry tomatoes.

lamb chops with rosemary

serves four

8 lamb chops

5 tbsp olive oil

2 tbsp lemon juice

1 garlic clove, crushed

⅓ tsp lemon pepper

salt

8 fresh rosemary sprigs

SALAD

4 tomatoes, sliced

4 scallions, diagonally sliced

DRESSING

2 tbsp olive oil

1 tbsp lemon juice

1 garlic clove, chopped

¼ tsp finely chopped fresh
   rosemary

NNUTRITION

Calories 560	Sugars 1g
Protein 48g	Fat 40g
Carbohydrate 1g	Saturates 13g

1 Preheat the grill. Trim the lamb by cutting away the flesh to expose the tips of the bones.

2 Place the oil, lemon juice, garlic, lemon pepper, and salt in a shallow nonmetallic dish and whisk with a fork to combine.

3 Lay the rosemary in the dish and place the lamb on top. Cover and let marinate in the refrigerator for at least 1 hour, turning once.

4 Remove the chops from the marinade and wrap foil around the exposed bones to stop them from burning.

5 Place the rosemary sprigs on the rack and place the lamb on top. Cook over hot coals for 10–15 minutes, turning once.

6 Meanwhile, make the salad and dressing. Arrange the tomatoes on a serving dish and sprinkle the scallions on top. Place all the ingredients for the dressing in a screw-top jar, then shake well and pour over the salad. Serve with the grilled lamb chops.

lamb with olives

serves four

2 lb 12 oz/1.25 kg boned leg
   of lamb

6 tbsp olive oil

2 garlic cloves, crushed

1 onion, sliced

1 small fresh red chili, seeded and
   finely chopped

¾ cup dry white wine

1 cup pitted black olives

salt

1 fresh flatleaf parsley sprig,
   to garnish

NUTRITION

Calories 577	Sugars 1g
Protein 62g	Fat 33g
Carbohydrate 1g	Saturates 10g

1 Preheat the oven to 350°F/180°C. Cut the lamb into 1-inch/2.5-cm cubes with a sharp knife.

2 Heat the oil in a skillet over medium heat. Add the garlic, onion, and chili and cook for 5 minutes.

3 Add the meat and wine and cook for an additional 5 minutes.

4 Stir in the olives, then transfer the mixture to a casserole. Cook in the preheated oven for 1 hour 20 minutes, or until the meat is tender. Season to taste with salt. Transfer to a serving plate, then garnish with a parsley sprig and serve.

lamb & anchovies with thyme

serves four

1 tbsp corn oil

1 tbsp butter

1 lb 5 oz/600 g boneless lamb
  (shoulder or leg), cut into 1-inch/
  2.5-cm chunks

4 garlic cloves, peeled

3 fresh thyme sprigs, stems removed

6 canned anchovy fillets, drained

⅔ cup red wine

⅓ cup lamb or vegetable stock

1 tsp sugar

scant ⅓ cup black olives, pitted
  and halved

2 tbsp chopped fresh parsley,
  to garnish

NUTRITION

Calories 577	Sugars 1g
Protein 62g	Fat 33g
Carbohydrate 1g	Saturates 10g

COOK'S TIP

This dish is excellent served with
Charbroiled Vegetables
(see page 193).

1 Heat the oil and butter in a large skillet. Add the lamb and cook for 4–5 minutes, stirring, until the meat is browned all over.

2 Using a pestle and mortar, grind the garlic, thyme, and anchovies together to make a smooth paste.

3 Add the wine and stock to the skillet. Stir in the garlic and anchovy paste together with the sugar.

4 Bring the mixture to a boil, then reduce the heat and let simmer, covered, for 30–40 minutes, or until the lamb is tender. For the last 10 minutes of the cooking time, remove the lid in order to let the sauce reduce slightly.

5 Stir the olives into the sauce and mix to combine.

6 Transfer the lamb and its sauce to a serving bowl and garnish with chopped parsley. Serve.

pork stir-fry with vegetables

serves four

2 tbsp vegetable oil

2 garlic cloves, crushed

½-inch/1-cm piece fresh gingerroot,
   cut into slivers

12 oz/350 g lean pork tenderloin,
   thinly sliced

1 carrot, cut into thin strips

1 red bell pepper, seeded and diced

1 fennel bulb, sliced

1 oz/25 g canned water chestnuts,
   drained and halved

1½ cups fresh bean sprouts

2 tbsp rice wine

1¼ cups pork or chicken stock

pinch of brown sugar

1 tsp cornstarch

2 tsp water

1 Heat the oil in a preheated wok. Add the garlic, ginger, and pork. Stir-fry for 1–2 minutes, or until the meat is sealed.

2 Add the carrot, bell pepper, fennel, and water chestnuts and stir-fry for 2–3 minutes.

NUTRITION

Calories 216	Sugars 3g
Protein 19g	Fat 12g
Carbohydrate 5g	Saturates 3g

3 Add the bean sprouts and stir-fry for 1 minute. Remove the pork and vegetables and keep warm.

4 Add the rice wine, stock, and sugar to the wok. Blend the cornstarch to a smooth paste with the water and stir it into the sauce. Bring to a boil, stirring constantly, and cook until thickened and clear.

5 Return the meat and vegetables to the wok and cook for 1–2 minutes, or until heated through and coated with the sauce. Serve immediately.

VARIATION

Use dry sherry instead of the rice wine if you have difficulty obtaining it.

---

baked ham with sauce

serves four–six

4 lb 8 oz–6 lb 8 oz/2–3 kg whole
   boneless cured ham

2 bay leaves

1–2 onions, cut into fourths

2 carrots, thickly sliced

6 cloves

GLAZE

1 tbsp red currant jelly

1 tbsp whole-grain mustard

CUMBERLAND SAUCE

1 orange

3 tbsp red currant jelly

2 tbsp lemon or lime juice

2 tbsp orange juice

2–4 tbsp port

1 tbsp whole-grain mustard

TO GARNISH

salad greens

orange slices

NUTRITION

Calories 414	Sugars 4g
Protein 70g	Fat 13g
Carbohydrate 4g	Saturates 5g

1 Place the ham in a large pan. Add the bay leaves, onions, carrots, and cloves and cover with cold water. Bring to a boil over low heat, then cover and simmer for half the cooking time. To calculate the cooking time, allow 30 minutes per 1 lb 2 oz/500 g plus 30 minutes.

2 Preheat the oven to 350°F/180°C. Drain the meat and remove the skin. Place the meat in a roasting pan and score the fat. To make the glaze, combine the ingredients and spread over the fat. Cook in the oven for the remainder of the cooking time. Baste at least once.

3 To make the sauce, pare the rind from half the orange and cut into strips. Cook in boiling water for 3 minutes. Drain.

4 Place all the remaining sauce ingredients in a small pan and heat gently, stirring occasionally, until the red currant jelly dissolves. Add the orange rind strips and simmer gently for an additional 3–4 minutes.

5 Slice the ham and place on a warmed serving platter. Garnish with salad greens and orange slices and serve with the Cumberland sauce.

121

griddled pork with orange sauce

serves four

4 tbsp freshly squeezed orange juice

4 tbsp red wine vinegar

2 garlic cloves, finely chopped

pepper

4 pork steaks, trimmed of all
    visible fat

olive oil, for brushing

GREMOLATA

3 tbsp finely chopped fresh parsley

grated rind of 1 lime

grated rind of ½ lemon

1 garlic clove, very finely chopped

NUTRITION

Calories 204	Sugars 1g
Protein 26g	Fat 10g
Carbohydrate 2g	Saturates 3g

1 Mix the orange juice, vinegar, and garlic together in a shallow, nonmetallic dish and season to taste with pepper. Add the pork, turning to coat. Cover and let marinate in the refrigerator for up to 3 hours.

2 Meanwhile, mix all the Gremolata ingredients together in a small mixing bowl, then cover with plastic wrap and let chill in the refrigerator until required.

3 Heat a nonstick grill pan and brush lightly with olive oil. Remove the pork from the marinade, reserving the marinade, and add to the pan. Cook over medium–high heat for 5 minutes on each side, or until the juices run clear when the meat is pierced with the tip of a sharp knife.

4 Meanwhile, pour the marinade into a small pan and let simmer over medium heat for 5 minutes, or until slightly thickened. Transfer the pork to a serving dish, then pour the orange sauce over it and sprinkle with the Gremolata. Serve immediately.

> **VARIATION**
> This dish would work equally well with chicken breast portions. Remove the skin from the cooked chicken before serving.

stuffed pork with prosciutto

serves four

1 lb 2 oz/500 g piece pork
    tenderloin, trimmed of excess fat
salt and pepper
small bunch of fresh basil
    leaves, washed
2 tbsp freshly grated Parmesan
    cheese
2 tbsp sun-dried tomato paste
6 thin slices prosciutto
1 tbsp olive oil
salad greens, to serve
OLIVE PASTE
⅓ cup pitted black olives
2 garlic cloves, peeled
4 tbsp olive oil

COOK'S TIP

Choose a good lean piece of pork
tenderloin for the best results.

NUTRITION

Calories 427	Sugars 0g
Protein 31g	Fat 34g
Carbohydrate 0.2g	Saturates 7g

1 Preheat the oven to 375°F/190°C. Slice the pork lengthwise down the center, taking care not to cut all the way through. Open out the pork and season the inside with salt and pepper.

2 Lay the basil leaves down the center of the pork. Mix the cheese and sun-dried tomato paste together and spread over the basil.

3 Press the pork back together. Wrap the prosciutto around the pork, overlapping, to cover. Place on a rack in a roasting pan, seam-side down, and brush with oil. Bake in the preheated oven for 30–40 minutes, depending on thickness, until cooked through. Let stand for 10 minutes.

4 To make the olive paste, place all the ingredients in a food processor and process until smooth. Alternatively, for a coarser paste, finely chop the olives and garlic and mix with the oil.

5 Drain the cooked pork and slice. Serve with the olive paste and salad greens.

pork & sage kabobs

serves twelve

1 lb/450 g ground lean pork

2 tbsp fresh bread crumbs

1 small onion, very finely chopped

1 tbsp chopped fresh sage

2 tbsp applesauce

¼ tsp ground nutmeg

salt and pepper

BASTE

3 tbsp olive oil

1 tbsp lemon juice

TO SERVE

6 tbsp thick plain yogurt

mixed salad greens

NUTRITION

Calories 96	Sugars 0g
Protein 8g	Fat 7g
Carbohydrate 2g	Saturates 2g

1 Place the ground pork in a large bowl. Add the bread crumbs, onion, sage, applesauce, and nutmeg, then season to taste with salt and pepper, and mix until well combined.

2 Using your hands, shape the mixture into balls, about the size of large marbles. Cover and let chill in the refrigerator for at least 30 minutes.

3 Preheat the grill. Soak 12 small wooden skewers in cold water for 30 minutes. Thread the meatballs onto the skewers.

4 To make the baste, mix the oil and lemon juice in a small bowl, whisking with a fork until blended.

5 Cook the kabobs over hot coals, turning and basting, for 8–10 minutes, or until the meat is cooked through.

6 Spoon some of the yogurt over the salad greens. Serve immediately with the grilled pork kabobs.

carnitas

serves four–six

2 lb 4 oz/1 kg pork, such as
   lean belly

1 onion, chopped

1 garlic bulb, cut in half

½ tsp ground cumin

2 meat stock cubes

2 bay leaves

salt and pepper

fresh chili strips, to garnish

salsa of your choice,
   to serve

NUTRITION

Calories 236	Sugars 1g
Protein 36g	Fat 9g
Carbohydrate 3g	Saturates 3g

1 Place the pork in a heavy-bottom skillet with the onion, garlic, cumin, stock cubes, and bay leaves. Add just enough water to cover. Bring to a boil, then reduce the heat to very low. Skim off the foam and scum that forms on the surface.

2 Simmer very gently for 2 hours, or until the meat is cooked through and tender. Remove the skillet from the heat and let the meat cool in the cooking liquid.

3 Remove the meat from the skillet with a slotted spoon. Cut off any rind (roast separately to make cracklings). Cut the meat into bite-size pieces and season to taste with salt and pepper. Reserve 1¼ cups of the cooking liquid.

4 Brown the meat in a heavy-bottom skillet for 15 minutes to cook out the fat. Add the reserved cooking liquid and reduce. Cover and cook for an additional 15 minutes, turning the meat occasionally.

5 Transfer the meat to a serving dish and garnish with chili strips. Serve with salsa.

pork with daikon

serves four

4 tbsp vegetable oil

1 lb/450 g lean pork tenderloin

1 eggplant

8 oz/225 g daikon

2 garlic cloves, crushed

3 tbsp light soy sauce

2 tbsp sweet chili sauce

NUTRITION

Calories 280	Sugars 1g
Protein 25g	Fat 19g
Carbohydrate 2g	Saturates 4g

COOK'S TIP

Daikon are long white vegetables common in Chinese cooking. Usually grated, they have a milder flavor than red radish. They are generally available in most large supermarkets.

1 Heat 2 tablespoons of the oil in a preheated wok or large heavy-bottom skillet.

2 Using a sharp knife, thinly slice the pork into even-size pieces.

3 Add the slices of pork to the wok and stir-fry for 5 minutes.

4 Using a sharp knife, trim and dice the eggplant. Peel and thinly slice the daikon.

5 Add the remaining vegetable oil to the wok.

6 Add the diced eggplant to the wok together with the garlic and stir-fry for 5 minutes.

7 Add the daikon to the wok and stir-fry for 2 minutes.

8 Stir the soy sauce and sweet chili sauce into the mixture in the wok and cook until heated through.

9 Transfer the pork to serving bowls and serve immediately.

ham steaks with apple rings

serves four

4 ham steaks, about 6 oz/
   175 g each
1–2 tsp whole-grain mustard
1 tbsp clear honey
2 tbsp lemon juice
1 tbsp corn oil
APPLE RINGS
2 green dessert apples
2 tsp raw brown sugar
¼ tsp ground nutmeg
¼ tsp ground cinnamon
¼ tsp ground allspice
1–2 tbsp melted butter

NUTRITION

Calories 358	Sugars 13g
Protein 31g	Fat 21g
Carbohydrate 13g	Saturates 8g

1 Preheat the grill. Using a pair of scissors, make a few cuts around the edges of the ham steaks to prevent them curling up as they cook. Spread a little whole-grain mustard over the steaks.

2 Mix the honey, lemon juice, and oil together in a bowl.

3 To prepare the apple rings, core the apples and cut them into thick slices. Mix the sugar with the spices and press the apple slices in the mixture until well coated on both sides.

4 Cook the ham steaks over hot coals for 3–4 minutes on each side, basting frequently with the honey and lemon mixture.

COOK'S TIP

Ham can be a little salty. If you have time, soak the steaks in cold water for 30–60 minutes before cooking—this process will remove the excess salt.

5 Meanwhile, brush the apple slices with melted butter and cook them over the hot coals, alongside the ham steaks, for 3–4 minutes, turning once and brushing with melted butter as they cook.

6 Serve the ham steaks with the cooked apple slices.

thai stir-fried chicken

serves four

3 tbsp sesame oil

12 oz/350 g skinless, boneless
   chicken breast, thinly sliced

salt and pepper

8 shallots, sliced

2 garlic cloves, finely chopped

2 tsp grated fresh gingerroot

1 fresh green chili, seeded and
   finely chopped

1 red bell pepper, seeded and
   thinly sliced

1 green bell pepper, seeded and
   thinly sliced

3 zucchini, thinly sliced

2 tbsp ground almonds

1 tsp ground cinnamon

1 tbsp oyster sauce

¾ oz/20 g creamed coconut, grated

1 Heat the oil in a preheated wok or heavy-bottom skillet. Add the chicken and season to taste with salt and pepper, then stir-fry over medium heat for 4 minutes.

2 Add the shallots, garlic, ginger, and chili and stir-fry for an additional 2 minutes.

NUTRITION

Calories 184	Sugars 6g
Protein 24g	Fat 5g
Carbohydrate 8g	Saturates 2g

3 Add the red and green bell peppers and zucchini and stir-fry for 1 minute.

4 Stir in the almonds, cinnamon, oyster sauce, and creamed coconut and season to taste with salt and pepper. Stir-fry for 1 minute to heat through, then serve immediately.

COOK'S TIP
Creamed coconut is sold in supermarkets and Asian stores. It is a useful pantry standby because it adds richness and depth of flavor.

sweet mango chicken

serves four

1 tbsp corn oil

6 skinless, boneless chicken thighs

1 ripe mango

2 garlic cloves, crushed

8 oz/225 g leeks, shredded

1¼ cups bean sprouts

⅓ cup mango juice

1 tbsp white wine vinegar

2 tbsp clear honey

2 tbsp tomato ketchup

1 tsp cornstarch

NUTRITION

Calories 244		Sugars 18g
Protein 27g		Fat 7g
Carbohydrate 2.1g		Saturates 2g

COOK'S TIP

Mango juice is available in jars from most supermarkets and is quite thick and sweet. If it is unavailable, purée and strain a ripe mango and add a little water to make up the required quantity.

1 Heat the oil in a preheated wok or large skillet.

2 Cut the chicken into bite-size cubes. Add to the wok and stir-fry over high heat for 10 minutes, tossing frequently until the chicken is cooked through and golden in color.

3 Peel, pit, and slice the mango and add to the wok with the garlic, leeks, and bean sprouts. Stir-fry for an additional 2–3 minutes, or until softened.

4 Mix the mango juice, vinegar, honey, ketchup, and cornstarch together. Pour into the wok and stir-fry for an additional 2 minutes, or until the juices begin to thicken.

5 Transfer to a warmed serving plate and serve immediately.

karahi chicken

serves four

2 tbsp ghee

3 garlic cloves, crushed

1 onion, finely chopped

2 tbsp garam masala

1 tsp coriander seeds, ground

½ tsp dried mint

1 bay leaf

1 lb 10 oz/750 g lean boneless
    chicken, diced

generous ¾ cup chicken stock

1 tbsp chopped cilantro

salt

mixed salad, to serve

NUTRITION	
Calories 270	Sugars 1g
Protein 41g	Fat 11g
Carbohydrate 1g	Saturates 2g

1 Heat the ghee in a preheated karahi, wok, or large heavy-bottom skillet. Add the garlic and onion and stir-fry for 4 minutes, or until the onion is golden.

2 Stir in the garam masala, coriander, mint, and bay leaf.

3 Add the diced chicken and cook over high heat, stirring occasionally, for 5 minutes. Add the stock, then reduce the heat and simmer for 10 minutes, or until the sauce has thickened and the chicken is thoroughly cooked and tender.

4 Stir in the cilantro and season to taste with salt, then mix well. Serve immediately with a mixed salad.

COOK'S TIP

It is important always to heat a karahi or wok before you add the oil to help maintain the high temperature.

minty lime chicken

serves six

3 tbsp finely chopped fresh mint

4 tbsp clear honey

4 tbsp lime juice

12 boneless chicken thighs

SAUCE

⅔ cup thick plain yogurt

1 tbsp finely chopped fresh mint

2 tsp finely grated lime rind

mixed salad, to serve

COOK'S TIP

Mint can be grown very easily in a garden or window box. It is a useful herb for marinades and salad dressings. Other useful herbs to grow are parsley and basil.

1 Mix the mint, honey, and lime juice together in a bowl.

2 Use wooden toothpicks to keep the chicken thighs in neat shapes and place in a large nonmetallic bowl. Add the marinade to the chicken and turn to coat evenly.

VARIATION

Use this marinade for chicken kabobs, alternating the chicken with lime and red onion wedges.

3 Cover and let marinate in the refrigerator for at least 30 minutes, or preferably overnight. Preheat the grill or broiler to medium. Cook the chicken over the hot coals or under the hot broiler, turning frequently and basting with the marinade, until the chicken is tender and the juices run clear when a skewer or tip of a knife is inserted into the thickest part of the meat.

4 Meanwhile, mix all the ingredients for the sauce together in a bowl. Remove the toothpicks from the chicken and serve immediately with the sauce and a mixed salad.

NUTRITION	
Calories 170	Sugars 12g
Protein 23g	Fat 3g
Carbohydrate 12g	Saturates 1g

chicken & ginger stir-fry

serves four

3 tbsp corn oil

1 lb 9 oz/700 g lean skinless,
    boneless chicken breasts, cut into
    2-inch/5-cm strips

3 garlic cloves, crushed

1½-inch/4-cm piece fresh
    gingerroot, cut into strips

1 tsp pomegranate seeds,
    crushed

½ tsp ground turmeric

1 tsp garam masala

2 fresh green chilies, sliced

½ tsp salt

4 tbsp lemon juice

grated rind of 1 lemon

6 tbsp chopped cilantro

½ cup chicken stock

COOK'S TIP

Stir-frying is perfect for lowfat diets, because only a little oil is needed. Cooking the food over high heat ensures that food is sealed and cooked quickly to hold in the flavor.

1 Heat the oil in a preheated wok or large skillet. Add the chicken and stir-fry until golden brown all over. Remove from the wok and reserve.

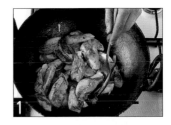

2 Add the garlic, ginger, and pomegranate seeds to the wok and cook in the oil for 1 minute, taking care not to let the garlic burn.

3 Stir in the turmeric, garam masala, and chilies and cook for 30 seconds.

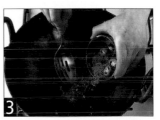

4 Return the chicken to the wok and add the salt, lemon juice and rind, cilantro, and stock. Stir the chicken well to make sure it is coated in the sauce.

5 Bring the mixture to a boil, then reduce the heat and simmer for 10–15 minutes, or until the chicken is cooked and tender. Serve.

NUTRITION	
Calories 291	Sugars 0g
Protein 41g	Fat 14g
Carbohydrate 0g	Saturates 3g

chicken in banana leaves

serves four–six

1 garlic clove, chopped

1 tsp finely chopped fresh
    gingerroot

¼ tsp pepper

2 cilantro sprigs

1 tbsp Thai fish sauce

1 tbsp whiskey

3 skinless, boneless chicken breasts

2–3 banana leaves, cut into 3-inch/
    7.5-cm squares

corn oil, for pan-frying

chili dipping sauce, to serve

NUTRITION

Calories 185	Sugars 0g
Protein 18g	Fat 12g
Carbohydrate 0.5g	Saturates 1g

1 Place the garlic, ginger, pepper, cilantro, fish sauce, and whiskey in a mortar and, using a pestle, grind to a smooth paste.

2 Cut the chicken into 1-inch/ 2.5-cm chunks and toss in the paste to coat. Cover and let marinate in the refrigerator for 1 hour.

3 Place a piece of chicken on a square of banana leaf and wrap it up like a package to enclose the chicken completely. Secure with wooden toothpicks or tie with string.

4 Heat a ⅛-inch/3–mm depth of oil in a large heavy-bottom skillet until hot.

5 Pan-fry the packages for 8–10 minutes, turning them over occasionally, until golden brown and the chicken is thoroughly cooked. Serve with a chili dipping sauce.

COOK'S TIP

To make a sweet chili dipping sauce to serve with the chicken pieces, mix together equal amounts of chili sauce and tomato ketchup, then stir in a dash of rice wine to taste.

green salsa chicken breasts

serves four

4 skinless chicken breast fillets

salt and pepper

all-purpose flour, for dusting

2–3 tbsp butter or a mixture of
butter and vegetable oil

2⅔ cups mild green salsa or
puréed tomatillos

1 cup chicken stock

1–2 garlic cloves, finely chopped

3–5 tbsp chopped cilantro

½ fresh green chili, seeded
and chopped

½ tsp ground cumin

TO SERVE

1 cup sour cream

romaine lettuce leaves, shredded

3–5 scallions, thinly sliced

coarsely chopped cilantro

1 Sprinkle the chicken with salt and pepper to taste, then dredge in flour. Shake off the excess.

2 Melt the butter or heat the butter and oil mixture in a large heavy-bottom skillet. Add the chicken and cook over medium–high heat, turning once, until the fillets are golden all over but not quite cooked through—they will continue to cook slightly in the sauce. Remove from the pan and reserve.

NUTRITION

Calories 349	Sugars 7g
Protein 34g	Fat 20g
Carbohydrate 10g	Saturates 12g

3 Place the salsa, stock, garlic, cilantro, chili, and cumin in a pan and bring to a boil. Reduce the heat to a low simmer. Add the chicken breasts to the sauce, spooning the sauce over the chicken. Continue to cook until the chicken is cooked through and tender.

4 Remove the chicken from the pan and season to taste with salt and pepper. Serve immediately with the sour cream, shredded lettuce, sliced scallions, and chopped cilantro.

chicken with balsamic vinegar

serves four

4 boneless chicken thighs

2 garlic cloves, crushed

generous ¾ cup red wine

3 tbsp white wine vinegar

salt and pepper

1 tbsp corn oil

1 tbsp butter

4 shallots

3 tbsp balsamic vinegar

2 tbsp chopped fresh thyme

NUTRITION

Calories 148	Sugars 0.2g
Protein 11g	Fat 8g
Carbohydrate 0.2g	Saturates 3g

1 Using a sharp knife, make a few slashes in the skin of the chicken. Brush the chicken with the crushed garlic and place in a nonmetallic dish.

2 Pour the wine and wine vinegar over the chicken and season to taste with salt and pepper. Cover with plastic wrap and let marinate in the refrigerator overnight.

COOK'S TIP

To make the chicken pieces look a little neater, use wooden skewers to hold them together or secure them with a length of string.

3 Remove the chicken pieces with a slotted spoon, draining well, and reserve the marinade.

4 Heat the oil and butter in a skillet. Add the shallots and cook, stirring, for 2–3 minutes, or until they begin to soften.

5 Add the chicken pieces to the skillet and cook for 3–4 minutes, turning, until browned all over. Reduce the heat and add half the reserved marinade. Cover and cook for 15–20 minutes, adding more marinade when necessary.

6 Once the chicken is tender, add the balsamic vinegar and thyme and cook for an additional 4 minutes.

7 Transfer the chicken and marinade to serving plates and serve.

chicken in spicy yogurt

serves four

3 dried red chilies

2 tbsp coriander seeds

2 tsp ground turmeric

2 tsp garam masala

4 garlic cloves, crushed

½ onion, chopped

1-inch/2.5-cm piece fresh
    gingerroot, grated

2 tbsp lime juice

1 tsp salt

½ cup lowfat plain yogurt

1 tbsp corn oil

4 lb 8 oz/2 kg skinless chicken,
    cut into 6 pieces, or
    6 chicken portions

fresh mint sprigs, to garnish

TO SERVE

chopped tomatoes

diced cucumber

sliced red onion

raita

NUTRITION

Calories 74	Sugars 2g
Protein 9g	Fat 4g
Carbohydrate 2g	Saturates 1g

1 Grind the chilies, coriander seeds, turmeric, garam masala, garlic, onion, ginger, lime juice, and salt together in a mortar using a pestle.

2 Gently heat a skillet and add the spice mixture. Stir-fry for 2 minutes, or until fragrant, then turn into a shallow nonmetallic dish.

3 Add the yogurt and oil to the spice paste and mix well.

4 Make 3 slashes in the flesh of each piece of chicken. Add to the yogurt and spice mixture and coat the pieces in the marinade. Cover and chill in the refrigerator for at least 4 hours. Remove from the refrigerator and let stand, covered, at room temperature for 30 minutes before cooking.

5 Preheat the grill. Wrap the chicken pieces in foil, sealing well so the juices cannot escape.

6 Cook the chicken over very hot coals for 15 minutes, turning once. Remove the foil and cook for an additional 5 minutes.

7 Garnish the chicken with mint sprigs and serve with tomatoes, cucumber, onion, and raita.

jerk chicken

serves four

4 lean chicken portions

1 bunch of scallions

1–2 fresh habanero
   chilies, seeded

1 garlic clove

2-inch/5-cm piece fresh gingerroot,
   coarsely chopped

½ tsp dried thyme

½ tsp paprika

¼ tsp ground allspice

pinch of ground cinnamon

pinch of ground cloves

4 tbsp white wine vinegar

3 tbsp light soy sauce

pepper

1 Place the chicken portions in a shallow nonmetallic dish.

2 Place the scallions, chilies, garlic, ginger, thyme, paprika, allspice, cinnamon, cloves, vinegar, soy sauce, and pepper to taste in a food processor and process until smooth.

3 Pour the spicy mixture over the chicken. Turn the chicken portions over so that they are well coated in the marinade.

4 Transfer the chicken portions to the refrigerator and let marinate for up to 24 hours.

5 Preheat the grill. Remove the chicken from the marinade and cook over medium–hot coals for 30 minutes, turning the chicken over and basting occasionally with any remaining marinade, until the chicken is browned and cooked through.

6 Transfer the chicken portions to individual serving plates and serve immediately.

NUTRITION	
Calories 158	Sugars 0.4g
Protein 29g	Fat 4g
Carbohydrate 2g	Saturates 1g

lemongrass skewers

serves four

2 long or 4 short lemongrass stems

2 large skinless, boneless chicken
 breasts, coarsely chopped

1 small egg white

1 carrot, finely grated

1 small fresh red chili, seeded and
 chopped

2 tbsp chopped fresh garlic chives

2 tbsp chopped cilantro

salt and pepper

1 tbsp corn oil

TO GARNISH

cilantro sprigs

lime slices

NUTRITION

Calories 140	Sugars 2g
Protein 19g	Fat 7g
Carbohydrate 2g	Saturates 1g

COOK'S TIP

If you can't find lemongrass
stems, use wooden or bamboo
skewers instead and add
½ teaspoon ground lemongrass
with the other flavorings.

1 If the lemongrass stems are long,
cut them in half across the center
to make 4 short lengths. Cut each stalk
in half lengthwise, so you have
8 lemongrass stems altogether.

2 Place the chicken pieces in a food
processor with the egg white.
Process to a smooth paste, then add
the carrot, chili, garlic chives, cilantro,
and salt and pepper to taste. Process
for a few seconds to mix well.

3 Cover and let the mixture chill in
the refrigerator for 15 minutes.
Preheat the broiler to medium. Divide
the mixture into 8 equal-size
portions and use your hands to
shape the mixture around the
lemongrass "skewers."

4 Brush the skewers with oil and
cook under the hot broiler, turning
them occasionally, for 4–6 minutes, or
until golden brown and thoroughly
cooked. Alternatively, grill over
medium–hot coals.

5 Garnish with cilantro sprigs and
lime slices and serve hot.

citrus duckling skewers

serves twelve

3 skinless, boneless duckling breasts

1 small red onion, cut into wedges

1 small eggplant, cut into cubes

MARINADE

grated rind and juice of 1 lemon

grated rind and juice of 1 lime

grated rind and juice of 1 orange

1 garlic clove, crushed

1 tsp dried oregano

2 tbsp olive oil, plus extra for oiling

dash of Tabasco sauce

COOK'S TIP

For more zing, add 1 teaspoon of chili sauce to the marinade. The meat can be marinated for several hours, but it is best to marinate the vegetables separately for only 30 minutes.

1 Cut the duckling into bite-size pieces. Place in a nonmetallic bowl with the prepared vegetables.

2 To make the marinade, place the lemon, lime, and orange rinds and juices, garlic, oregano, oil, and Tabasco in a screw-top jar and shake until well combined. Pour the marinade over the duckling and vegetables and toss to coat. Cover and let marinate in the refrigerator for 30 minutes.

3 Preheat the grill. Remove the duck and vegetables from the marinade and thread them onto presoaked wooden skewers, reserving the marinade.

4 Cook the skewers on an oiled rack over medium–hot coals, turning and basting frequently with the reserved marinade, for 15–20 minutes, or until the meat is cooked through. Alternatively, cook under a preheated broiler. Serve immediately.

NUTRITION	
Calories 205	Sugars 5g
Protein 24g	Fat 10g
Carbohydrate 5g	Saturates 2g

duck with berry sauce

serves four

1 lb/450 g boneless duck breasts

2 tbsp raspberry vinegar

2 tbsp brandy

1 tbsp clear honey

salt and pepper

1 tsp corn oil, for brushing

SAUCE

generous 1½ cups raspberries,
    thawed if frozen

1¼ cups rosé wine

2 tsp cornstarch blended with
    4 tsp cold water

TO SERVE

2 kiwifruit, peeled and thinly sliced

assorted vegetables

1 Skin and trim the duck breasts to remove any excess fat. Using a sharp knife, score the flesh in diagonal lines. Pound with a meat mallet or rolling pin until ¾ inch/2 cm thick.

2 Place the duck breasts in a shallow nonmetallic dish. Mix the vinegar, brandy, and honey together in a small bowl and spoon it over the duck. Cover and let chill in the refrigerator for 1 hour.

3 Preheat the broiler. Drain the duck breasts, reserving the marinade, and place on the broiler rack. Season to taste with salt and pepper and brush with a little oil. Cook for 10 minutes under the hot broiler and turn over, then season and brush with oil again. Cook for an additional 8–10 minutes, or until the meat is cooked through.

4 Meanwhile, make the sauce. Reserve about ⅓ cup raspberries and place the rest in a pan. Add the reserved marinade and the wine. Bring to a boil, then reduce the heat and simmer for 5 minutes, or until slightly reduced. Strain the sauce into a bowl, pressing the raspberries with the back of a spoon. Return the liquid to the pan and add the cornstarch paste. Heat through, stirring, until thickened. Add the reserved raspberries and season to taste with salt and pepper.

5 Thinly slice the duck breasts and alternate with slices of kiwifruit. on warmed serving plates. Spoon over the sauce and serve with vegetables.

NUTRITION	
Calories 293	Sugars 10g
Protein 28g	Fat 8g
Carbohydrate 13g	Saturates 2g

turkey stuffed with cheese

serves four

4 turkey breast pieces, about
    8 oz/225 g each

salt and pepper

4 portions soft cheese, such as
    Bel Paese, ½ oz/15 g each

4 fresh sage leaves or
    ½ tsp dried sage

8 lean bacon slices

4 tbsp olive oil

2 tbsp lemon juice

TO SERVE

salad greens

cherry tomatoes

NUTRITION

Calories 518	Sugars 0g
Protein 66g	Fat 28g
Carbohydrate 0g	Saturates 9g

VARIATION

You can vary the cheese you use
to stuff the turkey—try grated
mozzarella or slices of Brie or
Camembert. Also try 1 teaspoon
of red currant jelly or cranberry
sauce in each slit instead
of the sage.

1 Preheat the grill. Carefully cut a slit into the side of each turkey breast. Open out each breast a little and season inside to taste with salt and pepper.

2 Place a portion of cheese in each slit. Tuck a sage leaf into each slit or sprinkle with a little dried sage.

3 Stretch each bacon slice with the back of a knife. Wrap 2 pieces around each turkey breast, covering the slit.

4 Mix the oil and lemon juice together in a small bowl.

5 Cook the turkey over medium–hot coals, basting frequently with the oil and lemon mixture, for 10 minutes on each side, or until cooked through and tender.

6 Transfer the turkey to warmed serving plates. Serve with salad greens and cherry tomatoes.

Fish & Seafood

This selection of recipes exploits the contrasting characteristics of different fish and shellfish to the full. Fish that come in handy single-portion size are cooked whole for maximum succulence as well as ease of preparation, either with sealed-in seasonings in foil packages, such as Lemon Herrings, or directly on the grill rack in the case of Mediterranean Sardines. The firm texture of tuna, swordfish, and halibut, on the other hand, makes them ideally suited to the speedy searing of steaks in a ridged grill pan. Shrimp are also given the fast-food treatment, either stir-fried in Garlic Shrimp or deep-fried after initial marinating for enhanced flavor in Spicy Salt & Pepper Shrimp.

Lively, exotic flavorings abound in this chapter, from Mussels with Lemongrass to Indonesian-Style Spicy Cod.

lemon herrings

serves four

4 herrings, cleaned and scaled

4 bay leaves

salt

1 lemon, sliced

4 tbsp unsalted butter

2 tbsp chopped fresh parsley

½ tsp lemon pepper

NUTRITION

Calories 355	Sugars 0g
Protein 19g	Fat 31g
Carbohydrate 0g	Saturates 13g

1 Preheat the grill. Season the prepared herrings inside and out to taste with salt.

2 Place a bay leaf inside the cavity of each fish.

3 Place 4 squares of foil on the counter and divide the lemon slices evenly between them. Place a fish on top of the lemon slices on each of the foil squares.

4 Beat the butter until softened in a bowl, then mix in the parsley and lemon pepper. Dot the flavored butter liberally all over the fish.

5 Wrap the fish tightly in the foil and cook over medium–hot coals for 15–20 minutes, or until the fish is cooked through—the flesh should be white in color and firm to the touch (unwrap the foil to check if the fish is cooked, then rewrap).

6 Transfer the wrapped fish packages to warmed serving plates.

7 Open the foil packages just before serving, but serve the fish in their cooking juices still in the packages.

blackened fish

serves four

4 white fish steaks

1 tbsp paprika

1 tsp dried thyme

1 tsp cayenne pepper

1 tsp black pepper

½ tsp white pepper

½ tsp salt

¼ tsp ground allspice

3½ tbsp unsalted butter

3 tbsp corn oil

mixed salad greens, to serve

NUTRITION	
Calories 331	Sugars 0g
Protein 37g	Fat 20g
Carbohydrate 0g	Saturates 8g

COOK'S TIP

A whole fish—red snapper, for example—rather than steaks is also delicious cooked this way. The spicy seasoning can also be used to coat chicken portions, if you prefer.

1 Preheat the grill. Rinse the fish under cold running water and pat dry with paper towels.

2 Mix the paprika, thyme, cayenne, black and white peppers, salt, and allspice together in a shallow dish.

3 Place the butter and oil in a small pan and heat over low heat, stirring occasionally, until the butter has melted.

4 Brush the butter mixture liberally all over the fish steaks on both sides.

5 Dip the fish into the spicy mix until well coated on both sides.

6 Cook the fish over hot coals for 10 minutes on each side, turning once. Continue to baste the fish with the remaining butter mixture during the cooking time. Transfer the fish to 4 large serving plates and serve with mixed salad greens.

butterfly shrimp

serves two–four

1 lb 2 oz/500 g or 16 raw jumbo
   shrimp, shelled and tails
   left intact
juice of 2 limes
1 tsp cardamom seeds
2 tsp cumin seeds, ground
2 tsp coriander seeds, ground
½ tsp ground cinnamon
1 tsp ground turmeric
1 garlic clove, crushed
1 tsp cayenne pepper
2 tbsp corn oil
cucumber slices, to garnish

NUTRITION

Calories 183	Sugars 0g
Protein 28g	Fat 8g
Carbohydrate 0g	Saturates 1g

1 Soak 8 wooden skewers in a bowl of water for 20 minutes. Cut the shells lengthwise in half down to the tail and flatten out to form a symmetrical shape.

2 Thread a shrimp onto 2 presoaked wooden skewers, with the tail between them, so that, when laid flat, the skewers hold the shrimp in shape. Thread another 3 shrimp onto these 2 skewers in the same way.

3 Repeat until you have 4 sets of 4 shrimp each.

4 Lay the skewered shrimp in a nonmetallic dish and sprinkle over the lime juice.

5 Mix the spices and oil together, then coat the shrimp well in the mixture. Cover the shrimp and let chill in the refrigerator for 4 hours.

6 Preheat the grill or broiler. Cook over hot coals or place in a broiler pan lined with foil and cook under the hot broiler for 6 minutes, turning once.

7 Serve immediately, garnished with cucumber slices.

mackerel with lime & cilantro

serves four

4 small mackerel, cleaned and scaled

¼ tsp ground coriander

¼ tsp ground cumin

salt and pepper

3 tbsp chopped cilantro

1 fresh red chili, seeded and
    chopped

grated rind and juice of 1 lime

2 tbsp corn oil

TO GARNISH

fresh red chili flowers
    (see Cook's Tip—optional)

1 lime, sliced

salad greens, to serve

NUTRITION

Calories 302	Sugars 0g
Protein 21g	Fat 24g
Carbohydrate 0g	Saturates 4g

1 Preheat the grill. Make the chili flowers for the garnish (see Cook's Tip). Remove the heads from the prepared mackerel. Sprinkle the mackerel with the spices and season to taste with salt and pepper. Sprinkle 1 teaspoon of the cilantro inside the cavity of each fish.

2 Mix the remaining cilantro, chili, lime rind and juice, and oil together in a small bowl. Brush the mixture liberally over the fish.

3 Cook the fish cook over hot coals for 3–4 minutes on each side, turning once. Brush frequently with the basting mixture. Transfer the fish to serving plates and garnish with chili flowers, if using, and lime slices. Serve with salad greens.

COOK'S TIP

To make the chili flowers, cut the tip of 8 small chilies lengthwise into thin strips, leaving the chilies intact at the stem end. Remove the seeds and place the chilies in ice water until curled.

marinated fish

serves four

4 whole mackerel

4 tbsp chopped fresh marjoram

2 tbsp extra virgin olive oil

finely grated rind and juice of 1 lime

2 garlic cloves, crushed

salt and pepper

lime wedges, to garnish

salad greens, to serve

NUTRITION	
Calories 361	Sugars 0g
Protein 26g	Fat 29g
Carbohydrate 0g	Saturates 5g

1 Using a sharp knife, clean and scale the fish (see page 156), then cut 4–5 diagonal slashes on each side of the fish. Place the fish in a shallow nonmetallic dish.

2 To make the marinade, mix the marjoram, oil, lime rind and juice, garlic, and salt and pepper to taste together in a bowl.

3 Pour the mixture over the fish. Cover and let marinate in the refrigerator for 30 minutes.

4 Preheat the broiler, then cook the mackerel under the hot broiler for 5–6 minutes on each side, brushing occasionally with the reserved marinade, until golden.

5 Transfer the fish to serving plates. Pour over any remaining marinade, then garnish with lime wedges and serve with salad greens.

mediterranean sardines

serves four

8–12 whole fresh sardines

8–12 fresh thyme sprigs

salt and pepper

3 tbsp lemon juice

4 tbsp olive oil

TO GARNISH

lemon wedges

tomato slices

mixed salad

NUTRITION

Calories 857	Sugars 0g
Protein 88g	Fat 56g
Carbohydrate 0g	Saturates 11g

VARIATION

For a slightly different flavor and texture, give the sardines a crispy coating by tossing them in dried bread crumbs and basting them with a little olive oil.

1 Preheat the grill. Clean the fish if this has not already been done.

2 Remove the scales from the sardines by rubbing the back of a knife from tail to head along the body. Wash the sardines and pat dry with paper towels.

3 Tuck a thyme sprig into the body cavity of each sardine.

4 Transfer the sardines to a large nonmetallic dish and season to taste with salt and pepper.

5 Beat the lemon juice and oil together in a bowl and pour the mixture over the sardines. Cover and let marinate in the refrigerator for 30 minutes.

6 Remove the sardines from the marinade and place them in a hinged basket, if you have one, or on a rack. Cook the sardines over hot coals for 3–4 minutes on each side, basting frequently with any remaining marinade.

7 Serve the cooked sardines garnished with lemon wedges, tomato slices, and a mixed salad.

tuna with anchovy butter

serves four

4 thick tuna steaks, about 8 oz/
   225 g each and ¾ inch/2 cm thick
olive oil, for oiling
ANCHOVY BUTTER
8 anchovy fillets in oil, drained
4 scallions, finely chopped
1 tbsp finely grated orange rind
1 stick unsalted butter
¼ tsp lemon juice
salt and pepper
TO GARNISH
fresh flatleaf parsley sprigs
orange rind strips

NUTRITION

Calories 564	Sugars 0g
Protein 55g	Fat 38g
Carbohydrate 0g	Saturates 19g

VARIATION

If you like your food particularly
hot and spicy, add a pinch of
dried chili flakes to the anchovy
butter mixture for a little
extra punch.

1 Preheat the grill. To make the anchovy butter, very finely chop the anchovies and place them in a bowl with the scallions, orange rind, and softened butter. Beat until all the ingredients are blended well together, seasoning to taste with lemon juice and pepper.

2 Place the flavored butter on a sheet of parchment paper and roll up into a log shape. Fold over the ends and place in the freezer for 15 minutes to become firm.

3 Cook the tuna steaks for 2 minutes on an oiled grill rack over hot coals. Alternatively, cook in an oiled, ridged grill pan over high heat, in batches if necessary. Turn the steaks over and cook for 2 minutes for rare or up to 4 minutes for well done. Season to taste with salt and pepper.

4 Transfer the tuna steaks to warmed serving plates and place 2 thin slices of anchovy butter on each steak. Garnish with parsley sprigs and strips of orange rind and serve.

skate with black butter

serves four

2 lb/900 g skate wings, cut into 4

1½ sticks butter

4 tbsp red wine vinegar

½ oz/15 g capers, drained

1 tbsp chopped fresh parsley

salt and pepper

COURT-BOUILLON

3½ cups cold water

3½ cups dry white wine

3 tbsp white wine vinegar

2 large carrots, coarsely chopped

1 onion, coarsely chopped

2 celery stalks, coarsely chopped

2 leeks, coarsely chopped

2 garlic cloves, coarsely chopped

2 bay leaves

4 fresh parsley sprigs

4 fresh thyme sprigs

6 black peppercorns

1 tsp salt

green vegetables, to serve

NUTRITION

Calories 381	Sugars 0g
Protein 34g	Fat 27g
Carbohydrate 0g	Saturates 17g

1 Begin by making the court-bouillon. Place all the ingredients in a large pan and bring slowly to a boil. Reduce the heat, then cover and simmer gently for 30 minutes. Strain the liquid through a fine strainer into a clean pan. Return to a boil, then simmer fast, uncovered, for 15–20 minutes, or until reduced to 2½ cups.

2 Place the skate in a wide shallow pan and pour the court-bouillon over it. Bring to a boil, then reduce the heat and simmer very gently for 15 minutes or a little longer depending on the thickness of the skate. Drain the fish and put to one side, keeping it warm.

3 Meanwhile, melt the butter in a skillet. Cook over medium heat until the butter changes color to a dark brown and smells very nutty.

4 Add the vinegar, capers, and parsley and simmer for 1 minute. Season to taste with salt and pepper. Pour over the fish. Serve with seasonal fresh green vegetables of your choice.

smoky fish skewers

serves four

12 oz/350 g smoked cod fillet

12 oz/350 g cod fillet

8 large raw shrimp

8 bay leaves

fresh dill sprigs, to garnish (optional)

MARINADE

4 tbsp corn oil, plus extra

   for oiling

2 tbsp lemon or lime juice

grated rind of ½ lemon or lime

¼ tsp dried dill

salt and pepper

NUTRITION

Calories 221	Sugars 0g
Protein 33g	Fat 10g
Carbohydrate 0g	Saturates 1g

1 Skin both types of cod and cut the flesh into bite-size pieces. Shell the shrimp, leaving the tails intact.

2 To make the marinade, mix the oil, lemon juice and rind, dried dill, and salt and pepper to taste together in a shallow nonmetallic dish.

3 Place the prepared fish in the marinade and stir well until the fish is coated on all sides. Cover and let marinate in the refrigerator for 30 minutes.

4 Preheat the grill. Thread the seafood onto 4 metal skewers, alternating the fish with the shrimp and bay leaves.

COOK'S TIP

Cod fillet can be rather flaky, so choose the thicker end, which is easier to cut into chunky pieces. Cook the fish on foil rather than directly on the rack, so that if the fish breaks away from the skewer it is not wasted.

5 Cover the grill rack with lightly oiled foil. Place the fish skewers on top and cook over hot coals for 5–10 minutes, basting with any remaining marinade. Turn once.

6 Transfer the skewers to a warmed serving plate and garnish with dill sprigs, if using, then serve.

stuffed angler fish tail

serves six

1 lb 10 oz/750 g angler fish tail, skinned and trimmed

6 slices prosciutto

4 tbsp chopped fresh mixed herbs, such as parsley, chives, basil, and sage

1 tsp finely grated lemon rind

salt and pepper

2 tbsp olive oil

shredded stir-fried vegetables, to serve

NUTRITION

Calories 154	Sugars 0g
Protein 24g	Fat 6g
Carbohydrate 0g	Saturates 1g

1 Preheat the oven to 400°F/200°C. Using a sharp knife, carefully cut down each side of the central bone of the angler fish to leave 2 fillets. Rinse the fillets under cold running water and pat dry with paper towels.

2 Lay the prosciutto slices widthwise on a counter so that they overlap slightly. Lay the fish fillets lengthwise on top of the ham so that the 2 cut sides face each other.

3 Mix the chopped herbs and lemon rind together. Season well with salt and pepper. Pack this mixture onto the cut surface of 1 angler fish fillet. Press the 2 fillets together and wrap tightly with the prosciutto slices. Secure with string or wooden toothpicks.

4 Heat the oil in a large skillet over low heat. Place the fish in the pan, seam-side down first, and brown the wrapped fish all over.

5 Transfer the fish to a large ovenproof dish and cook in the preheated oven for 25 minutes, or until golden and the fish is tender. Remove from the oven and let rest for 10 minutes before slicing thickly. Serve with shredded stir-fried vegetables.

165

szechuan white fish

serves four

1 small egg, beaten

3 tbsp all-purpose flour

4 tbsp dry white wine

3 tbsp light soy sauce

12 oz/350 g white fish fillets, cut
    into 1½-inch/4-cm cubes

vegetable oil, for frying

1 garlic clove, cut into slivers

1 tsp finely chopped fresh
    gingerroot

1 onion, finely chopped

1 celery stalk, chopped

1 fresh red chili, chopped

3 scallions, chopped

1 tsp rice wine vinegar

½ tsp ground Szechuan pepper

¾ cup fish stock

1 tsp superfine sugar

1 tsp cornstarch

2 tsp water

NUTRITION

Calories 225	Sugars 3g
Protein 20g	Fat 8g
Carbohydrate 17g	Saturates 1g

1 Beat the egg, flour, wine, and 1 tablespoon of the soy sauce together in a bowl to make a batter. Dip the fish into the batter to coat well.

2 Heat the oil in a preheated wok or large heavy-bottom skillet. Reduce the heat slightly, then add the fish in batches and cook for 2–3 minutes, or until golden brown. Remove the fish with a slotted spoon and drain on paper towels. Keep warm.

3 Pour all but 1 tablespoon of the oil from the wok and return it to the heat. Add the garlic, ginger, onion, celery, chili, and scallions and stir-fry for 1–2 minutes. Stir in the remaining soy sauce and the vinegar.

4 Add the Szechuan pepper, stock, and sugar to the wok. Mix the cornstarch with the water to form a smooth paste and stir it into the stock. Bring to a boil and cook, stirring, for 1 minute, or until the sauce thickens and clears.

5 Return the fish to the wok and cook for 1–2 minutes. Serve immediately.

thai-spiced salmon

serves four

1-inch/2.5-cm piece fresh
   gingerroot, grated

1 tsp coriander seeds,
   crushed

½ tsp chili powder

1 tbsp lime juice

1 tsp sesame oil

4 pieces salmon fillet with skin,
   about 5½ oz/150 g each

2 tbsp vegetable oil

stir-fried vegetables, to serve

NUTRITION	
Calories 329	Sugars 0.1g
Protein 30g	Fat 23g
Carbohydrate 0.1g	Saturates 4g

COOK'S TIP

Use a heavy-bottom skillet or
grill pan so that the fish cooks
evenly throughout without
sticking. If it is very thick, turn it
over carefully to cook on the
other side for 2–3 minutes.

1 Mix the ginger, crushed coriander, chili powder, lime juice, and sesame oil together.

2 Place the salmon on a wide nonmetallic plate or dish and spoon the mixture over the flesh side of the fillets, spreading it to coat each piece of salmon evenly.

3 Cover the dish and chill in the refrigerator for 30 minutes.

4 Heat a wide heavy-bottom skillet or grill pan with the vegetable oil over high heat. Place the salmon in the hot pan, skin-side down.

5 Cook the salmon for 4–5 minutes, without turning, until the salmon is crusty underneath and the flesh flakes easily. Serve immediately with stir-fried vegetables.

baked sea bass

serves four

2 sea bass, about 2 lb 4 oz/1 kg
each, cleaned and scaled

2 scallions, green part only,
cut into strips

2-inch/5-cm piece fresh gingerroot,
cut into strips

2 garlic cloves, unpeeled and
lightly crushed

2 tbsp mirin or dry sherry

salt and pepper

TO SERVE

pickled sushi ginger (optional)

soy sauce

NUTRITION

Calories 140	Sugars 0.1g
Protein 29g	Fat 1g
Carbohydrate 0.1g	Saturates 0.2g

1 Preheat the grill. For each fish, lay out a double thickness of foil and oil the top piece well or lay a piece of parchment paper over the foil.

2 Place the fish in the center of the foil and expose the cavities. Divide the scallions, ginger, and garlic between each cavity.

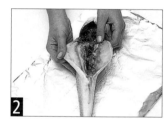

3 Pour the mirin over the fish and season to taste with salt and pepper.

4 Close the cavities and lay each fish on its side. Fold over the foil to encase the fish and seal the edges securely. Fold each end neatly.

5 Cook over medium–hot coals for 15 minutes, turning once.

6 To serve, remove the foil and cut each fish into 2–3 pieces. Serve with the pickled sushi ginger, if using, accompanied by soy sauce.

COOK'S TIP

Fresh sea bass is just as delicious when cooked very simply. Stuff the fish with garlic and chopped herbs and brush with olive oil, then bake in the oven.

salmon fillet with herbs

serves four

½ large bunch of dried thyme

5 fresh rosemary branches,
    6–8 inches/15–20 cm long

8 bay leaves

2 lb 4 oz/1 kg salmon fillet

1 fennel bulb, cut into 8 pieces

2 tbsp lemon juice

2 tbsp olive oil

fresh salad greens, to serve

NUTRITION

Calories 507	Sugars 0.4g
Protein 46g	Fat 35g
Carbohydrate 0.5g	Saturates 6g

1 Preheat the grill. Make a base on the hot grill with the thyme, rosemary, and bay leaves, overlapping them so that they cover a slightly larger area than the salmon.

2 Carefully place the salmon on top of the herbs.

VARIATION

Use whatever combination of herbs you may have to hand— but avoid the stronger tasting herbs, such as sage and marjoram, which are unsuitable for fish.

3 Arrange the fennel around the edge of the fish.

4 Mix the lemon juice and oil together, then brush the salmon with it. Cover the salmon loosely with a piece of foil, to keep it moist.

5 Cook over hot coals for 20–30 minutes, basting frequently with the lemon mixture.

6 Remove the cooked salmon from the grill and cut it into slices, then arrange the fennel around it. Serve with salad greens.

noisettes of salmon

COOK'S TIP

You can make cod steaks into noisettes in the same way. Cook them with butter flavored with fresh chives and basil.

1 Preheat the oven to 400°F/200°C. Carefully remove the central bone from the salmon steaks and cut them in half. Curl each piece around to form a noisette and tie with string. Blend the butter, garlic, mustard seeds, thyme, parsley, and salt and pepper to taste together in a bowl and reserve.

2 Heat the oil in a preheated ridged grill pan or large skillet over medium heat. Add the salmon noisettes and brown on both sides, in batches if necessary. Drain on paper towels and let cool.

3 Cut 4 pieces of parchment paper into 12-inch/30-cm squares. Place 2 salmon noisettes on top of each square and top with a little of the flavored butter and chopped tomato. Draw up the edges of the paper and fold together to enclose the fish. Place on a cookie sheet.

4 Cook in the preheated oven for 10–15 minutes, or until the salmon is cooked through. Serve while still warm with green vegetables or salad of your choice.

spicy salt & pepper shrimp

serves four

9 10½ oz/250–300 g raw shrimp
  in shells, thawed if frozen

1 tbsp light soy sauce

1 tsp rice wine or dry sherry

2 tsp cornstarch

vegetable oil, for deep-frying

2–3 scallions, to garnish

SPICY SALT & PEPPER

1 tbsp salt

1 tsp ground Szechuan peppercorns

1 tsp Chinese five-spice powder

NUTRITION

Calories 160	Sugars 0.2g
Protein 17g	Fat 10g
Carbohydrate 0.5g	Saturates 1g

1 Pull the soft legs off the shrimp, but keep the body shell on. Dry well on paper towels.

2 Place the shrimp in a bowl with the soy sauce, rice wine, and cornstarch. Turn the shrimp to coat thoroughly in the mixture, then cover and let marinate in the refrigerator for 25–30 minutes.

3 To make the Spicy Salt & Pepper, mix the salt, ground Szechuan peppercorns, and five-spice powder together in a bowl. Place in a dry skillet and stir-fry for 3–4 minutes over low heat, stirring constantly to prevent the spices burning on the bottom of the skillet. Remove from the heat and let cool.

4 Heat the oil in a preheated wok or large skillet until smoking. Add the shrimp, in batches, and deep-fry until golden brown. Remove the shrimp from the wok with a slotted spoon and drain on paper towels.

5 Place the scallions in a bowl, pour over 1 tablespoon of the hot oil, and let stand for 30 seconds. Serve the shrimp garnished with the scallions, with the Spicy Salt & Pepper as a dip.

173

fish with yucatan flavors

serves eight

4 tbsp annatto seeds, soaked in
    water overnight
3 garlic cloves, finely chopped
1 tbsp mild chili powder
1 tbsp paprika
1 tsp ground cumin
½ tsp dried oregano
2 tbsp beer or tequila
juice of 1 lime and 1 orange or
    3 tbsp pineapple juice
2 tbsp olive oil
2 tbsp chopped cilantro
¼ tsp ground cinnamon
¼ tsp ground cloves
2 lb 4 oz/1 kg swordfish steaks
banana leaves, for wrapping
    (optional)
cilantro sprigs, to garnish
orange wedges, to serve

NUTRITION	
Calories 179	Sugars 1g
Protein 24g	Fat 8g
Carbohydrate 1g	Saturates 2g

1 Drain the annatto, then crush them to a paste in a mortar using a pestle. Work in the garlic, chili powder, paprika, cumin, oregano, beer, fruit juice, oil, cilantro, cinnamon, and cloves.

2 Smear the paste over the fish, then cover and let marinate in the refrigerator for at least 3 hours or overnight.

3 Preheat the grill or broiler. Wrap the fish steaks in banana leaves, tying with string to make packages. Bring enough water to a boil in a steamer, then add a batch of packages to the top part of the steamer and steam for 15 minutes, or until the fish is cooked through.

4 Alternatively, cook the fish without wrapping in the banana leaves. To cook on the grill, place in a hinged basket or on a rack and cook over hot coals for 5–6 minutes on each side, or until cooked through. Alternatively, cook the fish under the hot broiler for 5–6 minutes on each side, or until cooked through.

5 Garnish with cilantro sprigs and serve with orange wedges for squeezing over the fish.

garlic shrimp

serves four

½ cup olive oil

4 garlic cloves, finely chopped

2 hot fresh red chilies, seeded and
  finely chopped

1 lb/450 g cooked jumbo shrimp

2 tbsp chopped fresh
  flatleaf parsley

salt and pepper

lemon wedges, to garnish

NUTRITION	
Calories 385	Sugars 0g
Protein 26g	Fat 31g
Carbohydrate 1g	Saturates 5g

COOK'S TIP

If you can get hold of raw
shrimp, cook them as above but
increase the cooking time to
5–6 minutes, or until the shrimp
are cooked through and turn
bright pink. If you are using
frozen shrimp, make sure they
are thoroughly thawed
before cooking.

1 Heat the oil in a large heavy-bottom skillet over low heat. Add the garlic and chilies and cook, stirring occasionally, for 1–2 minutes, or until softened but not colored.

2 Add the shrimp and stir-fry for 2–3 minutes, or until heated through and coated in the oil and garlic mixture.

3 Turn off the heat and add the chopped parsley, stirring well to mix. Season to taste with salt and pepper.

4 Divide the shrimp and garlic-flavored oil between warmed serving dishes. Garnish with lemon wedges and serve.

mussels with lemongrass

serves four

1 lb 10 oz/750 g live mussels

1 tbsp sesame oil

3 shallots, finely chopped

2 garlic cloves, finely chopped

1 lemongrass stem

2 fresh kaffir lime leaves

2 tbsp chopped cilantro

finely grated rind of 1 lime

2 tbsp lime juice

1¼ cups hot vegetable stock

cilantro, to garnish

NUTRITION

Calories 194	Sugars 0g
Protein 33g	Fat 7g
Carbohydrate 1g	Saturates 1g

COOK'S TIP

Mussels are now farmed, so they should be available throughout the year.

1 Clean the mussels thoroughly by scrubbing or scraping the shells and pulling out any beards that are attached to them. Discard any with broken shells or any that refuse to close when tapped.

2 Heat the oil in a large pan. Add the shallots and garlic and cook gently for 2 minutes, or until softened.

3 Bruise the lemongrass, using a meat mallet or rolling pin, and add to the pan with the lime leaves, cilantro, lime rind and juice, mussels, and stock. Cook, covered, over high heat for 3–4 minutes, shaking the pan occasionally, until the mussels have opened.

4 Lift the mussels out into 4 warmed soup plates, discarding any that remain closed. Boil the remaining liquid rapidly to reduce slightly. Remove and discard the lemongrass and lime leaves, then pour the liquid over the mussels. Garnish with cilantro and serve.

thai steamed mussels

serves two

2 lb 4 oz/1 kg live mussels

2 shallots, finely chopped

1 lemongrass stem, finely sliced

1 garlic clove, finely chopped

3 tbsp rice wine or dry sherry

2 tbsp lime juice

1 tbsp Thai fish sauce

4 tbsp chopped fresh basil

salt and pepper

2 tbsp butter

fresh basil leaves, to garnish

NUTRITION

Calories 252	Sugars 2g
Protein 22g	Fat 14g
Carbohydrate 8g	Saturates 8g

COOK'S TIP

If you prefer to serve this dish as an appetizer, this amount will be enough for 4 portions. Fresh clams in shells are also very good when cooked by this method.

1 Clean the mussels thoroughly by scrubbing or scraping the shells and pulling out any beards that are attached to them. Discard any with broken shells or any that refuse to close when tapped.

2 Place the shallots, lemongrass, garlic, rice wine, lime juice, and fish sauce in a large heavy-bottom pan and place over high heat.

3 Add the mussels, then cover and cook for 3–4 minutes, shaking the pan occasionally, until the mussels have opened.

4 Discard any mussels that remain closed, then stir in the chopped basil and season to taste with salt and pepper.

5 Scoop out the mussels with a slotted spoon and divide between 2 deep bowls. Quickly whisk the butter into the pan juices, then pour the juices over the mussels.

6 Garnish each bowl with basil leaves and serve.

red curry fish cakes

serves six

2 lb 4 oz/1 kg fish fillets or prepared
    seafood, such as cod, haddock,
    shrimp, crabmeat, or lobster

1 egg, beaten

2 tbsp chopped cilantro

6 tbsp Thai red curry paste

1 bunch of scallions,
    finely chopped

vegetable oil, for deep-frying

fresh red chili flowers, to garnish
    (see page 158)

CUCUMBER SALAD

1 large cucumber, peeled
    and grated

2 shallots, grated

2 fresh red chilies, seeded and very
    finely chopped

2 tbsp Thai fish sauce

2 tbsp dried powdered shrimp

1½–2 tbsp lime juice

NUTRITION

Calories 203	Sugars 1g
Protein 32g	Fat 8g
Carbohydrate 1g	Saturates 1g

1 Place the fish in a food processor with the egg, cilantro, and curry paste and process until smooth and well blended.

2 Transfer the mixture to a bowl, then add the scallions and mix well to combine.

3 Taking 2 tablespoons of the fish mixture at a time, shape into balls, then flatten them slightly with your fingers to make fish cakes.

4 Heat the oil in a preheated wok or skillet until hot.

5 Add a few fish cakes to the wok and deep fry for a few minutes until brown and cooked. Remove and drain on paper towels. Keep warm while cooking the remaining fish cakes.

6 To make the salad, mix the cucumber, shallots, chilies, fish sauce, dried shrimp, and lime juice together. Garnish the salad with a chili flower and serve with the fish cakes.

gingered angler fish

serves four

1 lb/450 g angler fish

1 tbsp grated fresh gingerroot

2 tbsp sweet chili sauce

1 tbsp corn oil

3½ oz/100 g fine asparagus

3 scallions, diagonally sliced

1 tsp sesame oil

NUTRITION

Calories 133	Sugars 0g
Protein 21g	Fat 5g
Carbohydrate 1g	Saturates 1g

1 Cut the angler fish into bite-size pieces. Mix the ginger and sweet chili sauce together in a small bowl until thoroughly blended. Brush the ginger and chili sauce mixture over the fish pieces using a pastry brush.

2 Heat the corn oil in a preheated wok or large heavy-bottom skillet.

3 Add the fish, asparagus, and scallions to the wok and stir-fry for 5 minutes, stirring gently so the fish and asparagus do not break up.

4 Remove the wok from the heat. Drizzle the sesame oil over the stir-fry and toss well to combine.

5 Transfer the fish mixture to warmed serving plates and serve immediately.

COOK'S TIP

Angler fish is quite expensive, but it is well worth using, because it has a wonderful flavor and texture. You could use cubes of chunky cod fillet instead.

swordfish steaks

serves four

4 swordfish steaks, about
 5½ oz/150 g each

4 tbsp olive oil

1 garlic clove, crushed

1 tsp lemon rind

parsley sprigs, to garnish

SALSA VERDE

scant ½ cup fresh flatleaf parsley

¼ cup mixed fresh herbs, such as
 basil, mint, and chives

1 garlic clove, chopped

1 tbsp capers, drained and rinsed

1 tbsp green peppercorns in
 brine, drained

4 canned anchovy fillets in oil,
 drained and coarsely chopped

1 tsp Dijon mustard

½ cup extra virgin olive oil

salt and pepper

NUTRITION

Calories 548	Sugars 0g
Protein 28g	Fat 48g
Carbohydrate 1g	Saturates 7g

1 Rinse the swordfish steaks under cold running water and pat dry with paper towels. Arrange the steaks in a nonmetallic dish. Mix the oil, garlic, and lemon rind together in a small bowl and pour over the swordfish steaks. Cover and let marinate in the refrigerator for 1 hour.

2 To make the Salsa Verde, place the parsley, mixed herbs, garlic, capers, green peppercorns, anchovies, mustard, and oil in a food processor and process to a smooth paste, adding a little warm water if necessary. Season to taste with salt and pepper and reserve.

3 Remove the swordfish steaks from the marinade. Transfer to a preheated ridged grill pan and cook for 2–3 minutes on each side, or until tender. Transfer the fish to 4 large serving plates and garnish with parsley sprigs, then serve immediately with the Salsa Verde.

COOK'S TIP

Firm-fleshed fish is ideal for this recipe. Try tuna or shark instead.

indonesian-style spicy cod

serves four

4 cod steaks

1 lemongrass stem

1 small red onion, chopped

3 garlic cloves, chopped

2 fresh red chilies, seeded
    and chopped

1 tsp grated fresh gingerroot

¼ tsp ground turmeric

salt and pepper

2 tbsp butter, cut into small cubes

8 tbsp canned coconut milk

2 tbsp lemon juice

fresh red chilies, to garnish
    (optional)

mixed salad greens, to serve

NUTRITION

Calories 146	Sugars 2g
Protein 19g	Fat 7g
Carbohydrate 2g	Saturates 4g

COOK'S TIP

If you prefer a milder flavor, omit
the chilies altogether. For a hotter
flavor, do not remove the seeds
from the chilies.

1 Preheat the grill. Rinse the cod steaks under cold running water and pat dry on paper towels.

2 Remove and discard the outer leaves from the lemongrass and thinly slice the inner section.

3 Place the lemongrass, onion, garlic, chilies, ginger, and turmeric in a food processor and process until finely chopped. Season to taste with salt and pepper. With the motor running, add the butter, coconut milk, and lemon juice and process until well blended.

4 Place the fish in a shallow nonmetallic dish. Pour over the coconut mixture and turn the fish until well coated.

5 If you have one, place the fish steaks in a hinged basket, which will make them easier to turn. Cook the fish steaks over hot coals for 15 minutes, or until the fish is cooked through, turning once. Transfer to 4 large serving plates and garnish with red chilies, if using, then serve with mixed salad greens.

pan-seared halibut

serves four

1 tsp olive oil

4 halibut steaks, skinned, about
  6 oz/175 g each

½ tsp cornstarch mixed with 2 tsp
  cold water

2 tbsp snipped fresh chives,
  to garnish

RED ONION RELISH

2 red onions

6 shallots

1 tbsp lemon juice

2 tsp olive oil

2 tbsp red wine vinegar

2 tsp superfine sugar

⅔ cup fish stock

salt and pepper

COOK'S TIP

If raw onions make your eyes
water, try peeling them under
cold running water. Alternatively,
stand or sit well back from the
onion so that your face isn't
directly over it.

1 To make the relish, shred the onions and shallots thinly, then place in a small bowl and toss in the lemon juice.

2 Heat the oil for the relish in a skillet over medium heat. Add the onions and shallots and cook for 3–4 minutes, or until just softened.

3 Add the vinegar and sugar and cook for an additional 2 minutes over high heat. Pour in the stock and season well with salt and pepper. Bring to a boil, then reduce the heat and simmer gently for an additional 8–9 minutes, or until the sauce has thickened and is slightly reduced.

4 Brush a nonstick ridged grill pan or skillet with oil and heat over medium–high heat until hot. Press the fish steaks into the pan to seal, then reduce the heat and cook for 4 minutes. Turn the fish over and cook for 4–5 minutes, or until cooked through. Drain the fish on paper towels and keep warm.

5 Stir the cornstarch paste into the onion relish and heat through, stirring, until thickened. Season to taste with salt and pepper.

6 Pile the relish onto 4 warmed serving plates and place a fish steak on top of each. Garnish with snipped chives and serve.

NUTRITION	
Calories 197	Sugars 1g
Protein 31g	Fat 7g
Carbohydrate 2g	Saturates 1g

trout in red wine

serves four

4 fresh trout, about 10½ oz/
   300 g each

generous 1 cup red or white
   wine vinegar

1¼ cups red or dry
   white wine

⅔ cup water

1 carrot, sliced

2–4 bay leaves

thinly pared rind of 1 lemon

1 small onion, very thinly sliced

4 fresh parsley sprigs

4 fresh thyme sprigs

1 tsp black peppercorns

6–8 whole cloves

salt and pepper

¾ stick butter

TO GARNISH

fresh parsley sprigs

lemon slices

mixed salad, to serve

NUTRITION

Calories 489		Sugars 0.6g	
Protein 48g		Fat 27g	
Carbohydrate 0.6g		Saturates 14g	

1 Clean the trout but leave their heads on. Dry on paper towels and lay the fish head to tail in a shallow container or baking pan large enough to hold them.

2 Bring the vinegar to a boil and pour slowly all over the fish. Cover and let the fish marinate in the refrigerator for 20 minutes.

3 Meanwhile, place the wine, water, carrot, bay leaves, lemon rind, onion, herbs, peppercorns, and cloves in a pan with a good pinch of salt and heat gently.

4 Drain the fish thoroughly, discarding the vinegar. Place the fish in a fish kettle or large skillet so they touch. When the wine mixture boils, strain gently over the fish so they are about half covered. Cover and simmer very gently for 15 minutes.

5 Carefully remove the fish from the kettle, draining off and reserving as much of the liquid as possible. Arrange the fish in a serving dish and keep warm.

6 Boil the cooking liquid until reduced to 4–6 tablespoons. Melt the butter in a pan and strain in the cooking liquor. Season and spoon over the fish. Garnish with parsley and lemon slices and serve with salad.

Vegetables

Vegetables are too good to be confined to a supporting role in your diet, especially in a low-carbohydrate eating plan. So here they take center stage in a range of imaginative, flavorful dishes. Enjoy the colorful medley of bell peppers, zucchini, and baby eggplants, threaded onto skewers, in the recipe for Charbroiled Vegetables, or savor the aromatic spices in the rich red Tomato Curry.

In other recipes in this chapter, you will find vegetables perfectly partnered with a choice protein, such as vegetarian smoked tofu in Marinated Brochettes and fluffy eggs in Spinach & Herb Frittata. You can even enjoy your vegetables with a limited amount of carbohydrates, with tender asparagus encased in crisp phyllo pastry and juicy mushrooms stuffed with a creamy potato filling.

marinated brochettes

serves four

1 lemon

1 garlic clove, crushed

4 tbsp olive oil

4 tbsp white wine vinegar

1 tbsp chopped fresh herbs, such as
    rosemary, parsley, and thyme

salt and pepper

10½ oz/300 g smoked tofu, drained

12 oz/350 g mushrooms

fresh herbs, to garnish

TO SERVE

mixed salad greens

cherry tomatoes

NUTRITION

Calories 192	Sugars 0.5g
Protein 11g	Fat 16g
Carbohydrate 1g	Saturates 2g

1 Finely grate the rind from the lemon and squeeze out the juice into a bowl.

2 Add the garlic, oil, vinegar, and chopped herbs and mix well. Season to taste with salt and pepper.

3 Slice the tofu into large chunks with a sharp knife. Thread the pieces onto presoaked wooden skewers, alternating them with the mushrooms.

4 Place the brochettes in a shallow nonmetallic dish and pour over the marinade. Cover and let chill in the refrigerator for 1–2 hours, turning in the marinade occasionally.

5 Preheat the grill or broiler. Remove the brochettes from the dish, reserving the marinade. Cook over medium–hot coals, brushing them frequently with the marinade and turning often, for 6 minutes, or until cooked through and golden brown. Alternatively, cook under the hot broiler, turning frequently and brushing with the reserved marinade.

6 Transfer to warmed serving plates and garnish with fresh herbs. Serve immediately with mixed salad greens and cherry tomatoes.

braised tofu home-style

serves four

3 packages tofu, about 8 oz/
   225 g each (drained weight)
4½ oz/125 g boneless pork
1 leek
few small dried whole chilies,
   soaked
vegetable oil, for deep-frying
1–2 scallions, cut into sections
2 tbsp crushed yellow bean sauce
1 tbsp light soy sauce
2 tsp rice wine or dry sherry
few drops of sesame oil

NUTRITION

Calories 218	Sugars 1g
Protein 17g	Fat 16g
Carbohydrate 2g	Saturates 2g

1 Split each package of tofu into 3 slices crosswise, then cut each slice diagonally into 2 triangles.

2 Cut the pork into small thin slices or shreds. Cut the leek into thin strips.

COOK'S TIP

Tofu is sold in three forms: firm tofu, which can be smoked, silken tofu, or marinated tofu. It is the solid kind that is used for braising and stir-frying. Silken tofu is usually added to soups or sauces.

3 Drain the chilies and remove the seeds using the tip of a knife and discard, then cut into small shreds.

4 Heat the vegetable oil in a preheated wok until smoking, then deep-fry the tofu triangles for 2–3 minutes, or until golden brown all over. Remove with a slotted spoon and drain on paper towels.

5 Pour off the hot oil, leaving about 1 tablespoon in the wok. Add the pork strips, scallions, and chilies and stir-fry for 1 minute, or until the pork changes color.

6 Add the leek, tofu, yellow bean sauce, soy sauce, and wine and cook for 2–3 minutes, stirring gently to blend well. Sprinkle over the sesame oil and serve immediately.

charbroiled vegetables

serves four

1 large red bell pepper

1 large green bell pepper

1 large orange bell pepper

1 large zucchini

4 baby eggplants

2 red onions

2 tbsp lemon juice

1 tbsp olive oil

1 garlic clove, crushed

1 tbsp chopped fresh rosemary or
   1 tsp dried rosemary

salt and pepper

Fresh Tomato Relish (see page 107),
   to serve

NUTRITION

Calories 66	Sugars 7g
Protein 2g	Fat 3g
Carbohydrate 7g	Saturates 0.5g

1 Preheat the grill or broiler. Halve and seed the bell peppers. Cut into pieces 1 inch/2.5 cm wide.

2 Cut the zucchini in half lengthwise and slice into 1-inch/2.5-cm pieces. Place the bell peppers and zucchini in a bowl.

3 Cut the eggplants into fourths lengthwise. Cut the onions into 8 even-size wedges. Add the eggplants and onions to the bell peppers and zucchini.

4 Whisk the lemon juice, oil, garlic, and rosemary together in a small bowl. Season to taste with salt and pepper. Pour the mixture over the vegetables and stir to coat them evenly.

5 Thread the vegetables onto 8 metal or presoaked wooden skewers. Cook over hot coals, turning frequently, for 8–10 minutes, or until softened and beginning to char. Alternatively, arrange the kabobs on the broiler rack and cook under the hot broiler, turning frequently, for 10–12 minutes, or until the vegetables are lightly charred and just softened.

6 Drain the vegetable kabobs and serve them immediately, accompanied by Fresh Tomato Relish.

eggplant bake

serves four

3–4 tbsp olive oil

2 garlic cloves, crushed

2 large eggplants

3½ oz/100 g mozzarella cheese,
   thinly sliced

generous ¾ cup strained tomatoes

½ cup freshly grated
   Parmesan cheese

mixed salad greens, to serve

NUTRITION

Calories 232	Sugars 8g
Protein 10g	Fat 18g
Carbohydrate 8g	Saturates 6g

1 Preheat the oven to 400°F/200°C. Heat 2 tablespoons of the oil in a large heavy-bottom skillet. Add the garlic and cook, stirring constantly, for 30 seconds.

2 Slice the eggplants lengthwise. Add the slices to the pan and cook for 3–4 minutes on each side, or until tender. (You will probably have to cook them in batches, so add the remaining oil as necessary.)

3 Remove the eggplants from the pan and drain on paper towels.

4 Place a layer of eggplant in a shallow ovenproof dish. Cover with a layer of mozzarella cheese, then pour over a third of the strained tomatoes. Continue layering in the same order, finishing with a layer of strained tomatoes on top.

5 Generously sprinkle the grated Parmesan cheese over the top and bake in the preheated oven for 25–30 minutes.

6 Transfer to serving plates and let cool, then serve warm or cold with salad greens.

asparagus packages

serves four

3½ oz/100 g fine tip asparagus

1 red bell pepper, seeded and
thinly sliced

1 cup bean sprouts

2 tbsp plum sauce

1 egg yolk

8 sheets phyllo pastry

corn oil, for deep-frying

chili dipping sauce, to serve

NUTRITION

Calories 194	Sugars 2g
Protein 3g	Fat 16g
Carbohydrate 11g	Saturates 4g

1 Place the asparagus, bell pepper, and bean sprouts in a large bowl. Add the plum sauce to the vegetables and mix well.

2 Beat the egg yolk in a small bowl and reserve until required.

3 Lay the sheets of phyllo pastry out on a clean counter and cover with a damp dish towel to prevent them drying out.

4 Working with 1 sheet of phyllo pastry at a time, place a small quantity of the asparagus and bell pepper filling at the top end of the sheet. Brush all the edges of the phyllo pastry with a little of the beaten egg yolk. Roll up the sheet, tucking in the ends to enclose the filling like a spring roll. Continue filling and rolling the remaining phyllo pastry sheets.

5 Heat the oil for deep-frying in a preheated wok. Carefully cook the packages, 2 at a time, in the hot oil for 4–5 minutes, or until crispy.

6 Remove the packages with a slotted spoon and let drain on paper towels. Transfer the packages to warmed serving plates and serve immediately with a chili dipping sauce.

bell peppers with chestnuts

serves four

8 oz/225 g leeks

corn oil, for deep-frying

1 yellow bell pepper, seeded
and diced

1 green bell pepper, seeded and diced

1 red bell pepper, seeded and diced

7 oz/200 g canned water chestnuts,
drained and sliced

2 garlic cloves, crushed

3 tbsp light soy sauce

NUTRITION

Calories 192	Sugars 5g
Protein 3g	Fat 14g
Carbohydrate 13g	Saturates 13g

1 Thinly shred the leeks. Heat the oil for deep-frying in a preheated wok or large heavy-bottom pan.

2 Add the leeks to the wok and cook for 2–3 minutes, or until crispy. Remove with a slotted spoon and drain on paper towels. Reserve.

3 Pour all but 3 tablespoons of the oil from the wok. Add the yellow, green, and red bell peppers and stir-fry over high heat for 5 minutes, or until they begin to brown at the edges and have softened.

4 Add the water chestnuts, garlic, and soy sauce to the wok and stir-fry the vegetables for an additional 2–3 minutes.

5 Spoon the stir-fry onto warmed serving plates, then sprinkle with the reserved crispy leek and serve.

mixed bean pan-fry

serves four

12 oz/350 g mixed fresh beans,
    such as green and fava beans

2 tbsp vegetable oil

2 garlic cloves, crushed

1 red onion, halved and sliced

8 oz/225 g marinated tofu pieces
    (drained weight)

1 tbsp lemon juice

½ tsp ground turmeric

1 tsp ground allspice

⅔ cup vegetable stock

2 tsp sesame seeds

NUTRITION

Calories 179	Sugars 4g
Protein 10g	Fat 11g
Carbohydrate 10g	Saturates 1g

VARIATION

Add lime juice instead of lemon
for an alternative citrus flavor.
Use smoked tofu instead of
marinated tofu, if you prefer.

1 Slice the green beans, then shell the fava beans and reserve until required.

2 Heat the oil in a large skillet. Add the garlic and onion and cook for 2 minutes, stirring well.

3 Add the tofu and cook for 2–3 minutes, or until just beginning to brown.

4 Add the reserved green beans and fava beans. Stir in the lemon juice, turmeric, allspice, and stock and bring to a boil.

5 Reduce the heat and simmer for 5 7 minutes, or until the beans are tender. Sprinkle with sesame seeds and serve immediately.

vegetable stir-fry with eggs

serves four

2 eggs

8 oz/225 g carrots

12 oz/350 g white cabbage

2 tbsp vegetable oil

1 red bell pepper, seeded and
   thinly sliced

3 cups fresh bean sprouts

1 tbsp tomato ketchup

2 tbsp soy sauce

½ cup salted peanuts, chopped

peanut sauce, to serve

NUTRITION

Calories 269		Sugars 12g	
Protein 12g		Fat 19g	
Carbohydrate 14g		Saturates 3g	

COOK'S TIP

The eggs are cooled in cold
water after cooking in order to
prevent the egg yolks turning
black around the edges.

1 Bring a small pan of water to a boil. Add the eggs and cook for 7 minutes. Remove the eggs from the pan and cool under cold running water for 1 minute. Shell the eggs, then cut into fourths.

2 Coarsely grate the carrots and finely shred the cabbage. Heat the oil in a preheated wok or large heavy-bottom skillet.

3 Add the carrots, cabbage, and bell pepper to the wok and stir-fry for 3 minutes.

4 Add the bean sprouts to the wok and stir-fry for 2 minutes.

5 Mix the ketchup and soy sauce together in a small bowl and add to the wok, stirring well to combine.

6 Add the chopped peanuts to the wok and stir-fry for 1 minute.

7 Transfer the stir-fry to warmed serving plates and garnish with the hard-cooked egg fourths. Serve with a peanut sauce.

vegetable chop suey

serves four

1 yellow bell pepper, seeded

1 red bell pepper, seeded

1 carrot

1 zucchini

1 fennel bulb

1 onion

generous ½ cup snow peas

2 tbsp peanut oil

3 garlic cloves, crushed

1 tsp grated fresh gingerroot

2 cups bean sprouts

2 tsp brown sugar

2 tbsp light soy sauce

½ cup vegetable stock

NUTRITION

Calories 155	Sugars 6g
Protein 4g	Fat 12g
Carbohydrate 9g	Saturates 2g

1 Cut the bell peppers, carrot, zucchini, and fennel into thin slices. Cut the onion into fourths, then cut each fourth in half. Slice the snow peas diagonally to create the maximum surface area.

2 Heat the oil in a preheated wok. Add the garlic and ginger and stir fry for 30 seconds. Add the onion and stir-fry for an additional 30 seconds.

VARIATION

Use any combination of colorful vegetables that you have to hand to make this versatile dish.

3 Add the bell peppers, carrot, zucchini, fennel, and snow peas to the wok and stir-fry for 2 minutes.

4 Add the bean sprouts to the wok and stir in the sugar, soy sauce, and stock. Reduce the heat to low and simmer for 1–2 minutes, or until the vegetables are tender and coated in the sauce.

5 Transfer the vegetables and sauce to a serving dish and serve immediately.

dolmades

8 oz/225 g grape leaves preserved
in brine, about 40 in total

⅔ cup olive oil

4 tbsp lemon juice

1¼ cups water

lemon wedges, to serve

FILLING

generous ½ cup long-grain rice,
not basmati

1½ cups water

salt and pepper

generous ⅓ cup currants

½ cup pine nuts, chopped

2 scallions, very finely chopped

1 tbsp very finely chopped
cilantro

1 tbsp very finely chopped
fresh parsley

1 tbsp very finely chopped fresh dill

finely grated rind of ½ lemon

NUTRITION

Calories 82	Sugars 2g
Protein 1g	Fat 7g
Carbohydrate 5g	Saturates 1g

1 Rinse the vine leaves in cold water and place them in a heatproof bowl. Cover with boiling water and soak for 5 minutes. Drain.

2 To make the filling, place the rice and water in a pan. Add a pinch of salt and cook for 10–12 minutes, or until the liquid is absorbed. Drain and let cool.

3 Stir the currants, pine nuts, scallions, herbs, lemon rind, and salt and pepper to taste into the rice.

4 Line the bottom of a large skillet with 3–4 of the thickest grape leaves or with any that are torn. Place a grape leaf on the counter, vein-side upward, with the pointed end facing away from you. Place a small, compact roll of the rice filling at the base of the leaf. Fold up the bottom end of the leaf.

5 Fold in each side of the leaf to overlap in the center. Roll up the leaf around the filling and squeeze lightly in your hand to shape and seal it. Continue with the remaining grape leaves and filling mixture.

6 Place the rolls in a single layer in the skillet, seam-side down. Combine the oil, lemon juice, and water and pour into the pan.

7 Fit a heatproof plate over the rolls and cover the skillet. Simmer for 30 minutes, then remove the skillet from the heat and let the stuffed grape leaves cool in the liquid. Serve chilled with lemon wedges.

cantonese garden vegetables

serves four

2 tbsp peanut oil

1 tsp Chinese five-spice powder

2¾ oz/75 g baby carrots,
   halved

2 celery stalks, sliced

2 baby leeks, sliced

½ cup snow peas

4 baby zucchini, halved
   lengthwise

8 baby corn cobs

8 oz/225 g marinated tofu pieces
   (drained weight)

4 tbsp fresh orange juice

1 tbsp clear honey

TO GARNISH

celery leaves

orange zest

NUTRITION

Calories 130	Sugars 8g
Protein 6g	Fat 8g
Carbohydrate 8g	Saturates 1g

1 Heat the oil in a preheated wok until almost smoking. Add the five-spice powder, carrots, celery, leeks, snow peas, zucchini, and baby corn cobs and stir-fry for 3–4 minutes.

2 Add the tofu and cook for an additional 2 minutes, stirring.

3 Stir in the orange juice and honey, then reduce the heat and stir-fry for 1–2 minutes.

4 Transfer the stir-fry to a serving dish and garnish with celery leaves and orange zest. Serve immediately.

COOK'S TIP

Chinese five-spice powder is a mixture of fennel, star anise, cinnamon bark, cloves, and Szechuan pepper. It is very pungent, so it should be used sparingly. If kept in an airtight container, it will keep indefinitely.

oven-baked risotto

serves four

4 tbsp olive oil

14 oz/400 g portobello mushrooms, thickly sliced

4 oz/115 g pancetta or thick-cut smoked bacon, diced

1 large onion, finely chopped

2 garlic cloves, finely chopped

1¾ cups risotto rice

1 quart chicken stock, simmering

2 tbsp chopped fresh tarragon or flatleaf parsley

salt and pepper

¾ cup freshly grated Parmesan cheese, plus extra for sprinkling

NUTRITION	
Calories 428	Sugars 2g
Protein 15g	Fat 18g
Carbohydrate 14g	Saturates 6g

1 Preheat the oven to 350°F/ 180°C. Heat 2 tablespoons of the oil in a large heavy-bottom skillet over high heat. Add the mushrooms and stir-fry for 2–3 minutes, or until golden and tender. Transfer to a plate.

2 Add the pancetta to the skillet and cook for 2 minutes, stirring frequently, until crisp and golden. Remove with a slotted spoon and add to the mushrooms on the plate.

3 Heat the remaining oil in a heavy-bottom pan over medium heat. Add the onion and cook for 2 minutes. Add the garlic and rice and cook, stirring, for 2 minutes, or until the rice is well coated with the oil.

4 Gradually stir the stock into the rice, then add the mushroom and pancetta mixture and the tarragon. Season to taste with salt and pepper. Bring to a boil.

5 Remove the pan from the heat and transfer to a casserole.

6 Cover and bake in the preheated oven for 20 minutes, or until the rice is almost tender and most of the liquid has been absorbed. Uncover and stir in the Parmesan cheese. Bake for an additional 15 minutes, or until the rice is tender but still firm to the bite. Serve immediately with extra Parmesan cheese for sprinkling.

baked eggplant gratin

serves four–six

1 large eggplant, about
   1 lb 12 oz/800 g

10½ oz/300 g mozzarella cheese

3 oz/85 g Parmesan cheese

olive oil

about 1 cup Tomato Sauce
   (see page 78) or good quality
   bottled tomato sauce for pasta

salt and pepper

NUTRITION	
Calories 261	Sugars 5g
Protein 20g	Fat 18g
Carbohydrate 6g	Saturates 10g

1 Trim the eggplant and, using a sharp knife, cut it into ¼-inch/5-mm slices crosswise. Arrange the eggplant slices on a large plate, then sprinkle with salt and let drain for 30 minutes.

2 Preheat the oven to 400°F/200°C. Drain and grate the mozzarella cheese and finely grate the Parmesan cheese.

3 Rinse the eggplant slices under cold running water and pat dry with paper towels. Lightly brush a cookie sheet with oil and arrange the eggplant slices in a single layer. Brush the tops with oil.

4 Roast in the preheated oven for 5 minutes. Using tongs, turn the slices over, then brush with a little more oil and bake for an additional 5 minutes, or until the eggplant is cooked through and tender. Do not turn off the oven.

5 Spread about 1 tablespoon of oil over the bottom of a gratin dish or other ovenproof serving dish. Add a layer of eggplant slices, about a fourth of the Tomato Sauce, and top with a fourth of the mozzarella. Season to taste with salt and pepper.

6 Continue layering until all the ingredients are used, ending with a layer of sauce. Sprinkle the Parmesan cheese over the top. Bake for 30 minutes, or until bubbling. Let stand for 5 minutes before serving.

tomato curry

serves four

14 oz/400 g canned tomatoes

1 tsp finely chopped fresh
   gingerroot

1 tsp crushed garlic

1 tsp chili powder

1 tsp salt

½ tsp ground coriander

½ tsp ground cumin

4 tbsp corn oil

½ tsp onion seeds

½ tsp mustard seeds

½ tsp fenugreek seeds

pinch of white cumin seeds

3 dried red chilies

2 tbsp lemon juice

3 hard-cooked eggs

cilantro leaves, to garnish

NUTRITION

Calories 170	Sugars 3g	
Protein 6g	Fat 15g	
Carbohydrate 3g	Saturates 2g	

1 Place the tomatoes in a large bowl. Add the ginger, garlic, chili powder, salt, coriander, and ground cumin and blend well.

2 Heat the oil in a pan. Add the onion, mustard, fenugreek, and white cumin seeds, and the dried red chilies and stir-fry for 1 minute, or until they give off their aroma. Remove the pan from the heat.

3 Add the tomato mixture to the spicy oil mixture and return the pan to the heat. Stir-fry for 3 minutes.

4 Reduce the heat and continue to cook, partially covered and stirring frequently, for 7–10 minutes.

5 Sprinkle over 1 tablespoon of the lemon juice. Taste and add the remaining lemon juice if required.

6 Transfer the tomato curry to a warmed serving dish and keep warm until required.

7 Shell the hard-cooked eggs and cut them into fourths. Add them to the tomato curry, pushing them in gently, yolk-end downward. Garnish with cilantro leaves and serve.

creamy stuffed mushrooms

serves four

1 oz/25 g dried cèpes

8 oz/225 g mealy potatoes, diced

salt and pepper

2 tbsp butter, melted

4 tbsp heavy cream

2 tbsp snipped fresh chives

8 large open-cap mushrooms

¼ cup grated Emmental cheese

⅔ cup vegetable stock

fresh chives, to garnish

salad greens, to serve

1 Preheat the oven to 425°F/220°C. Place the dried cèpes in a small heatproof bowl. Pour over enough boiling water to cover and let soak for 20 minutes.

2 Meanwhile, cook the potatoes in a pan of lightly salted boiling water for 10 minutes, or until cooked through and tender. Drain them well and mash until smooth.

3 Drain the soaked cèpes and chop them finely. Mix them into the mashed potato.

4 Thoroughly blend the butter, cream, and chives together in a pitcher and pour the mixture into the potato mixture, stirring well to blend. Season to taste with salt and pepper.

5 Remove the stems from the open-cap mushrooms. Chop the stems and stir them into the potato mixture. Spoon the mixture into the open-cap mushrooms and sprinkle the grated cheese over the top.

6 Arrange the filled mushrooms in a shallow ovenproof dish and pour the stock around them.

7 Cover the dish and cook in the preheated oven for 20 minutes. Remove the lid and cook for an additional 5 minutes, or until the tops are golden.

8 Garnish with chives and serve with salad greens.

NUTRITION	
Calories 214	Sugars 1g
Protein 5g	Fat 17g
Carbohydrate 11g	Saturates 11g

broccoli in oyster sauce

serves four

9–10½ oz/250–300 g broccoli

3 tbsp vegetable oil

3–4 small slices fresh gingerroot

½ tsp salt

½ tsp sugar

3–4 tbsp water

1 tbsp oyster sauce

NUTRITION

Calories 100		Sugars 1g	
Protein 3g		Fat 9g	
Carbohydrate 2g		Saturates 1g	

COOK'S TIP

The broccoli stems have to be peeled and cut diagonally to ensure that they will cook evenly. If they are thin stems, the pieces can be added to the wok at the same time as the florets, but otherwise add the stems first, to ensure that they will be tender.

1 Using a sharp knife, cut the broccoli spears into small florets. Trim the stems and peel off the rough skin, then cut the stems diagonally into diamond-shaped chunks.

2 Heat the oil in a preheated wok until really hot.

3 Add the pieces of broccoli stem and the slices of ginger to the wok and stir-fry for 30 seconds, then add the florets and continue to stir-fry for an additional 2 minutes.

4 Add the salt, sugar, and water, and stir-fry for an additional 1 minute.

5 Blend in the oyster sauce. Transfer the broccoli to a serving dish and serve hot or cold.

spinach frittata

serves four

1 lb/450 g fresh spinach leaves

2 tsp water

4 eggs, beaten

2 tbsp light cream

2 garlic cloves, crushed

⅓ cup canned corn kernels, drained

1 celery stalk, chopped

1 fresh red chili, seeded and chopped

2 tomatoes, seeded and diced

2 tbsp olive oil

2 tbsp butter

4 tbsp pecan nut halves

2 tbsp grated romano cheese

1 oz/25 g fontina cheese, cubed

pinch of paprika

COOK'S TIP

Be careful not to burn the underside of the frittata during the initial cooking stage—this is why it is important to use a heavy-bottom skillet. Add a little extra oil to the pan when you turn the frittata over, if required.

1 Cook the spinach in the water in a covered pan for 5 minutes. Drain thoroughly and pat dry on paper towels.

2 Beat the eggs in a bowl and stir in the spinach, cream, garlic, corn, celery, chili, and tomatoes until the ingredients are well mixed together.

NUTRITION	
Calories 307	Sugars 4g
Protein 15g	Fat 25g
Carbohydrate 6g	Saturates 8g

3 Heat the oil and butter in an 8-inch/20-cm heavy-bottom skillet over medium heat.

4 Spoon the egg mixture into the skillet and sprinkle with the pecan nut halves, romano and fontina cheeses, and paprika. Cook, without stirring, over medium heat for 5–7 minutes, or until the underside of the frittata is brown.

5 Place a large plate over the skillet and invert to turn out the frittata. Slide it back into the skillet and cook the other side for an additional 2–3 minutes. Serve the frittata straight from the skillet or transfer to a serving plate and serve immediately.

ratatouille

serves four–six

1 large eggplant, about
   10½ oz/300 g

salt and pepper

5 tbsp olive oil

2 large onions, thinly sliced

2 large garlic cloves, crushed

4 zucchini, sliced

1 lb 12 oz/800 g canned
   chopped tomatoes

1 tsp sugar

1 bouquet garni of 2 fresh
   thyme sprigs, 2 large fresh
   parsley sprigs, 1 fresh basil sprig,
   and 1 bay leaf, tied in a 3-inch/
   7.5-cm piece of celery

fresh basil leaves, to garnish

NUTRITION	
Calories 157	Sugars 11g
Protein 4g	Fat 9g
Carbohydrate 14g	Saturates 1g

1 Coarsely chop the eggplant, then place in a colander. Sprinkle with salt and let stand for 30 minutes to drain. Rinse well under cold running water to remove all traces of the salt and pat dry with paper towels.

2 Heat the oil in a large heavy-bottom flameproof casserole over medium heat. Add the onions, then reduce the heat and cook, stirring occasionally, for 10 minutes, or until softened and light golden brown.

3 Add the garlic and cook for an additional 2 minutes, or until the onions are tender.

4 Add the eggplant, zucchini, tomatoes with their can juices, sugar, and bouquet garni. Season to taste with salt and pepper. Bring to a boil, then reduce the heat to very low and simmer, covered, for 30 minutes.

5 Taste and adjust the seasoning if necessary. Remove and discard the bouquet garni. Garnish the vegetable stew with basil leaves and serve immediately.

spinach & herb frittata

serves six–eight

4 tbsp olive oil

6 scallions, sliced

9 oz/250 g young spinach
  leaves, any coarse stems
  removed, rinsed

6 large eggs

salt and pepper

3 tbsp finely chopped mixed fresh
  herbs, such as flatleaf parsley,
  thyme, and cilantro

2 tbsp freshly grated Parmesan
  cheese, plus extra for garnishing

fresh parsley sprigs, to garnish

NUTRITION

Calories 145	Sugars 1g
Protein 8g	Fat 12g
Carbohydrate 1g	Saturates 13g

1 Preheat the broiler. Heat a 10-inch/25-cm skillet, preferably nonstick with a flameproof handle, over medium heat. Add the oil and heat. Add the scallions and cook for 2 minutes.

2 Add the spinach and cook until it is just wilted.

3 Beat the eggs and season to taste with salt and pepper. Using a slotted spoon, transfer the spinach and onions to the eggs and stir in the herbs. Pour the excess oil left in the skillet into a heatproof pitcher, then scrape off the bits from the bottom of the pan.

4 Reheat the skillet. Add 2 tablespoons of the reserved oil. Pour in the egg mixture, smoothing it into an even layer. Cook, shaking the skillet occasionally, for 6 minutes, or until the bottom is set when you lift up the side with a spatula.

5 Sprinkle the top of the frittata with the Parmesan cheese. Place the pan under the hot broiler and cook for 3 minutes, or until the excess liquid is set and the cheese is golden.

6 Remove the skillet from the heat and slide the frittata out onto a warm serving plate. Let the frittata stand for at least 5 minutes before cutting and garnishing with extra Parmesan cheese and parsley. The frittata can be served hot, warm, or at room temperature.

215

thai-spiced mushrooms

serves four

8 large flat mushrooms

3 tbsp corn oil

2 tbsp light soy sauce

1 garlic clove, crushed

¾-inch/2-cm piece fresh galangal or
    gingerroot, grated

1 tbsp Thai green curry paste

8 baby corn cobs, sliced

3 scallions, chopped

2 cups bean sprouts

3½ oz/100 g firm tofu (drained
    weight), diced

2 tsp sesame seeds, toasted

TO SERVE

chopped cucumber

sliced red bell pepper

NUTRITION

Calories 147	Sugars 2g
Protein 6g	Fat 12g
Carbohydrate 4g	Saturates 1g

1 Preheat the broiler to high. Remove the stems from the mushrooms and reserve. Place the caps on a cookie sheet. Mix 2 tablespoons of the oil with 1 tablespoon of the soy sauce and brush over the mushrooms.

2 Cook the mushroom caps under the hot broiler until golden and tender, turning them over once.

3 Meanwhile, chop the mushroom stems finely. Heat the remaining oil in a large skillet or preheated wok. Add the mushroom stems, garlic, and galangal and stir-fry for 1 minute.

4 Stir in the curry paste, baby corn cobs, and scallions and stir-fry for 1 minute. Add the bean sprouts and stir-fry for an additional 1 minute.

5 Add the tofu and remaining soy sauce, then toss lightly to heat. Spoon the mixture into the mushroom caps.

6 Sprinkle with sesame seeds and serve with chopped cucumber and sliced red bell pepper.

vegetable rolls

serves four

8 large Napa cabbage leaves

FILLING

2 baby corn cobs, sliced

1 carrot, finely chopped

1 celery stalk, chopped

4 scallions, chopped

4 water chestnuts, chopped

2 tbsp unsalted cashews, chopped

1 garlic clove, chopped

1 tsp grated fresh gingerroot

1 oz/25 g canned bamboo shoots, drained, rinsed, and chopped

1 tsp sesame oil

2 tsp soy sauce

NUTRITION

Calories 69	Sugars 1g
Protein 2g	Fat 5g
Carbohydrate 3g	Saturates 1g

1 Place the Napa cabbage leaves in a large heatproof bowl and pour over boiling water to soften them. Let them stand for 1 minute and drain thoroughly.

2 Mix the baby corn cobs, carrot, celery, scallions, water chestnuts, cashew nuts, garlic, ginger, and bamboo shoots together in a large bowl.

3 Whisk the oil and soy sauce together in a separate bowl. Add this to the vegetables and stir well until all the vegetables are thoroughly coated in the mixture.

4 Spread out the Napa cabbage leaves on a cutting board and divide the filling mixture between them, carefully spooning an equal quantity of the mixture on to each leaf.

5 Roll up the Napa cabbage leaves, folding in the sides, to make neat packages. Secure the packages with wooden toothpicks.

6 Place in a small heatproof dish in a steamer, then cover and cook for 15–20 minutes, or until the packages are cooked.

7 Transfer the vegetable rolls to a warmed serving dish and serve immediately.

Desserts

You can still enjoy a dessert or a sweet treat on a low-carbohydrate diet, as the following recipes prove. Some, of course, are higher in carbs than others, so be sure to consult the nutritional information alongside each recipe when making your choice, so that you can limit the "naughtier" ones to an occasional indulgence.

As with vegetables, eating as wide a variety of fruits as possible is the healthy approach, and here you can feast on luscious summer berries in Balsamic Strawberries, fragrant tropical fruits in Pineapple with Tequila & Mint, and no less enticing tree fruits in Peaches in White Wine and Figs with Orange Cream.

But if a hit of chocolate is what you crave, try the moreish Mini Florentines, or the truly wicked Rich Chocolate Loaf.

balsamic strawberries

serves four–six

3 cups fresh strawberries

2–3 tbsp balsamic vinegar

pepper

fresh mint leaves, torn, plus extra to
decorate (optional)

4–6 oz/115–175 g mascarpone
cheese

NUTRITION	
Calories 132	Sugars 5g
Protein 1g	Fat 12g
Carbohydrate 5g	Saturates 7g

COOK'S TIP

This is most enjoyable when it is made with the best quality balsamic vinegar, one that has aged slowly and has turned thick and syrupy. Unfortunately, the genuine mixture is always expensive—cheaper versions are artificially sweetened and colored.

1 Wipe the strawberries with a damp cloth, rather than rinsing them, so they do not become soggy. Using a paring knife, cut off the stems at the top, then use the tip to remove the core.

2 Cut each strawberry in half or into fourths if large. Transfer to a large nonmetallic bowl.

3 Add ½ tablespoon of the vinegar per person. Add several twists of pepper, then gently stir together. Cover with plastic wrap and let chill in the refrigerator for 4 hours.

4 Just before serving, stir in the mint leaves to taste. Spoon the mascarpone cheese into bowls and spoon the berries on top.

5 Decorate the balsamic strawberries with a few mint leaves, if desired. Sprinkle with extra pepper to taste.

rich chocolate loaf

makes sixteen slices

½ cup whole almonds

5 squares semisweet chocolate

6 tbsp unsalted butter

generous ¾ cup condensed milk

2 tsp ground cinnamon

3 oz/85 g amaretti cookies, broken

⅓ cup no-soak dried apricots,
    coarsely chopped

NUTRITION

Calories 118	Sugars 16g
Protein 3g	Fat 12g
Carbohydrate 18g	Saturates 6g

COOK'S TIP

To melt chocolate, first break it
into manageable pieces. The
smaller the pieces, the quicker it
will melt.

1 Line a 1-lb 8 oz/675-g loaf pan with a sheet of foil.

2 Using a sharp knife, coarsely chop the almonds.

3 Place the chocolate, butter, condensed milk, and cinnamon in a heavy-bottom pan.

4 Heat the chocolate mixture over low heat for 3–4 minutes, stirring constantly with a wooden spoon, until the chocolate has melted. Beat the mixture well.

5 Stir the chopped almonds, broken cookies, and apricots into the chocolate mixture, stirring with a wooden spoon until well mixed.

6 Pour the mixture into the prepared pan. Cover and let chill in the refrigerator for 1 hour, or until set. Cut the loaf into slices to serve.

coconut candy

serves four–six

scant ¾ stick butter

2 cups dry unsweetened coconut

¾ cup condensed milk

few drops of pink food coloring
(optional)

NUTRITION

Calories 338	Sugars 5g
Protein 4g	Fat 34g
Carbohydrate 5g	Saturates 26g

COOK'S TIP

Coconut is used extensively in Indian cooking to add flavor and creaminess to various dishes. The best flavor comes from freshly grated coconut, although ready-prepared dry unsweetened coconut, as used here, makes an excellent standby. Freshly grated coconut freezes successfully, so it is well worth preparing when you have the time.

1 Place the butter in a heavy-bottom pan and melt over low heat, stirring constantly.

2 Add the coconut to the melted butter, stirring to mix.

3 Stir in the condensed milk and the food coloring, if using, and mix constantly for 7–10 minutes.

4 Remove the pan from the heat and let the coconut mixture cool slightly.

5 Once cool enough to handle, shape the coconut mixture into long blocks and cut into equal-size rectangles. Let set for 1 hour, then serve.

mini florentines

makes forty

6 tbsp butter, plus extra for greasing

all-purpose flour, for dusting

generous ⅓ cup superfine sugar

2 tbsp golden raisins or raisins

2 tbsp chopped candied cherries

2 tbsp chopped candied ginger

¼ cup sunflower seeds

scant 1 cup slivered almonds

2 tbsp heavy cream

6 squares semisweet chocolate

NUTRITION

Calories 75		Sugars 6g	
Protein 1g		Fat 5g	
Carbohydrate 6g		Saturates 2g	

1 Preheat the oven to 350°F/180°C. Grease and flour 2 cookie sheets.

2 Place the butter in a pan and heat until melted. Add the sugar and stir until dissolved, then bring to a boil. Remove from the heat and stir in the golden raisins, cherries, ginger, sunflower seeds, and almonds. Mix well, then beat in the cream.

3 Place small teaspoons of the fruit and nut mixture onto the prepared cookie sheets, leaving plenty of space for the mixture to spread. Bake in the preheated oven for 10–12 minutes, or until light golden.

4 Remove from the oven and, while still hot, use a circular cookie cutter to pull in the edges to form perfect circles. Let cool and go crisp before removing from the cookie sheets.

5 Break the chocolate into pieces, then place in a heatproof bowl over a pan of simmering water and stir until melted. Spread most of the chocolate onto a sheet of parchment paper. When the chocolate is on the point of setting, place the cookies flat-side down on the chocolate and let it harden completely.

6 Cut around the florentines and remove from the parchment paper. Spread a little more melted chocolate on the coated side of the florentines and use a fork to mark waves in the chocolate. Let set. Arrange the florentines on a plate (or in a presentation box for a gift) with alternate sides facing upward. Keep them cool.

lavender hearts

makes about forty-eight

1½ cups all-purpose flour, plus extra
for dusting

scant ¾ stick chilled butter, diced

generous ⅓ cup superfine sugar

1 large egg

1 tbsp dried lavender flowers, very
finely chopped

TO DECORATE

about 4 tbsp confectioners' sugar

about 1 tsp cold water

about 2 tbsp fresh lavender flowers

NUTRITION	
Calories 36	Sugars 2g
Protein 1g	Fat 1g
Carbohydrate 5g	Saturates 1g

1 Preheat the oven to 350°F/180°C.
Line 2 cookie sheets with
parchment paper. Place the flour in a
bowl, then add the butter and cut it in
until the mixture resembles bread
crumbs. Stir in the superfine sugar.

2 Lightly beat the egg, then add it
to the flour and butter mixture
along with the dried lavender flowers.
Stir the mixture until a stiff paste
is formed.

3 Turn out the dough onto a lightly
floured counter and roll out until
about ¼ inch/5 mm thick.

4 Using a 2-inch/5-cm heart-shaped
cookie cutter, press out
48 cookies, occasionally dipping the
cutter into extra flour, and re-rolling the
trimmings as necessary. Transfer the
pastry hearts to the cookie sheets.

5 Prick the surface of each heart
with a fork. Bake in the preheated
oven for 10 minutes, or until lightly
browned. Transfer to a wire rack set
over parchment paper to cool.

6 Sift the confectioners' sugar into a
bowl. Add the water and stir until
a thin, smooth frosting forms, adding a
little extra water if necessary.

7 Drizzle the frosting from the tip of
the spoon over the cooled cookie
in a random pattern. Immediately
sprinkle with the fresh lavender flower
while the frosting is still soft so that
they stick in place. Let stand for at least
15 minutes, or until the frosting has
set. Store the cookies for up to 4 days
in an airtight container.

zabaglione

4 egg yolks

⅓ cup superfine sugar

½ cup Marsala wine

amaretti cookies, to serve (optional)

NUTRITION

Calories 110		Sugars 13g
Protein 2g		Fat 4g
Carbohydrate 13g		Saturates 1g

COOK'S TIP

Decorate the zabaglione
with a slit strawberry,
placed on the rim of the glass,
or serve with ladyfingers
or crisp cookies.

---

1 Half fill a pan with water and bring to a boil. Reduce the heat so that the water is barely simmering.

2 Beat the egg yolks and sugar together in a heatproof bowl with an electric whisk until pale and creamy. Set the bowl over the pan of water. Do not let the bottom of the bowl touch the surface of the water, or the egg yolks will scramble.

3 Gradually add the Marsala wine, beating constantly with the electric whisk. Continue beating until the mixture is thick and has increased in volume. Pour into heatproof glasses or bowls and serve immediately with amaretti cookies.

italian chocolate truffles

makes twenty-four

6 squares semisweet chocolate

2 tbsp almond-flavored liqueur or
orange-flavored liqueur

3 tbsp unsalted butter

scant ½ cup confectioners' sugar

½ cup ground almonds

1¾ squares milk chocolate, grated

NUTRITION

Calories 82	Sugars 7g
Protein 1g	Fat 5g
Carbohydrate 8g	Saturates 3g

1 Melt the semisweet chocolate with the liqueur in a heatproof bowl set over a pan of hot water, stirring until well combined.

2 Add the butter and stir until it has melted. Stir in the sugar and the ground almonds.

3 Let the mixture stand in a cool place until firm enough to roll into 24 balls.

4 Place the grated milk chocolate on a plate and roll the truffles in the chocolate to coat them.

5 Place the truffles in paper candy cases and let chill.

VARIATION

Almond-flavored liqueur gives these truffles an authentic Italian flavor. The original almond liqueur, Amaretto di Saronno, comes from Saronno in Italy.

exotic fruit packages

serves four

1 papaya

1 mango

1 carambola

1 tbsp grenadine

3 tbsp orange juice

lowfat plain yogurt or light cream,
   to serve

NNUTRITION

Calories 43	Sugars 9g	
Protein 2g	Fat 0.3g	
Carbohydrate 9g	Saturates 0.1g	

1 Cut the papaya in half, then scoop out the seeds and discard them. Peel the papaya and cut the flesh into thick slices.

2 Prepare the mango by cutting it in half lengthwise and cutting carefully away from the flat central pit with a sharp knife.

3 Score each mango half in a criss-cross pattern. Push each mango half inside out to separate the cubes, and cut them away from the skin.

4 Using a sharp knife, thickly slice the carambola.

5 Place all the fruits in a bowl and mix them together.

6 Mix the grenadine and orange juice together and pour over the fruits. Let marinate for at least 30 minutes.

7 Preheat the grill. Divide the fruits between 4 double-thickness squares of foil and gather the edges to form a package that encloses the fruits.

8 Place the foil packages on a rack set over warm coals and cook for 15–20 minutes.

9 Serve the fruits in their packages with plain yogurt.

rose ice

serves four

1¾ cups water

2 tbsp coconut cream

4 tbsp sweetened condensed milk

2 tsp rose water

few drops of pink food coloring
(optional)

pink rose petals, to decorate

NUTRITION	
Calories 76	Sugars 9g
Protein 2g	Fat 4g
Carbohydrate 9g	Saturates 3g

1 Place the water in a small pan
and add the coconut cream. Heat
the mixture gently without boiling,
stirring constantly.

COOK'S TIP

To prevent the ice thawing too
quickly at the table, nestle the
bottom of the serving dish in
another dish filled with
crushed ice.

2 Remove from the heat and let
cool. Stir in the sweetened
condensed milk, rose water, and food
coloring, if using.

3 Pour into a freezerproof container
and freeze for 1–1½ hours, or
until slushy.

4 Remove from the freezer and
break up the ice crystals with a
fork. Return to the freezer and freeze
until firm.

5 Spoon the ice roughly into a pile
on a serving dish and sprinkle
with rose petals to decorate.

mocha swirl mousse

serves four

1 tbsp coffee and chicory extract

2 tsp unsweetened cocoa, plus extra
    for dusting

1 tsp lowfat drinking
    chocolate powder

⅔ cup lowfat sour cream, plus 4 tsp
    to serve

2 tsp powdered gelozone
    (vegetarian gelatin)

2 tbsp boiling water

2 large egg whites

2 tbsp superfine sugar

4 chocolate coffee beans, to serve

NUTRITION

Calories 136	Sugars 5g
Protein 5g	Fat 8g
Carbohydrate 11g	Saturates 5g

COOK'S TIP

The vegetarian equivalent of
gelatin, called gelozone, is
available from healthfood stores.

1 Place the coffee and chicory
extract in one bowl and the cocoa
and drinking chocolate in another
bowl. Divide the sour cream between
the 2 bowls and mix both well.

2 Dissolve the gelozone in the
boiling water in a heatproof bowl
and reserve. Whisk the egg whites and
sugar in a greasefree bowl until stiff
and divide this evenly between the
2 mixtures.

3 Divide the dissolved gelozone
between the 2 mixtures and,
using a large metal spoon, gently fold
in until well mixed.

4 Spoon small amounts of the
2 mousses alternately into
4 serving glasses and swirl together
gently. Let chill in the refrigerator for
1 hour, or until set.

5 To serve, top each mousse
with a teaspoonful of sour cream,
a chocolate coffee bean, and a light
dusting of cocoa.

figs with orange cream

serves four

8 large fresh figs

4 large fresh fig leaves, if available,
　rinsed and dried

CREME FRAICHE

2 tbsp buttermilk

1¼ cups heavy cream

ORANGE BLOSSOM CREAM

½ cup Crème Fraîche

about 4 tbsp orange blossom water

1 tsp orange blossom honey

finely grated rind of ½ orange

2 tbsp slivered almonds,
　to decorate (optional)

1 Begin making the Crème Fraîche at least a day ahead. Place the buttermilk in a preserving jar or a jar with a screw top. Add the cream, then close securely and shake to blend. Let stand at room temperature for 6–8 hours, or until set, then chill for at least 8 hours and up to 4 days. It will develop a slight tangy flavor. Lightly beat the Crème Fraîche before using.

2 To toast the almonds for the decoration, place in a dry skillet over medium heat and stir until lightly browned. Take care that they do not burn. Immediately tip the almonds out of the pan. Reserve.

3 To make the Orange Blossom Cream, place the Crème Fraîche in a small bowl and stir in the orange blossom water with the orange blossom honey and orange rind. Taste and add a little extra orange blossom water if necessary.

4 To serve, cut the stems off the figs, but do not peel them. Stand the figs upright with the pointed end upward. Cut each fig into fourths without cutting all the way through, so that you can open them out into attractive "flowers."

5 If you are using fig leaves, place one in the center of each serving plate. Arrange 2 figs on top of each leaf and spoon a small amount of the orange-flavored cream alongside them. Sprinkle the cream with the toasted almonds, if desired, just before serving.

NUTRITION

Calories 20	Sugars 13g
Protein 3g	Fat 18g
Carbohydrate 14g	Saturates 9g

paper-thin fruit pies

serves four

1 dessert apple

1 ripe pear

2 tbsp lemon juice

4 tbsp lowfat spread

8 oz/225 g phyllo pastry, thawed
   if frozen

2 tbsp low-sugar apricot jelly

1 tbsp unsweetened orange juice

1 tbsp finely chopped pistachio nuts

2 tsp confectioners' sugar, for dusting

lowfat custard, to serve

NUTRITION

Calories 158	Sugars 12g
Protein 2g	Fat 10g
Carbohydrate 14g	Saturates 2g

VARIATION

Other combinations of fruit are
equally delicious. Try peach and
apricot, raspberry, and apple, or
pineapple and mango.

2 Melt the spread in a small pan over low heat. Cut the sheets of phyllo pastry into fourths and cover with a clean, damp dish towel. Brush 4 nonstick shallow pans, measuring 4 inches/10 cm across, with a little of the spread.

3 Working on each pie separately, brush 4 sheets of phyllo with spread. Press a small sheet of phyllo into the bottom of 1 pan. Arrange the other sheets of phyllo on top at slightly different angles. Repeat with the remaining sheets of phyllo to make another 3 pies. Arrange the apple and pear slices alternately in the center of each pastry shell and lightly crimp the edges of the dough of each pie.

1 Preheat the oven to 400°F/200°C. Core and thinly slice the apple and pear and toss them in the lemon juice to prevent discoloration.

4 Mix the jelly and orange juice together until smooth and brush over the fruits. Bake in the preheated oven for 12–15 minutes. Sprinkle with the pistachio nuts and dust lightly with sugar, then serve with custard.

peaches in white wine

serves four

4 large peaches

2 tbsp confectioners' sugar, sifted

1 orange

generous ¾ cup medium or sweet
white wine, chilled

NUTRITION

Calories 89	Sugars 14g
Protein 1g	Fat 0g
Carbohydrate 14g	Saturates 0g

COOK'S TIP

There is absolutely no need to
use expensive wine in this recipe,
so it can be quite economical
to make.

1 Using a sharp knife, halve the
peaches, then remove the pits
and discard them. Peel the peaches, if
you prefer. Slice into thin wedges.

2 Place the peach wedges in a glass
serving bowl and sprinkle over
the sugar.

3 Using a sharp knife, pare the rind
from the orange. Cut the orange
rind into short thin sticks and place
them in a bowl of cold water. Reserve.

4 Squeeze the juice from the orange
and pour over the peaches,
together with the chilled wine.

5 Cover and place the bowl in the
refrigerator for at least 1 hour to
let the peaches marinate and chill.

6 Remove the orange rind sticks
from the water and pat them dry
with paper towels.

7 Decorate the chilled marinated
peaches with the strips of orange
rind and serve immediately.

tropical salad

serves eight

1 papaya

2 tbsp fresh orange juice

3 tbsp rum

2 bananas

2 guavas

1 small pineapple or 2 baby
    pineapples

2 passion fruit

pineapple leaves, to decorate

NUTRITION

Calories 69	Sugars 13g
Protein 1g	Fat 0.3g
Carbohydrate 14g	Saturates 0g

COOK'S TIP

Guavas have a heavenly smell
when ripe—their scent will fill a
whole room. They should give to
gentle pressure when ripe, and
their skins should be yellow. The
canned varieties are very good
and have a pink tinge to
the flesh.

1 Cut the papaya in half and remove and discard the seeds. Peel and slice the flesh into a bowl.

2 Pour over the orange juice together with the rum.

3 Peel and slice the bananas, and peel and slice the guavas, then add both to the bowl.

4 Cut the top and base from the pineapple, then cut off the skin.

5 Slice the pineapple flesh, discarding the core, then cut into pieces and add to the bowl.

6 Halve the passion fruit and scoop out the flesh with a teaspoon. Add to the bowl and stir well to mix.

7 Spoon the salad into glass bowls and decorate with pineapple leaves. Serve.

chocolate biscotti

makes sixteen

butter, for greasing

1 egg

½ cup superfine sugar

1 tsp vanilla extract

scant 1 cup all-purpose flour, plus
extra for dusting

½ tsp baking powder

1 tsp ground cinnamon

1¾ squares semisweet chocolate,
coarsely chopped

scant ½ cup toasted slivered almonds

scant ½ cup pine nuts

NUTRITION

Calories 113	Sugars 9g
Protein 2g	Fat 5g
Carbohydrate 15g	Saturates 1g

1 Preheat the oven to 350°F/180°C.
Grease a cookie sheet with butter.

2 Whisk the egg, sugar, and vanilla
extract in a large bowl with an
electric mixer until it is thick and
pale—ribbons of mixture should trail
from the whisk as you lift it.

3 Sift the flour, baking powder, and
cinnamon into a separate bowl,
then sift into the egg mixture and
fold in gently. Stir in the chocolate,
almonds, and pine nuts.

4 Turn out onto a floured counter
and shape into a flat log
9 inches/23 cm long and ¾ inch/
2 cm wide. Transfer to the prepared
cookie sheet.

5 Bake in the preheated oven for
20–25 minutes, or until golden.
Remove from the oven and let cool for
5 minutes, or until firm.

6 Transfer the log to a cutting
board. Using a serrated bread
knife, cut the log on the diagonal into
slices about ½ inch/1 cm thick and
arrange them on the cookie sheet.
Cook for 10–15 minutes, turning
halfway through the cooking time.

7 Let cool for 5 minutes. Transfer to
a wire rack to cool completely.

creamy fruit parfait

serves four–six

8 oz/225 g cherries

2 large peaches

2 large apricots

3 cups strained plain yogurt or thick
   plain yogurt

½ cup walnut halves

2 tbsp flower-scented honey

fresh red currants or berries,
   to decorate (optional)

NUTRITION

Calories 261	Sugars 17g
Protein 10g	Fat 18g
Carbohydrate 17g	Saturates 7g

1 To prepare the fruits, use a cherry or olive pitter to remove the cherry pits. Cut each cherry in half. Cut the peaches and apricots in half from top to bottom and remove and discard the pits, then finely chop the flesh of all the fruits.

2 Place the finely chopped cherries, peaches, and apricots in a bowl and gently stir together.

3 Spoon one-third of the yogurt into an attractive glass serving bowl. Top with half the fruit mixture.

4 Repeat with another layer of yogurt and fruits and, finally, top with the remaining yogurt.

5 Place the walnuts in a small food processor and pulse until they are chopped into quite small pieces but not finely ground. Alternatively, chop them with a sharp knife. Sprinkle the walnuts over the top of the yogurt.

6 Drizzle the honey over the nuts and yogurt. Cover with plastic wrap and let chill in the refrigerator for at least 1 hour. Decorate the bowl with a small bunch of fresh red currants, if desired, just before serving.

lemon & lime syllabub

serves four

¼ cup superfine sugar

grated rind and juice of

   1 small lemon

grated rind and juice of 1 small lime

4 tbsp Marsala or

   medium sherry

1¼ cups heavy cream

lime and lemon rind, to decorate

NUTRITION

Calories 403	Sugars 16g
Protein 2g	Fat 36g
Carbohydrate 16g	Saturates 22g

1 Place the sugar, citrus juices and rind, and Marsala in a bowl, then mix well and let infuse for 2 hours.

2 Add the cream to the mixture and whisk until it just holds its shape.

3 Spoon the mixture into 4 tall serving glasses and let chill in the refrigerator for 2 hours.

4 Decorate with lime and lemon rind and serve.

COOK'S TIP

Do not overwhip the cream when adding it to the lemon and lime mixture, or it may curdle. Replace the heavy cream with lowfat plain yogurt for a lighter, healthier version of this dessert, or alternatively, use half quantities of both yogurt and cream. Whip the cream before adding it to the yogurt.

1

2

3

VARIATION

For an alternative citrus flavor, substitute 2 oranges for the lemon and lime, if you prefer.

lime mousse with mango

serves four

generous 1 cup mascarpone cheese

grated rind of 1 lime

1 tbsp superfine sugar

⅓ cup heavy cream

MANGO SAUCE

1 mango

juice of 1 lime

4 tsp superfine sugar

TO DECORATE

4 cape gooseberries

strips of lime rind

NUTRITION

Calories 254	Sugars 17g
Protein 5g	Fat 19g
Carbohydrate 17g	Saturates 12g

COOK'S TIP

Cape gooseberries have a tart and mildly scented flavor and make an excellent decoration for many desserts. Peel back the papery husks to expose the bright orange fruits.

1 Place the mascarpone cheese, lime rind, and sugar in a large bowl and mix together.

2 Whip the cream in a separate bowl and fold into the mixture.

3 Line 4 decorative molds or ramekin dishes with cheesecloth or plastic wrap and divide the mixture evenly between them. Fold the cheesecloth or plastic wrap over the top and press down firmly. Let chill in the refrigerator for 30 minutes.

4 To make the sauce, slice through the mango on each side of the large flat pit, then cut the flesh from the pit. Remove the skin.

5 Cut off 12 thin slices of mango and reserve. Chop the remaining mango and place in a food processor or blender with the lime juice and sugar. Blend until smooth. Alternatively, push the mango through a strainer, then mix with the lime juice and sugar.

6 Turn the molds out onto serving plates. Arrange 3 slices of mango on each plate and pour some sauce around, then decorate and serve.

melon & kiwifruit salad

serves four

½ Galia melon

2 kiwifruit

4½ oz/125 g white seedless grapes

1 papaya, halved

3 tbsp orange-flavored liqueur, such
as Cointreau

1 tbsp chopped fresh lemon
verbena, lemon balm, or mint

TO DECORATE

fresh lemon verbena sprigs

cape gooseberries

NUTRITION

Calories 88	Sugars 17g
Protein 1g	Fat 0.2g
Carbohydrate 17g	Saturates 0g

1 Remove the seeds from the melon and cut it into 4 slices, then carefully cut away the skin. Cut the flesh into cubes and place in a bowl.

2 Peel the kiwifruit and slice widthwise. Add to the melon with the grapes.

3 Remove the seeds from the papaya and discard and cut off the skin. Slice the flesh thickly and cut into diagonal pieces. Add to the fruit bowl and mix well.

4 Mix the liqueur and the chopped lemon verbena together, then pour over the fruits and let macerate for 1 hour, stirring occasionally.

5 Spoon the fruit salad into glasses and pour over the juices, then decorate with lemon verbena sprigs and cape gooseberries.

COOK'S TIP

Lemon balm or sweet balm is a fragrant lemon-scented plant with slightly hairy serrated leaves and a pronounced lemon flavor. Lemon verbena can also be used—this has an even stronger lemon flavor and smooth elongated leaves.

mini frangipane tartlets with lime

makes twelve

scant 1 cup all-purpose flour, plus
  extra for dusting
generous ¾ stick butter, softened
1 tsp grated lime rind
1 tbsp lime juice
¼ cup superfine sugar
1 egg
¼ cup ground almonds
¼ cup confectioners' sugar, sifted
½ tbsp water

1 Preheat the oven to 400°F/200°C. Reserve 5 teaspoons of the flour and 3 teaspoons of the butter.

2 Cut the remaining butter into the remaining flour until the mixture resembles fine bread crumbs. Stir in the lime rind, followed by the lime juice, then bring the mixture together with your fingers to form a soft dough.

3 Roll out the dough thinly on a floured counter. Stamp out 12 circles, 3 inches/7.5 cm wide, with a fluted cutter, and line a tartlet pan.

4 Cream the reserved butter and the superfine sugar together in a large bowl.

5 Mix in the egg, then the ground almonds and the reserved flour.

6 Divide the almond mixture between the pastry shells.

7 Bake in the preheated oven for 15 minutes, or until set and lightly golden. Turn the tartlets out onto a wire rack to cool.

8 Mix the confectioners' sugar with the water. Drizzle a little of the frosting over each tartlet and serve.

NUTRITION	
Calories 149	Sugars 9g
Protein 2g	Fat 9g
Carbohydrate 17g	Saturates 5g

pink syllabubs

serves two

5 tbsp white wine

2–3 tsp black currant liqueur

finely grated rind of ½ lemon
   or orange

1 tbsp superfine sugar

generous ¾ cup heavy cream

TO DECORATE

fresh fruits, such as strawberries,
   raspberries, or red currants, or
   pecan or walnut halves

fresh mint sprigs

NUTRITION

Calories 536	Sugars 17g
Protein 2g	Fat 48g
Carbohydrate 17g	Saturates 30g

COOK'S TIP

These syllabubs will keep in the refrigerator for 48 hours, so it is worth making more than you need and keeping the extra for another day.

1 Mix the wine, black currant liqueur, lemon rind, and sugar together in a bowl and let stand for at least 30 minutes.

2 Add the cream to the wine mixture and whip until the mixture has thickened enough to stand in soft peaks.

3 For a decorative effect, place the mixture into a pastry bag fitted with a large star or plain tip and pipe into 2 glasses. Alternatively, simply pour the syllabub into the glasses. Chill in the refrigerator until ready to serve.

4 Before serving, decorate each syllabub with slices or small pieces of fresh soft fruits or nuts and mint sprigs.

poached allspice pears

COOK'S TIP

The Chinese do not usually have desserts to finish off a meal, except at banquets and special occasions. Sweet dishes are usually served in between main meals as snacks, but fruit is refreshing at the end of a big meal.

1 Using an apple corer, core the pears. Using a sharp knife, peel the pears and cut them in half.

2 Place the pear halves in a large heavy-bottom pan.

3 Add the orange juice, allspice, raisins, and sugar to the pan and heat gently, stirring, until the sugar has dissolved. Bring the mixture to a boil for 1 minute.

NNUTRITION	
Calories 157	Sugars 17g
Protein 5g	Fat 19g
Carbohydrate 17g	Saturates 12g

4 Reduce the heat to low and let simmer for 10 minutes, or until the pears are cooked but still fairly firm—test them by inserting the tip of a small sharp knife.

5 Remove the cooked pears from the pan with a slotted spoon and transfer to serving plates. Decorate with the grated orange rind and serve hot with the syrup.

chocolate cheese pots

serves four

1¼ cups lowfat cream cheese

⅔ cup lowfat plain yogurt

2 tbsp confectioners' sugar

4 tsp lowfat drinking
   chocolate powder

4 tsp unsweetened cocoa

1 tsp vanilla extract

2 tbsp dark rum (optional)

2 egg whites

4 chocolate cake decorations,
   to decorate

assorted fruits, such as pieces of
   kiwifruit, orange, and banana,
   strawberries, and raspberries

NUTRITION

Calories 117	Sugars 17g
Protein 9g	Fat 1g
Carbohydrate 18g	Saturates 1g

1 Mix the cream cheese and yogurt together in a bowl. Sift in the sugar, drinking chocolate, and cocoa and mix well. Add the vanilla extract and rum, if using.

2 Whisk the egg whites in a clean bowl until stiff. Using a metal spoon, gently fold the egg whites into the chocolate mixture.

3 Spoon the cream cheese and chocolate mixture into 4 small china dessert pots and let chill in the refrigerator for 30 minutes.

4 Decorate each chocolate cheese pot with a chocolate decoration and serve with an assortment of fresh fruits, such as kiwifruit, orange, banana, strawberries, and raspberries.

COOK'S TIP

This would make a great filling for a cheesecake. Make the base out of crushed amaretti cookies and egg white. Set the filling with 2 tablespoons gelozone (vegetarian gelatin) dissolved in 2 tablespoons of boiling water.

pineapple with tequila & mint

serves four–six

1 ripe pineapple

sugar, to taste

juice of 1 lemon

2–3 tbsp tequila or a few drops of
vanilla extract

several fresh mint sprigs, leaves
removed and cut into thin strips

fresh mint sprig, to decorate

NUTRITION	
Calories 87	Sugars 19g
Protein 1g	Fat 0g
Carbohydrate 19g	Saturates 0g

COOK'S TIP

Make sure you slice off the
"eyes" when removing the skin
from the pineapple.

1 Using a sharp knife, cut off the top and bottom of the pineapple. Place upright on a board, then slice off the skin, cutting downward. Cut in half, and remove the core if wished, then cut the flesh into chunks.

2 Place the pineapple in a bowl and sprinkle with the sugar, lemon juice, and tequila.

3 Toss the pineapple to coat well, then cover and let chill until ready to serve.

4 To serve, arrange on a large serving plate and sprinkle with the mint strips. Decorate the dish with a mint sprig.

VARIATION

Substitute 3 peeled sliced
mangoes for the pineapple. To
prepare mango, slice off a large
piece of flesh on either side of
the pit, then peel and cut into
chunks. Slice off the remaining
flesh attached to the pit.

raspberry fool

COOK'S TIP

Although this dessert is best made with fresh raspberries, an acceptable result can be achieved with frozen raspberries, available from supermarkets.

1 Place the raspberries and sugar in a food processor or blender and process until smooth. Alternatively, press through a strainer with the back of a spoon.

2 Reserve 4 tablespoons of sour cream for decorating.

3 Place the vanilla extract and remaining sour cream in a bowl and stir in the raspberry mixture.

4 Whisk the egg whites in a separate mixing bowl until stiff peaks form. Gently fold the egg whites into the raspberry mixture using a metal spoon, until fully incorporated.

5 Spoon the raspberry fool into serving dishes and let chill for at least 1 hour. Decorate with the reserved sour cream, raspberries, and lemon balm leaves and serve.

Quick & Easy

Introduction

This book is designed to appeal to anyone who wants a wholesome but quick and easy diet, and includes many recipes suitable for vegetarians and vegans. Its main aim is to show people that, with a little forethought, it is possible to spend very little time in the kitchen while still enjoying  appetizing food. The recipes collected together come from all over the world; some of the Asian and barbecue dishes featured require marinating, often overnight, but it is worth remembering that their actual cooking time is very short once the marinade has been absorbed.

The more exotic dishes on offer are balanced by some traditional dishes, which are sure to become firm family favorites. If you want fast food for everyday meals, or you are short on time and want to prepare a tasty dinner party treat, there is something for everybody in this book. To save time in the kitchen, always make sure that you have a stock of staple foodstuffs such as rice, pasta, spices, and herbs, so that you can easily turn your hand to any number of these recipes.

Flour

You will need to keep a selection of flour: Self-rising and whole-wheat are the most useful. You may also like to keep rice flour and cornstarch for thickening sauces and to add to cakes, and desserts.

Grains and Rice

A good variety of grains is essential. For rice, choose from long-grain, basmati, Italian risotto, short-grain, and wild rice. Other grains add variety to the diet. Try to include barley millet, bulgar wheat, polenta, oats, semolina, and tapioca.

Pasta

Pasta is very popular and there are many types and shapes to choose from. Keep a good selection, such as tagliatelle, fettuccine, and fusilli.

Herbs

A good selection of herbs is important for adding variety to your cooking. You should store dried basil, thyme, bay leaves, oregano, rosemary, mixed herbs, and bouquet garni.

Spices

Your basic stock of spices should include fresh chiles, ginger root and garlic, chili powder, turmeric, paprika, cloves, cardamom, black pepper, ground coriander, and ground cumin. The powdered spices will keep very well in airtight containers, while the fresh chile, ginger root and garlic will keep for 7–10 days in the refrigerator.

Legumes

Legumes are a valuable source of protein, vitamins, and minerals. Stock up on dried or canned soybeans, navy beans, red kidney beans, cannellini beans, garbanzo beans, lentils, split peas, and wax beans.

Dried Fruits

Currants, raisins, golden raisins, dates, apples, apricots, figs, pears, peaches, prunes, papayas, mangoes, figs, bananas, and pineapples can all be used in many different recipes.

Oils and Fats

Oils add subtle flavorings to foods, so it is a good idea to have a selection in your cupboard. Use a light olive oil for cooking and extra virgin olive oil for salad dressings. Use corn oil as a general-purpose oil. Sesame oil is wonderful in stir-fries; hazelnut and walnut oils are superb in salad dressings.

Vinegars

Choose three or four vinegars – red or white wine, cider, light malt, tarragon, sherry, or balsamic vinegar, to name just a few. Each will add its own character to your recipes.

Mustards

Mustards are made from black, brown, or white mustard seeds which are ground and mixed with spices. Meaux mustard has a grainy texture with a warm taste. Dijon mustard has a sharp flavor while American mustard is mild and sweet.

Basic Recipes

Fresh Chicken Bouillon

MAKES 7½ CUPS

2 lb 4 oz/1 kg chicken, skinned

2 celery stalks

1 onion

2 carrots

1 garlic clove

few fresh parsley sprigs

9 cups water

salt and pepper

1 Put all the ingredients into a large pan and bring to a boil over a medium heat.

2 Using a slotted spoon, skim away any scum on the surface. Reduce the heat to a gentle simmer, partially cover, and cook for 2 hours. Let cool.

3 Line a strainer with clean cheesecloth and put over a large pitcher or bowl. Pour the bouillon through the strainer. The cooked chicken can be used in another recipe. Discard the other solids. Cover the bouillon and chill in the refrigerator.

4 Skim away any fat that forms before using. Store in the refrigerator for 3–4 days, until required, or freeze in small batches.

Fresh Vegetable Bouillon

This can be kept chilled for up to 3 days or frozen for up to 3 months. Salt is not added when cooking the bouillon: it is better to season it according to the dish in which it is to be used.

MAKES 6¼ CUPS

9 oz/250 g shallots

1 large carrot, diced

1 celery stalk, chopped

½ fennel bulb

1 garlic clove

1 bay leaf

few fresh parsley and tarragon sprigs

8¾ cups water

pepper

1 Put all the ingredients into a large pan and bring to a boil over a medium heat.

2 Using a slotted spoon, skim away any scum on the surface. Reduce the heat to a gentle simmer, partially cover, and cook for 45 minutes. Let cool.

3 Line a strainer with clean cheesecloth and put over a large pitcher or bowl. Pour the bouillon through the strainer). Discard the herbs and vegetables.

4 Cover and store in small quantities in the refrigerator for up to 3 days.

Fresh Lamb Bouillon

MAKES 7½ CUPS

about 2 lb 4 oz/1 kg bones from
    a cooked joint or raw chopped
    lamb bones

2 onions, studded with 6 cloves, or
    sliced or chopped coarsely

2 carrots, sliced

1 leek, sliced

1–2 celery stalks, sliced

1 bouquet garni

about 2 quarts water

1 Chop or break up the bones and put into a large pan with the other ingredients.

2 Bring to a boil over a medium heat. Using a slotted spoon, skim away any scum on the surface. Reduce the heat, partially cover, and cook gently for 3–4 hours. Strain the bouillon and let cool.

3 Remove any fat from the surface and chill in the refrigerator. If stored for more than 24 hours the bouillon must be boiled every day, cooled quickly and chilled again. The bouillon may be frozen for up to 2 months; put into a large plastic bag and seal, leaving at least 1 inch/2.5 cm of headspace to allow for expansion.

Fresh Fish Bouillon

MAKES 7½ CUPS

1 head of a cod or salmon, etc. plus
    the trimmings, skin and bones or
    just the trimmings, skin and bones

1–2 onions, sliced

1 carrot, sliced

1–2 celery stalks, sliced

good squeeze of lemon juice

1 bouquet garni or 2 bay leaves

1 Wash the fish head and trimmings and put into a pan. Cover with water and bring to a boil over a medium heat.

2 Using a slotted spoon, skim away any scum on the surface, then add the remaining ingredients. Cover and simmer for 30 minutes.

3 Strain and let cool. Store in the refrigerator and use within 2 days.

Cornstarch Paste

Cornstarch paste is made by mixing 1 part cornstarch with about 1½ parts of cold water. Stir until smooth. The paste is used to thicken sauces.

Soups

The soups in this chapter combine a variety of

flavors and textures from all over the world.

There are thicker soups, thin clear consommés,

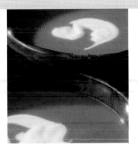

and soups to appeal to vegetarians. The range of soups include thick and

creamy winter warmers, and light and spicy Asian recipes. Many have been

chosen because of their nutritional content and may be eaten as part of a low-

fat diet. All, however, can be eaten as starters or as a light meal with fresh

bread. The recipes are taken from all over the world, with special emphasis on

Mediterranean, Indian, and Asian soups—something to please everybody.

artichoke soup

serves four

1 tbsp olive oil

1 onion, chopped

1 garlic clove, minced

1 lb/12 oz/ 800 g canned artichoke
hearts, drained

2½ cups hot vegetable bouillon

⅔ cup light cream

2 tbsp fresh thyme, stalks removed

2 sun-dried tomatoes, cut into strips

COOK'S TIP

Try adding 2 tbsp of dry
vermouth, such as Martini, to the
soup in step 5.

---

1 Heat the oil in a large pan over a
medium heat. Add the onion and
garlic, then cook until just softened.

2 Using a sharp knife, coarsely chop
the artichoke hearts. Add the
artichoke pieces to the onion and garlic
mixture in the pan. Pour in the hot
vegetable bouillon, stirring.

3 Bring the mixture to a boil over a
medium heat, then reduce the
heat, cover and simmer for 3 minutes.

4 Transfer the soup to a food
processor or blender and process
until smooth. Alternatively, push
through a strainer to remove lumps.

5 Return the soup to the pan and
stir in the cream and thyme.

6 Transfer the soup to a large bowl,
cover and chill in the refrigerator
for about 3–4 hours.

7 Ladle the chilled soup into 4 soup
bowls and garnish with strips of
sun-dried tomato. Serve immediately.

red bell pepper soup

serves four

8 oz/225 g red bell peppers, seeded
    and sliced

1 onion, sliced

2 garlic cloves, minced

1 fresh green chile, chopped

1¼ cups strained tomatoes

2½ cups vegetable bouillon

2 tbsp chopped fresh basil

fresh basil sprigs, to garnish

VARIATION

This soup is also delicious
served cold with ⅔ cup
plain yogurt swirled into it.

1 Put the red bell peppers in a large pan with the onion, garlic, and chili. Add the strained tomatoes and vegetable bouillon, then bring to a boil over a medium heat, stirring constantly.

2 Reduce the heat and simmer for 20 minutes, or until the peppers have softened. Drain and set aside the liquid and vegetables separately.

3 Puree the vegetables by pressing through a strainer with the back of a spoon. Alternatively, process in a food processor until smooth.

4 Return the vegetable puree to a clean pan and add the cooking liquid. Add the chopped basil and heat until hot. Ladle the soup into 4 bowls and garnish with basil sprigs. Serve.

mushroom noodle soup

serves four

4½ oz/125 g flat or open
  cup mushrooms

½ cucumber

2 scallions

1 garlic clove, peeled

2 tbsp vegetable oil

2½ cups water

1 oz/25 g Chinese rice noodles

¾ tsp salt

1 tbsp soy sauce

COOK'S TIP

Scooping the seeds out from the
cucumber gives it a prettier effect
when sliced, and also helps to
reduce any bitterness, but if you
prefer, you can leave them in.

1 Wash the mushrooms and pat
them dry on paper towels. Slice
thinly. Do not remove the mushroom
peel as this adds more flavor.

2 Cut the cucumber in half
lengthwise. Taking care not to
damage the flesh, scoop out the seeds,
using a teaspoon, then slice the
cucumber thinly.

3 Chop the scallions finely and cut
the garlic into thin strips.

4 Heat the oil in a large pan or wok
over a medium heat.

5 Add the scallions and garlic
to the pan or wok and cook for
30 seconds. Add the mushrooms and
cook for an additional 2–3 minutes.

6 Stir in the water. Break the noodles
into short lengths and add to the
pan. Bring the soup to a boil over a
medium heat, stirring occasionally.

7 Add the cucumber slices, salt, and
soy sauce and simmer for about
2–3 minutes.

8 Ladle the mushroom noodle
soup into 4 large, warmed soup
bowls, distributing the noodles and
vegetables evenly. Serve immediately.

mushroom & ginger soup

serves four

15 g/½ oz dried Chinese
    mushrooms or 4½ oz/125 g field
    or crimini mushrooms
4 cups hot vegetable bouillon
4½ oz/125 g egg thread noodles
2 tsp corn oil
3 garlic cloves, minced
1-inch/2.5-cm piece fresh
    gingerroot, shredded finely
½ tsp mushroom catsup
1 tsp light soy sauce
4½ oz/125 g bean sprouts
fresh cilantro leaves, to garnish

COOK'S TIP

Rice noodles contain no fat
and are ideal for for anyone
on a lowfat diet.

---

1 Soak the dried mushrooms (if
using) for at least 30 minutes in
1¼ cups of the bouillon. Remove and
discard the stalks from the fresh
mushrooms, then slice. Drain the dried
mushrooms and set aside the bouillon.

2 Bring a large pan of water to a
boil over a medium heat. Add the
noodles and cook for 2–3 minutes.
Drain thoroughly and rinse. Set aside.

3 Heat a large wok over a high
heat. Add the oil and when hot,
add the garlic and ginger. Stir and add
the mushrooms. Stir for 2 minutes.

4 Add the remaining vegetable
bouillon with the reserved
bouillon and bring to a boil over a high
heat. Add the catsup and soy sauce.

5 Stir in the bean sprouts and cook
until tender. Put some noodles
into each bowl and ladle the soup on
top. Garnish with cilantro and serve.

lettuce & beancurd soup

serves four

7 oz/200 g beancurd,
(drained weight)

2 tbsp vegetable oil

1 carrot, sliced thinly

½-inch/1-cm piece fresh gingerroot,
cut into thin shreds

3 scallions, sliced diagonally

5 cups vegetable bouillon

2 tbsp soy sauce

2 tbsp dry sherry

1 tsp sugar

4½ oz/125 g romaine lettuce, shredded

COOK'S TIP

For a pretty effect, score grooves along the length of the carrot with a sharp knife before slicing. This will create a flower effect as the carrot is cut into rounds.

---

1 Using a sharp knife, cut the beancurd into small cubes.

2 Heat a large wok over a high heat. Add the oil and when hot, add the beancurd and cook until browned. Remove with a slotted spoon and drain on paper towels.

3 Add the carrot, ginger, and scallions to the wok and cook for 2 minutes.

4 Add the vegetable bouillon, soy sauce, sherry, and sugar to the wok. Stir well to mix. Bring to a boil over a medium heat and simmer for 1 minute. Add the romaine lettuce to the wok and stir until it wilts.

5 Return the beancurd to the wok to heat through. Season to taste with salt and pepper and ladle into 4 warmed bowls and serve.

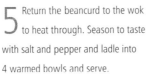

spicy dhal & carrot soup

serves six

⅔ cup split red lentils

5 cups vegetable bouillon

12 oz/350 g carrots, sliced

2 onions, chopped

8 oz/225 g canned
    chopped tomatoes

2 garlic cloves, chopped

2 tbsp ghee or vegetable oil

1 tsp ground cumin

1 tsp ground coriander

1 fresh green chile, seeded and
    chopped or 1 tsp minced chile

½ tsp ground turmeric

1 tbsp lemon juice

salt

1¼ cups milk

2 tbsp chopped fresh cilantro

unsweetened plain yogurt, to serve

COOK'S TIP

Lentils play an important part in ensuring that a healthy diet is maintained and provide energy-rich carbohydrates. Current guidelines recommend that 50% of our daily energy requirements come from carbohydrates.

1 Put the lentils into a strainer and rinse well under cold running water. Drain and put into a large pan, together with 2½ cups of the bouillon, the carrots, onions, tomatoes, and garlic. Bring the mixture to a boil over a medium heat, then cover and simmer for 30 minutes, or until the vegetables and lentils are tender.

2 Meanwhile, heat the ghee or oil in a small pan over a low heat. Add the cumin, ground coriander, chile, and turmeric and cook for 1 minute. Remove from the heat and stir in the lemon juice. Season with salt to taste.

3 Working in batches, transfer the soup to a blender and process until smooth. Return to the pan, add the spice mixture and the remaining 2½ cups of bouillon and cook over a low heat for 10 minutes.

4 Add the milk, taste, and adjust the seasoning, if necessary. Stir in the chopped cilantro and heat gently. Ladle the soup into 6 warmed bowls, and serve hot with a swirl of yogurt.

garbanzo bean soup

serves four

2 tbsp olive oil

2 leeks, sliced

2 zucchini, diced

2 garlic cloves, minced

1 lb 12 oz/800 g canned
    chopped tomatoes

1 tbsp tomato paste

1 bay leaf

3 cups vegetable bouillon

14 oz/400 g canned garbanzo
    beans, drained and rinsed

8 oz/225 g spinach

TO SERVE

freshly grated Parmesan cheese

sun-dried tomato bread

1 Heat the oil in a large pan over a medium heat. Add the leeks and zucchini and cook them for 5 minutes, stirring constantly.

2 Add the garlic, tomatoes, tomato paste, bay leaf, vegetable bouillon, and garbanzo beans.

3 Bring to a boil, then reduce the heat and simmer for 5 minutes.

4 Shred the spinach finely, add to the soup and cook for 2 minutes. Season to taste with salt and pepper.

5 Remove the bay leaf and discard. Ladle the soup into 4 bowls and serve with the Parmesan cheese and warmed sun-dried tomato bread.

COOK'S TIP

Garbanzo beans are used extensively in North African cuisine and are also found in Spanish and Asian cooking. They have a nutty flavor with a firm texture and are excellent canned.

tomato & pasta soup

serves four

4 tbsp unsalted butter

1 large onion, chopped

2½ cups vegetable bouillon

2 lb/900 g Italian plum tomatoes,
   peeled and chopped coarsely

pinch of baking soda

2 cups dried fusilli

1 tbsp superfine sugar

⅝ cup heavy cream

salt and pepper

fresh basil leaves, to garnish

1 Melt the butter in a large pan over a medium heat. Add the onion and cook for 3 minutes. Add 1¼ cups of vegetable bouillon to the pan, with the tomatoes, and baking soda. Bring to a boil, then reduce the heat and simmer for 20 minutes.

2 Remove the pan from the heat and let cool. Transfer the soup to a blender and process until smooth. Pour through a fine strainer back into the rinsed out pan.

3 Add the remaining vegetable bouillon and the pasta, and season to taste with salt and pepper.

4 Add the sugar to the pan and bring to a boil over a medium heat, then reduce the heat and simmer for about 15 minutes.

5 Ladle the soup into a warmed tureen, swirl the cream on top of the soup and garnish with fresh basil leaves. Serve immediately.

275

pumpkin soup

serves four

2 tbsp olive oil

2 medium onions, chopped

2 garlic cloves, chopped

2 lb/900 g pumpkin, peeled and cut
into 1-inch/2.5-cm chunks

6¾ cups boiling vegetable or
chicken bouillon

finely grated peel and juice of
1 orange

3 tbsp fresh thyme leaves

⅔ cup milk

salt and pepper

crusty bread, to serve

COOK'S TIP

Pumpkins are usually
large vegetables. To make
things a little easier, ask the
grocer to cut a chunk off for you.
Alternatively, make double the
quantity and freeze the soup
for up to 3 months.

1 Heat the oil in a large pan over a medium heat. Add the onions and cook, stirring occasionally, for 3–4 minutes, or until softened. Add the garlic and pumpkin and cook, stirring, for an additional 2 minutes.

2 Add the boiling bouillon, orange peel and juice, and 2 tablespoons of the fresh thyme to the pan. Cover and simmer for 20 minutes, or until the pumpkin is tender.

3 Transfer to a blender and process until smooth. Alternatively, put the mixture into a bowl and mash with a potato masher until smooth. Season to taste with salt and pepper.

4 Return the soup to the pan and add the milk. Heat through for 3–4 minutes, or until piping hot, but not boiling.

5 Sprinkle with the remaining fresh thyme just before serving.

6 Ladle the soup into 4 warmed soup bowls and serve with lots of fresh crusty bread.

spinach & mascarpone soup

serves four

4 tbsp butter

1 bunch scallions, trimmed
and chopped

2 celery stalks, chopped

12 oz/350 g spinach or sorrel
or arugula

3 cups vegetable bouillon

8 oz/225 g mascarpone cheese

1 tbsp olive oil

2 slices thick-cut bread, cut
into cubes

½ tsp caraway seeds

salt and pepper

sesame grissini, to serve

1 Melt half the butter in a very large pan over a medium heat. Add the scallions and celery, and cook, stirring frequently, for about 5 minutes, or until softened.

2 Pack the spinach, sorrel, or arugula into the pan. Add the bouillon and bring to a boil over a medium heat, then reduce the heat, cover, and cook for 15–20 minutes.

3 Transfer the soup to a blender or food processor and process until smooth. Alternatively, rub through a strainer with the back of a spoon. Return to the pan.

4 Add the mascarpone cheese to the soup and heat gently, stirring constantly, until smooth and blended. Season to taste with salt and pepper.

5 Heat the remaining butter with the oil in a skillet over a medium heat. Add the bread cubes and cook, turning frequently, until golden brown, adding the caraway seeds toward the end of cooking, so they do not burn.

6 Ladle the soup into 4 warmed bowls. Sprinkle with the croutons and serve with the sesame grissini.

beet & potato soup

serves six

1 onion, chopped

12 oz/350 g potatoes, diced

1 small cooking apple, peeled, cored, and grated

3 tbsp water

1 tsp cumin seeds

1 lb 2 oz/500 g cooked beet, peeled and diced

1 bay leaf

pinch of dried thyme

1 tsp lemon juice

2½ cups hot vegetable bouillon

4 tbsp sour cream

salt and pepper

fresh dill sprigs, to garnish

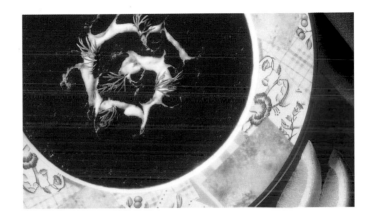

1 Put the onion, potatoes, apple, and water in a large bowl. Cover and cook on HIGH for 10 minutes.

2 Stir in the cumin seeds and cook on HIGH for 1 minute.

3 Stir in the beet, bay leaf, thyme, lemon juice, and bouillon. Cover and cook on HIGH for 12 minutes, stirring halfway through. Set aside, uncovered, for 5 minutes.

4 Remove the bay leaf and discard. Strain the vegetables and set aside the liquid in a pitcher.

5 Put the vegetables with a little of the reserved liquid in a blender and process until smooth.

6 Pour the vegetable puree into a clean bowl with the reserved liquid and mix well. Season to taste with salt and pepper. Cover and cook on HIGH for 4–5 minutes, or until piping hot.

7 Ladle the soup into 6 warmed bowls. Swirl 1 tablespoon of sour cream into each serving and garnish with a few fresh dill sprigs.

sweet & sour cabbage soup

serves four–six

½ cup golden raisins

½ cup orange juice

1 tbsp olive oil

1 large onion, chopped

9 oz/250 g cabbage, shredded

2 apples, peeled and diced

½ cup apple juice

14 oz/400 g canned
    peeled tomatoes

1 cup tomato or vegetable juice

3½ oz/100 g pineapple flesh,
    chopped finely

5 cups water

2 tsp wine vinegar

salt and pepper

fresh mint leaves, to garnish

COOK'S TIP

You can use green or white
cabbage to make this soup,
but red cabbage would require
a much longer cooking time.
Savoy cabbage has too
powerful a flavor.

1 Put the golden raisins into a
bowl, pour the orange juice over
them, and let soak for 15 minutes.

2 Heat the oil in a large pan over a
medium heat. Add the onion and
cook, stirring occasionally, for about
3–4 minutes, or until just soft. Add the
cabbage and cook for an additional
2 minutes, but do not let it brown.

3 Add the apples and apple juice,
cover, and cook for 5 minutes.
Stir in the tomatoes, tomato juice,
pineapple, and water. Season to taste
with salt and pepper and add the
vinegar. Add the golden raisins with
the orange juice. Bring to a boil over a
medium heat, reduce the heat, partially
cover, and cook for 1 hour, or until the
fruit and vegetables are tender.

4 Remove the pan from the heat
and let cool slightly. Working in
batches, transfer the soup to a blender
or food processor and process until
smooth. (If using a food processor,
strain off the cooking liquid and set
aside. Puree the solids with enough
cooking liquid to moisten them, then
mix with the remaining liquid.)

5 Return the soup to the pan and
simmer for about 10 minutes to
heat through. Ladle into warmed
bowls and garnish with fresh mint
leaves. Serve immediately.

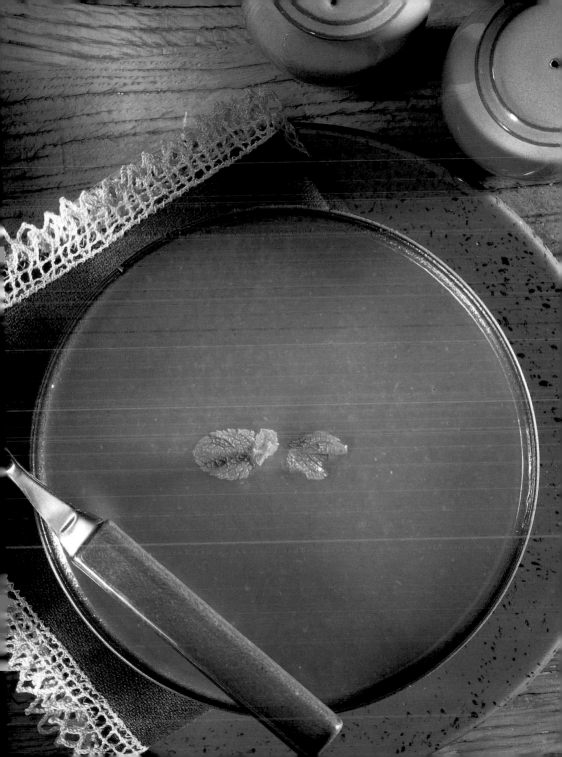

fresh mushroom soup

serves four

3 tbsp butter

1 lb 9 oz/700 g mushrooms, sliced

1 onion, chopped finely

1 shallot, chopped finely

3 tbsp all-purpose flour

2–3 tbsp sherry or dry white wine

6 cups vegetable bouillon

⅔ cup light cream

2 tbsp chopped fresh parsley

fresh lemon juice, optional

salt and pepper

TO GARNISH

4 tbsp sour cream

4 fresh herb sprigs

1 Melt half the butter in a large skillet over a medium heat. Add the mushrooms and season with salt and pepper. Cook for 8 minutes, or until golden, stirring occasionally at first, then more often after they start to color. Remove from the heat.

2 Melt the remaining butter in a pan over a medium heat. Add the onion and shallot, and cook for 2–3 minutes, or until just softened. Stir in the flour and cook for 2 minutes. Add the wine and bouillon and stir.

3 Set aside about one-quarter of the mushrooms and add the remainder to the pan. Reduce the heat, cover, and cook for 20 minutes.

4 Let cool slightly, then working in batches, transfer the soup to a blender or food processor and process until smooth. (If using a food processor, strain off the cooking liquid and set aside. Puree the soup solids with enough cooking liquid to moisten them, then mix well with the remaining liquid.)

5 Return the soup to the pan and stir in the reserved mushrooms, the cream, and parsley. Cook for about 5 minutes to heat through, taste and

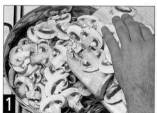

adjust the seasoning, adding a little lemon juice if you wish. Ladle the soup into 4 large, warmed bowls and garnish with sour cream and fresh herb sprigs. Serve immediately.

parsnip soup with ginger

serves six

2 tsp olive oil

1 large onion, chopped

1 large leek, sliced

1 lb 12 oz/800 g parsnips, sliced

2 carrots, sliced thinly

4 tbsp grated fresh gingerroot

2–3 garlic cloves, chopped finely

grated peel of ½ orange

6¼ cups water

1 cup orange juice

salt and pepper

TO GARNISH

snipped fresh chives

finely grated orange peel

VARIATION

You could make the soup using equal amounts (1 lb/450 g each) of carrots and parsnips.

1 Heat the oil in a large pan over a medium heat. Add the onion and leek and cook, stirring occasionally, for about 5 minutes, or until softened.

2 Add the parsnips, carrots, ginger, garlic, grated orange peel, water, and a pinch of salt. Reduce the heat, cover, and simmer, stirring occasionally, for about 40 minutes, or until the vegetables have softened.

3 Remove from the heat and let cool slightly, then working in batches, transfer the soup to a blender or food processor, and process until a smooth puree forms.

4 Return the soup to the pan and stir in the orange juice. Add a little water or more orange juice, if you prefer a thinner consistency. Season to taste with salt and pepper.

5 Simmer for about 10 minutes to heat through. Ladle the soup into 6 warmed bowls, garnish with chives and finely grated orange peel. Serve.

283

thick onion soup

serves four

6 tbsp butter

1 lb 2 oz/500 g onions, chopped finely

1 garlic clove, minced

⅓ cup all-purpose flour

2½ cups vegetable bouillon

2½ cups milk

2–3 tsp lemon or lime juice

good pinch of ground allspice

1 bay leaf

1 carrot, grated coarsely

4–6 tbsp heavy cream

2 tbsp chopped parsley

salt and pepper

CHEESE BISCUITS

½ cup whole-wheat flour

2 tsp baking powder

4 tbsp butter

4 tbsp freshly grated Parmesan cheese

1 egg, beaten

about 5 tbsp milk

1 Melt the butter in a pan over a low heat. Add the onions and garlic and cook, stirring frequently, for 10–15 minutes, or until softened, but not colored. Stir in the flour and cook, stirring, for 1 minute, then gradually stir in the bouillon and bring to a boil over a medium heat, stirring frequently. Add the milk, then bring back to a boil.

2 Season to taste with salt and pepper and add 2 teaspoons of the lemon juice, allspice, and bay leaf. Cover and simmer for 25 minutes, or until the vegetables are tender. Remove the bay leaf and discard.

3 Meanwhile, make the biscuits. Mix the flour, baking powder, and seasoning together. Rub in the butter until the mixture resembles fine bread crumbs, then stir in 3 tablespoons of the Parmesan cheese, the egg, and enough milk to mix to a soft dough.

4 Shape into a bar about ¾-inch/ 2-cm thick. Put onto a floured cookie sheet and mark into slices. Sprinkle with the remaining cheese and cook in a preheated oven at 425°F/220°C, for about 20 minutes, or until risen and golden brown.

5 Stir the carrot into the soup and simmer for 2–3 minutes. Add more lemon juice, if necessary. Stir in the cream and heat through. Garnish and serve with the biscuits.

gardener's broth

serves six

3 tbsp butter

1 onion, chopped

1–2 garlic cloves, minced

1 large leek

8 oz/225 g Brussels sprouts

4½ oz/125 g green beans

5 cups vegetable bouillon

1¼ cups frozen peas

1 tbsp lemon juice

½ tsp ground coriander

4 tbsp heavy cream

salt and pepper

MELBA TOAST

4–6 slices white bread

1 Melt the butter in a pan over a low heat. Add the onion and garlic and cook, stirring occasionally, until just soft, but not colored.

2 Slice the white part of the leek very thinly and set aside; slice the remaining leek. Slice the Brussels sprouts and thinly slice the beans.

3 Add the green part of the leeks, the Brussels sprouts, and beans to the pan. Add the bouillon and bring to a boil over a medium heat, then reduce the heat and simmer for 10 minutes.

4 Add the peas and seasoning. Add the lemon juice and cilantro, and continue to simmer for 10–15 minutes, or until the vegetables are tender.

5 Let cool slightly, then transfer the soup to a blender or food processor and process until smooth. Alternatively, rub through a strainer until smooth. Pour into a clean pan.

6 Add the reserved slices of leek, bring back to a boil, and simmer for about 5 minutes, or until the leek is tender. Adjust the seasoning, stir in the cream, and heat through gently.

7 To make the Melba toast, toast the bread on both sides under a preheated hot broiler. Cut horizontally through the slices, then toast the uncooked sides until they curl up. Serve immediately with the soup.

creamy onion & fava bean soup

serves five-six

1 tbsp butter

1 tsp oil

2 large onions, chopped finely

1 leek, sliced thinly

1 garlic clove, minced

5 cups water

6 tbsp white rice

1 bay leaf

½ tsp chopped fresh
  rosemary leaves

½ tsp chopped fresh thyme leaves

12 oz/350 g fresh or frozen fava
  beans, thawed if frozen

3½ oz/100 g rindless lean bacon,
  chopped finely

1½ cups milk, plus extra if needed

freshly grated nutmeg

salt and pepper

fresh herb sprigs, to garnish

1 Heat the butter and oil in a large pan over a medium heat. Add the onions, leek, and garlic. Season to taste with salt and pepper and cook for 10–15 minutes, stirring frequently, until the onion is soft.

2 Add the water, rice, and herbs with a large pinch of salt to the pan. Bring just to a boil over a medium heat, then reduce the heat to low. Cover and simmer for 15 minutes.

3 Add the fava beans, cover again and continue simmering for an additional 15 minutes, or until the vegetables are tender.

4 Remove the bay leaf and discard. let cool slightly, then, working in batches, transfer the soup to a blender or food processor and process until smooth. (If using a food processor, strain off the cooking liquid and set aside. Puree the solids with enough cooking liquid to moisten them, then mix with the remaining liquid.)

5 Put the bacon onto a large cookie sheet and put under a preheated hot broiler. Cook until crispy, turning the bacon over halfway through. Drain thoroughly on paper towels.

6 Return the soup to the pan and stir in the milk, adding extra, if you prefer a thinner consistency. Taste and adjust the seasoning, if necessary, then add a good grating of nutmeg. Cook over a low heat for 10 minutes, or until heated through, stirring occasionally. Ladle the soup into warmed bowls, sprinkle with bacon and garnish with herb sprigs. Serve.

chicken & pasta broth

serves six

12 oz/350 g boneless
   chicken breasts

2 tbsp corn oil

1 medium onion, diced

1½ cups carrots, diced

9 oz/250 g cauliflower flowerets

3¾ cups chicken bouillon

2 tsp dried mixed herbs

1¼ cups small pasta shapes

salt and pepper

freshly grated Parmesan
   cheese, optional

VARIATION

Broccoli flowerets can be
used to replace the cauliflower
flowerets. Substitute 2 tbsp
of chopped fresh mixed herbs for
the dried mixed herbs, if
you wish.

1 Finely dice the chicken breasts with a sharp knife. Remove and discard any skin.

2 Heat the oil in a large heavy-bottomed pan or skillet over a medium-high heat. Add the diced chicken and the vegetables and quickly cook until they are lightly colored.

3 Stir in the bouillon and herbs. Bring to a boil and add the pasta shapes. Return to a boil, cover, and simmer for 10 minutes, stirring occasionally to prevent the pasta shapes sticking together.

4 Season to taste with salt and pepper, sprinkle with Parmesan cheese (if using) and serve.

chicken & leek soup

serves six

12 oz/350 g boneless
   chicken breasts

12 oz/350 g leeks

2 tbsp butter

5 cups chicken bouillon

1 bouquet garni

8 pitted prunes

cooked rice and diced bell
   peppers, optional

salt and white pepper

VARIATION

Instead of the bouquet garni
sachet, you can use a bunch
of fresh, mixed herbs, tied
together with string. Choose
herbs such as parsley, thyme,
and rosemary.

1 Cut the chicken and leeks into
1-inch/2.5-cm pieces.

2 Melt the butter in a large pan
over a medium heat. Add the
chicken and leeks and cook for about
8 minutes, stirring occasionally.

3 Add the chicken bouillon and
bouquet garni to the mixture in
the pan, and season to taste with salt
and pepper.

4 Bring the soup to a boil over a
medium heat, then reduce the
heat and simmer for 45 minutes.

5 Add the pitted prunes with some
cooked rice and diced bell peppers
(if using), and simmer for 20 minutes.
Remove the bouquet garni and
discard. Ladle the soup into a warmed
tureen or individual bowls and serve.

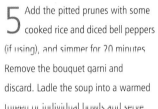

chunky potato & beef soup

serves four

2 tbsp vegetable oil

8 oz/225 g lean braising or frying
    steak, cut into strips

8 oz/225 g new potatoes, halved

1 carrot, diced

2 celery stalks, sliced

2 leeks, sliced

3¾ cups beef bouillon

8 baby corn cobs, sliced

1 bouquet garni

2 tbsp dry sherry

salt and pepper

chopped fresh parsley, to garnish

crusty bread, to serve

COOK'S TIP

Make double the quantity of
soup and freeze the remainder in
a rigid container for later use.
When ready to use, put in the
refrigerator to thaw thoroughly,
then heat until piping hot.

---

1 Heat the oil in a large pan over a medium heat. Add the strips of steak to the pan and cook for about 3 minutes, turning constantly.

2 Add the potatoes, carrot, and celery and leeks. Cook, stirring constantly, for an additional 5 minutes.

3 Pour in the beef bouillon and bring to a boil over a medium heat. Reduce the heat until the liquid is simmering gently, then add the sliced baby corn cobs and the bouquet garni.

4 Cook the soup for an additional 20 minutes, or until the meat and all the vegetables are tender.

5 Remove the bouquet garni from the pan and discard. Stir the dry sherry into the soup, then season to taste with salt and pepper.

6 Ladle the soup into 4 warmed soup bowls and garnish with the chopped fresh parsley. Serve with lots of crusty bread.

lamb & rice soup

serves four

5½ oz/150 g lean lamb

¼ cup rice

3¾ cups lamb bouillon

1 leek, sliced

1 garlic clove, sliced thinly

2 tsp light soy sauce

1 tsp rice wine vinegar

1 large open cap mushroom, sliced

salt

chopped fresh parsley, to garnish

1 Using a sharp knife, trim any fat from the lamb and cut the meat into thin strips. Set aside until required.

2 Bring a large pan of lightly salted water to a boil over a medium heat. Add the rice, bring back to a boil, stir once, reduce the heat and cook for 10–15 minutes, or until tender. Drain, rinse and drain again. Set aside.

3 Meanwhile, put the lamb bouillon into a large pan and bring to a boil over a medium heat.

4 Add the lamb strips, leek, garlic, soy sauce, and rice wine vinegar to the bouillon in the pan. Reduce the heat, then cover and simmer for about 10 minutes, or until the lamb is tender and cooked through.

5 Add the mushroom slices and the rice to the pan and cook for an additional 2–3 minutes, or until the mushroom is cooked through and the soup is piping hot.

6 Ladle the soup into 4 large, warmed soup bowls and garnish with chopped fresh parsley. Serve immediately.

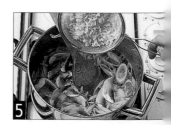

bacon, bean & garlic soup

serves four

8 oz/225 g lean smoked back
    bacon slices

1 carrot, sliced thinly

1 celery stalk, sliced thinly

1 onion, chopped

1 tbsp oil

3 garlic cloves, sliced

3 cups hot vegetable bouillon

7 oz/200 g canned
    chopped tomatoes

1 tbsp chopped fresh thyme

about 14 oz/400 g canned
    cannellini beans, drained

1 tbsp tomato paste

salt and pepper

freshly grated cheddar cheese,
    to garnish

1 Chop 2 slices of the bacon and put into a bowl. Cook in the microwave on HIGH for 3–4 minutes, until the fat runs out and the bacon is well cooked. Stir the bacon halfway through cooking to separate the pieces. Transfer to a large plate lined with paper towels and let cool. When cool, the bacon pieces should be crisp and dry.

2 Put the carrot, celery, onion and oil into a large bowl. Cover and cook on HIGH for 4 minutes.

3 Chop the remaining bacon and add to the bowl with the garlic. Cover and cook on HIGH for 2 minutes.

4 Add the bouillon, the chopped tomatoes, thyme, beans, and tomato paste. Cover and cook on HIGH for 8 minutes, stirring halfway through. Season to taste with salt and pepper. Ladle the soup into 4 warmed bowls and sprinkle with the crisp bacon and grated cheese. Serve immediately.

beef & noodle soup

serves four

8 oz/225 g lean beef

1 garlic clove, minced

2 scallions, chopped

3 tbsp soy sauce

1 tsp sesame oil

8 oz/225 g egg noodles

3¾ cups beef bouillon

3 baby corn cobs, sliced

½ leek, shredded

4½ oz/125 g broccoli, cut
   into flowerets

pinch of chili powder

VARIATION

Vary the vegetables used or use those to hand. If preferred, use a few drops of chili sauce instead of chili powder, but remember it is very hot!

1 Using a sharp knife, cut the beef into thin strips and put into a large bowl with the garlic, scallions, soy sauce, and sesame oil.

2 Mix the ingredients together in the bowl, turning the beef to coat. Cover and set aside to marinate in the refrigerator for 30 minutes.

3 Bring a pan of water to a boil over a medium heat. Add the noodles and cook for 3–4 minutes. Drain thoroughly and set aside.

4 Put the beef bouillon into a large pan and bring to a boil over a medium heat. Add the beef, with the marinade, the corn, shredded leek, and broccoli. Reduce the heat, cover and simmer for 7–10 minutes, or until the beef and vegetables are tender.

5 Stir in the cooked noodles and chili powder and cook for an additional 2–3 minutes.

6 Ladle the soup into 4 warmed bowls and serve immediately.

clear chicken & egg soup

serves four

1 tsp salt

1 tbsp rice wine vinegar

4 eggs

3¾ cups chicken bouillon

1 leek, sliced

4½ oz/125 g broccoli flowerets

1 cup shredded cooked chicken

2 open cap mushrooms, sliced

1 tbsp dry sherry

dash of chilli sauce, or to taste

chilli powder, for sprinkling

VARIATION

You could use 4 dried
Chinese mushrooms, rehydrated
according to the package
instructions, instead
of the open cap mushrooms,
if you prefer.

1 Bring a large pan of water to a
boil over a medium heat, Add the
salt and rice wine vinegar.

2 Reduce the heat so it is just
simmering and carefully break the
eggs into the water, one at a time.
Poach the eggs for 1 minute.

3 Remove the poached eggs with a
slotted spoon and set aside.

4 Bring the bouillon to a boil in a
separate pan over a medium
heat. Add the leek, broccoli, chicken,
mushrooms, and sherry. Add chilli
sauce and cook for 10–15 minutes.

5 Add the poached eggs to the
soup and cook for 2 minutes.
Carefully Ladle the soup and poached
eggs into 4 soup bowls. Sprinkle over
a little chilli powder and serve.

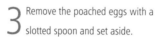

shrimp soup

serves four

2 tbsp corn oil

2 scallions, thinly sliced diagonally

1 carrot, grated coarsely

125 g/4½ oz large closed cup
mushrooms, sliced thinly

4 cups fish or vegetable bouillon

½ tsp Chinese five-spice powder

1 tbsp light soy sauce

125 g/4½ oz large, shelled shrimp
or shelled jumbo shrimp, thawed
if frozen

½ cup arugula, chopped coarsely

1 egg, well beaten

salt and pepper

4 large shrimp in shells, to
garnish (optional)

2 Add the bouillon and bring to a boil. Add the Chinese five-spice powder and soy sauce, and season to taste with salt and pepper. Simmer for 5 minutes.

3 If the shrimp are large, cut them in half before adding to the wok and simmer for 3–4 minutes.

4 Add the arugula and mix, then slowly pour in the beaten egg in a circular movement so it cooks in threads. Adjust the seasoning. Ladle the soup into 4 warmed bowls, top each with a whole shrimp and serve.

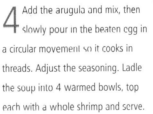

1 Heat a wok over a medium heat and when hot, add the oil and swirl it around. Add the scallions and cook for 1 minute. Add the carrots and mushrooms, then cook for 2 minutes.

partan bree

1 Remove all the brown and white meat from the cooked crab with a sharp knife and set aside until required. Carefully crack the claws, remove all the meat and chop coarsely. Set aside the claw meat.

2 Put the rice and milk into a pan and bring slowly to a boil over a medium heat. Cover and simmer gently for about 20 minutes.

3 Add the white and brown crab meat and season to taste with salt and pepper. Simmer for 5 minutes.

4 Let cool slightly, then transfer to a blender or food processor and process until smooth.

5 Pour the soup into a clean pan and add the fish bouillon and the claw meat. Bring slowly to a boil, then add the anchovy paste and lime juice. Adjust the seasoning.

6 Simmer for 2–3 minutes. Stir in the parsley. Ladle the soup into 6 bowls, swirl sour cream (if using) on the top, garnish with chives and serve.

smoked haddock soup

8 oz/225 g smoked haddock fillet

1 onion, chopped finely

1 garlic clove, minced

2¼ cups water

2½ cups skim milk

2⅔–4 cups hot mashed potatoes

2 tbsp butter

about 1 tbsp lemon juice

6 tbsp lowfat plain yogurt

4 tbsp chopped fresh parsley

salt and pepper

1 Put the fish, onion, garlic, and water into a pan. Bring to a boil, cover, and simmer over a low heat for 15–20 minutes.

2 Remove the fish from the pan. Strip off the skin and remove all the bones, and set both aside. Flake the flesh finely with a fork.

3 Return the skin and bones to the cooking liquid and simmer for 10 minutes. Strain, discarding the skin and bones. Pour the cooking liquid into a clean pan.

4 Add the milk and flaked fish, then season to taste with salt and pepper. Bring to a boil and simmer for about 3 minutes.

5 Gradually whisk in enough mashed potato to give a fairly thick soup, then stir in the butter, and sharpen to taste with lemon juice.

6 Add the plain yogurt and 3 tablespoons of the chopped parsley. Heat through gently and adjust the seasoning, if necessary. Ladle the soup into 4 warmed bowls, sprinkle with the remaining parsley and serve.

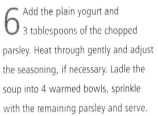

curried chicken & corn soup

serves four

1 cup canned corn, drained

3¾ cups chicken bouillon

12 oz/350 g cooked, lean chicken,
cut into strips

16 baby corn cobs

1 tsp Chinese curry powder

½-inch/1-cm piece fresh
gingerroot, grated

3 tbsp light soy sauce

2 tbsp snipped fresh chives

COOK'S TIP

Prepare the soup up to
24 hours in advance without
adding the chicken. Let cool,
cover, and store in the
refrigerator. Add the chicken
and heat the soup through
thoroughly before serving.

---

1 Put the canned corn in a food
processor, with ⅔ cup of the
chicken bouillon and process until a
smooth puree forms.

2 Pass the corn puree through a
fine strainer, pressing with the
back of a spoon to remove any husks.

3 Pour the remaining chicken
bouillon into a large pan and add
the strips of cooked chicken. Stir in the
corn puree and mix well.

4 Add the baby corn cobs and bring
the soup to a boil over medium
heat. Cook for 10 minutes.

5 Add the Chinese curry powder,
grated ginger, and light soy sauce
and stir well. Cook the soup for an
additional 10–15 minutes.

6 Stir in the snipped chives, then
ladle the soup into 4 warmed
soup bowls. Serve immediately.

avocado & mint soup

serves six

3 tbsp butter

6 scallions, sliced

1 garlic clove, minced

2 tbsp all-purpose flour

2½ cups vegetable bouillon

2 ripe avocados

2–3 tsp lemon juice

pinch of grated lemon peel

⅔ cup milk

⅔ cup light cream

1–1½ tbsp chopped fresh mint

salt and pepper

6 fresh mint sprigs, to garnish

MINTED GARLIC BREAD

5 tbsp butter

1–2 tbsp chopped fresh mint

1–2 garlic cloves, minced

1 whole-wheat or white French
    bread stick

1 Melt the butter in a large pan over a low heat. Add the scallions and garlic to the pan and cook, stirring occasionally, for about 3 minutes, or until soft and translucent.

2 Stir in the flour and cook, stirring, for 1–2 minutes. Gradually stir in the bouillon, then bring to a boil over a medium heat. Simmer gently while preparing the avocados.

3 Peel the avocados, discard the pits, and chop. Add to the soup with the lemon juice and peel. Season with salt and pepper. Cover and cook for 10 minutes, or until tender.

4 Let cool slightly, then transfer the soup to a blender and process until smooth. Alternatively, press through a strainer with the back of a spoon. Pour into a bowl.

5 Stir in the milk and cream, adjust the seasoning, then stir in the mint. Cover and chill thoroughly.

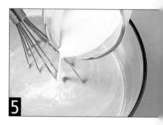

6 To make the minted garlic bread, soften the butter and beat in the mint and garlic. Cut the loaf into slanting slices, but leave a hinge on the bottom crust. Spread each slice with the butter and reassemble the loaf. Wrap in foil and put into a preheated oven, 350°F/180°C, for about 15 minutes.

7 Ladle the soup into 6 bowls and garnish with mint sprigs. Serve with the minted garlic bread.

Appetizers & Snacks

All of these recipes are easy to prepare and appetizing. They are colorful and flavorsome, providing an excellent beginning to any dinner party or just for an everyday snack. Depending on the main course, whet your guests' appetite with a tasty Eggplant Dipping Platter, Chinese Omelets, a Pâté, or delicious vegetable nibbles. Other quick and tasty snacks provide interesting colors and textures, and can all be rustled up at speed. In addition, all these quick recipes will satisfy your hunger pangs and tastebuds. All of these dishes are sure to get your meal off to the right start.

mint & cannellini bean dip

serves six

scant 1 cup dried cannellini beans
1 small garlic clove, minced
1 bunch of scallions,
   chopped coarsely
handful of fresh mint leaves
2 tbsp sesame seed paste
2 tbsp olive oil
1 tsp ground cumin
1 tsp ground coriander
lemon juice
salt and pepper
fresh mint sprigs, to garnish
TO SERVE
fresh vegetable crudités, such as
   cauliflower flowerets, carrots,
   cucumber, radishes, and
   bell peppers

1 Put the cannellini beans into a bowl and pour over enough cold water to cover. Let soak for at least 4 hours, or overnight.

2 Drain the beans and rinse under cold running water. put them into a large pan, and cover with cold water. Bring to a boil over a high heat and boil rapidly for 10 minutes. Reduce the heat, cover, and simmer until tender.

3 Drain the beans thoroughly and transfer them to a food processor. Add the garlic, scallions, mint, sesame seed paste, and oil and process for 15 seconds. Alternatively, mash with a potato masher until smooth.

4 Scrape the mixture into a bowl, if necessary, and stir in the cumin, coriander, and lemon juice. Season to taste with salt and pepper. Mix thoroughly, cover with plastic wrap, and set aside in a cool place, but not the refrigerator, for 30 minutes to let the flavors develop.

5 Spoon the dip into small serving bowls and garnish with fresh mint sprigs. Put the bowls onto plates and surround them with vegetable crudités. Serve at room temperature.

tzatziki & black olive dips

serves four

½ cucumber

225 g/8 oz thick plain yogurt

1 tbsp chopped fresh mint

salt and pepper

4 pocket breads

DIP

2 garlic cloves, minced

⅔ cup pitted ripe black olives

4 tbsp olive oil

2 tbsp lemon juice

1 tbsp chopped fresh parsley

TO GARNISH

1 fresh mint sprig

1 fresh parsley sprig

1 To make the tzatziki, peel the cucumber and chop it coarsely. Sprinkle with salt and let stand for 15–20 minutes. Rinse under cold running water and drain thoroughly.

2 Mix the cucumber, yogurt, and mint together. Season to taste with salt and pepper and transfer to a serving bowl. Cover and chill in the refrigerator for 20–30 minutes.

3 To make the black olive dip, put the garlic and olives into a blender or food processor and process for 15–20 seconds. Alternatively, chop them very finely.

4 Add the oil, lemon juice, and parsley to the blender or food processor and process for a few more seconds. Alternatively, mix with the garlic and olives, and mash together. Season with salt and pepper.

5 Wrap the pocket breads in foil and either put over a barbecue grill for 2–3 minutes, turning once to warm through, or heat in a preheated oven or under a preheated broiler. Cut into pieces and serve with the tzatziki and black olive dips, garnished with fresh mint and parsley sprigs.

eggplant dipping platter

serves four

1 eggplant, peeled and cut into
　　1-inch/2.5-cm cubes

3 tbsp sesame seeds, roasted in a
　　dry pan over low heat

1 tsp sesame oil

grated peel and juice of ½ lime

1 small shallot, diced

1 tsp sugar

1 fresh red chile, seeded and sliced

4 oz/115 g broccoli flowerets

2 carrots, cut into batons

8 baby corn cobs, cut in
　　half lengthwise

2 celery stalks, cut into batons

1 baby red cabbage, cut into
　　8 wedges, the leaves of each
　　wedge held together by the core

salt and pepper

VARIATION

You can vary the selection of vegetables depending on your preference or whatever you have to hand. Other vegetables you could use are cauliflower flowerets and cucumber batons.

1 Bring a pan of water to a boil over a medium heat. Add the eggplant and cook for 7–8 minutes. Drain thoroughly and let cool slightly.

2 Meanwhile, grind the sesame seeds with the oil in a food processor or in a mortar with a pestle.

3 Add the eggplant, lime peel and juice, shallot, sugar, and chile to the sesame seeds. Season to taste with salt and pepper, then process until smooth. Alternatively, chop and mash by hand.

4 Adjust the seasoning to taste, then spoon the dip into a bowl.

5 Serve the eggplant dipping platter surrounded by the prepared broccoli, carrots, baby corn, celery, and red cabbage.

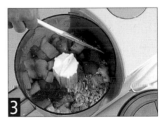

heavenly garlic dip

serves four

2 garlic bulbs

6 tbsp olive oil

1 small onion, chopped finely

2 tbsp lemon juice

3 tbsp sesame seed paste

2 tbsp chopped fresh parsley

salt and pepper

TO SERVE

fresh vegetable crudités

French bread or warmed
    pocket breads

VARIATION

If you come across smoked garlic, use it in this recipe—it tastes wonderful. There is no need to roast the smoked garlic, so omit the first step. This dip can also be used to baste vegetarian burgers.

---

1 Separate the garlic bulbs into individual cloves. Put them onto a large cookie sheet and roast in a preheated oven at 400°F/200°C, for about 8–10 minutes, then let cool for a few minutes.

2 When they are cool enough to handle, peel the garlic cloves and then chop them finely.

3 Heat the oil in a skillet over a low heat. Add the garlic and onion and cook, stirring occasionally, for 8–10 minutes, or until softened. Remove the pan from the heat.

4 Mix in the lemon juice, sesame seed paste, and chopped parsley. Season to taste with salt and pepper. Transfer the dip to a small bowl and keep warm while you prepare the vegetable crudites.

5 When ready to serve, garnish the dip with a parsley sprig and serve with vegetable crudités, with French bread or warm pocket breads.

mixed bean pâté

serves four

14 oz/400 g canned mixed
  beans, drained

2 tbsp olive oil

juice of 1 lemon

2 garlic cloves, minced

1 tbsp chopped fresh cilantro

2 scallions, chopped

salt and pepper

shredded scallions, to garnish

1 Rinse the mixed beans thoroughly under cold running water and drain well.

2 Transfer the beans to a food processor or blender and process until smooth. Alternatively, put the beans into a bowl and mash with a fork or potato masher.

3 Add the oil, lemon juice, garlic, cilantro, and scallions and blend until fairly smooth. Season to taste with salt and pepper.

4 Transfer the pâté to a serving bowl, cover, and chill in the refrigerator for at least 30 minutes.

5 Garnish the pâté with shredded scallions and serve.

lentil pâté

serves four

1 tbsp vegetable oil, plus extra
   for oiling
1 onion, chopped
2 garlic cloves, minced
1 tsp garam masala
½ tsp ground coriander
3 cups vegetable bouillon
1 cup red split lentils
1 small egg
2 tbsp milk
2 tbsp mango chutney
2 tbsp chopped fresh parsley
chopped fresh parsley, to garnish
TO SERVE
salad greens
warm toast

VARIATION

Use other spices, such as chili
powder or Chinese five-spice
powder, to flavor the pâté,
and add tomato relish or chili
relish instead of the mango
chutney, if you prefer.

---

1 Heat the oil in a large pan over a medium heat. Add the onion and garlic and cook for 2–3 minutes, stirring. Add the spices and cook for an additional 30 seconds. Stir in the vegetable bouillon and lentils, and bring the mixture to a boil. Reduce the heat and simmer for 20 minutes, or until the lentils are cooked and soft. Remove the pan from the heat and drain off any excess moisture.

2 Transfer the mixture to a food processor and add the egg, milk, mango chutney, and chopped parsley. Blend until smooth.

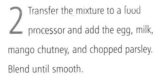

3 Oil and line the bottom of a 1 lb/450 g loaf pan. Spoon the mixture into the pan, cover and cook in a preheated oven at 400°F/200°C, for 40–45 minutes, or until firm.

4 Let the pâté cool in the pan for 20 minutes, then transfer to the refrigerator to cool completely. Turn out onto a serving plate, garnish with parsley sprigs and serve in slices with salad greens and warm toast.

smoked fish & potato pâté

serves four

1 lb 7 oz/650 g mealy potatoes,
    peeled and diced

10½ oz/300 g smoked mackerel,
    skinned and flaked

3 oz/85 g cooked gooseberries

2 tsp lemon juice

2 tbsp low-fat sour cream

1 tbsp capers, rinsed

1 gherkin, chopped

1 tbsp chopped dill pickle

1 tbsp chopped fresh dill

salt and pepper

lemon wedges, to garnish

toast or warm crusty bread, to serve

COOK'S TIP

Use stewed, canned, or bottled
cooked gooseberries for
convenience and to save time,
or when fresh gooseberries
are out of season.

1 Bring a large pan of water to a boil over a medium heat. Add the potatoes and cook for 10 minutes, or until tender. Drain thoroughly.

2 Put the cooked potatoes into a food processor or blender. Add the skinned and flaked smoked mackerel and process for 30 seconds until fairly smooth. Alternatively, put the ingredients into a large bowl and mash with a fork.

3 Add the cooked gooseberries, lemon juice, and sour cream to the fish and potato mixture. Blend for an additional 10 seconds or mash well.

4 Stir in the capers, gherkin, dill pickle, and fresh dill. Season to taste with salt and pepper.

5 Turn the fish pâté into a serving dish and garnish with lemon wedges. Serve with slices of toast or warm bread cut into chunks or slices.

walnut, egg & cheese pâté

serves two

1 celery stalk

1–2 scallions

¼ cup shelled walnuts

1 tbsp chopped fresh parsley

1 tsp chopped fresh dill or

    ½ tsp dried dill

1 garlic clove, minced

dash of Worcestershire sauce

½ cup cottage cheese

2 oz/55 g blue cheese

1 hard-cooked egg

2 tbsp butter

salt and pepper

fresh herbs, to garnish

crackers, toast, or crusty bread,

    to serve

3 Grate the blue cheese finely into the pâté mixture. Finely chop the hard-cooked egg and stir it into the mixture. Season to taste with salt and pepper.

1 Finely chop the celery, slice the scallions very thinly, and chop the walnuts evenly. Put into a bowl.

2 Add the chopped herbs, garlic and Worcestershire sauce to taste and mix well. Stir in the cottage cheese into the mixture and blend thoroughly.

4 Melt the butter in a small pan over a low heat, then stir it into the pate. Spoon into a serving dish or 2 individual dishes. Smooth the top, but do not press down firmly. Chill in the refrigerator until set.

5 Garnish with mixed herbs and serve with crackers, toast, or fresh crusty bread.

cheese, garlic & herb pâté

serves four

1 tbsp butter

1 garlic clove, minced

3 scallions, chopped finely

⅝ cup full-fat soft cheese

2 tbsp chopped mixed fresh herbs,
    such as parsley, chives,
    marjoram, oregano, and basil

1½ cups finely grated sharp
    cheddar cheese

pepper

4–6 slices of white bread from a
    medium-cut sliced loaf

TO GARNISH

ground paprika

1 fresh Italian parsley sprigs

TO SERVE

mixed salad greens

cherry tomatoes

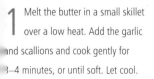

1 Melt the butter in a small skillet over a low heat. Add the garlic and scallions and cook gently for 3–4 minutes, or until soft. Let cool.

2 Beat the soft cheese in a large mixing bowl until smooth, then add the garlic and scallions. Stir in the chopped mixed herbs and mix well.

3 Add the cheddar cheese and work the mixture together to form a stiff paste. Cover and chill in the refrigerator until ready to serve.

4 Toast the slices of bread on both sides, then cut off the crusts. Using a sharp bread knife, cut through the slices horizontally to make very thin slices. Cut into triangles, then lightly toast the untoasted sides under a preheated hot broiler until golden.

5 Arrange the mixed salad greens on 4 serving plates with the cherry tomatoes. Pile the cheese pâté on top and sprinkle with a little paprika. Garnish with a parsley sprig and serve with the toast.

crostini alla fiorentina

serves four

3 tbsp olive oil

1 onion, chopped

1 celery stalk, chopped

1 carrot, chopped

1–2 garlic cloves, minced

125 g/4½ oz chicken livers

4½ oz/125 g calf's, lamb's or
   pig's liver

⅔ cup red wine

1 tbsp tomato paste

2 tbsp chopped fresh parsley

3–4 canned anchovy fillets,
   chopped finely

2 tbsp bouillon or water

2–3 tbsp butter

1 tbsp capers

salt and pepper

chopped fresh parsley, to garnish

toasted bread, to serve

1 Heat the oil in a skillet over a low heat. Add the onion, celery, carrot, and garlic. Cook gently for 4–5 minutes, or until the onion is soft.

2 Meanwhile, rinse the chicken livers and pat dry on paper towels. Rinse the calf's or other liver and pat dry. Slice into strips. Add the liver to the skillet and cook gently for a few minutes, or until the strips are well sealed on all sides.

3 Add half the wine and cook until it has mostly evaporated. Add the rest of the wine, tomato paste, half the parsley, anchovies, bouillon or water, a little salt and plenty of pepper.

4 Cover the pan and simmer, stirring occasionally, for about 15–20 minutes, or until tender and most of the liquid has been absorbed.

5 Let the mixture cool slightly, then either coarsely mince or put into a food processor and process to a chunky puree.

6 Return to the pan and add the butter, capers, and remaining parsley. Heat through gently until the butter melts. Adjust the seasoning, if necessary. Spoon into a bowl and sprinkle with chopped parsley. Serve warm or cold spread on slices of toasted bread.

hummus & garlic toasts

serves four

14 oz/400 g canned garbanzo beans

juice of 1 large lemon

6 tbsp sesame seed paste

2 tbsp olive oil

2 garlic cloves, chopped finely

salt and pepper

GARLIC TOASTS

1 ciabatta loaf, sliced

2 garlic cloves, chopped finely

1 tbsp chopped fresh cilantro

4 tbsp olive oil

TO GARNISH

1 tbsp chopped fresh cilantro

pitted ripe black olives

1 To make the hummus, firstly drain the garbanzo beans and set aside a little of the liquid. Put the garbanzo beans and liquid into a food processor and blend, gradually adding the reserved liquid and lemon juice. Blend well after each addition until smooth.

2 Stir in the sesame seed paste and all but 1 teaspoon of the oil. Add the garlic, season to taste with salt and pepper, and blend again until smooth.

3 Spoon the hummus into a dish. Drizzle the remaining oil over the top and chill in the refrigerator.

4 To make the garlic toasts. Lay the slices of ciabatta on a broiler rack in a single layer.

5 Mix the garlic, cilantro, and oil together and drizzle over the bread slices. Cook under a preheated medium-hot broiler for 2–3 minutes until golden, turning once. To serve, garnish the hummus with cilantro and olives, then serve with the toasts..

pork sesame toasts

serves four

9 oz/250 g lean pork

⅔ cup raw shrimp, shelled
    and deveined

4 scallions, trimmed

1 garlic clove, minced

1 tbsp chopped fresh cilantro leaves
    and stems

1 tbsp fish sauce

1 egg

8–10 slices of thick-cut white bread

3 tbsp sesame seeds

⅔ cup vegetable oil

salt and pepper

TO GARNISH

fresh cilantro sprigs

½ red bell pepper, sliced finely

1 Put the pork, shrimp, scallions, garlic, cilantro, fish sauce, and egg into a food processor or blender. Season with salt and pepper and process for a few seconds until the ingredients are finely chopped. Transfer the mixture to a bowl. Alternatively, chop the pork, shrimp, and scallions very finely, and mix with the garlic, cilantro, fish sauce, and beaten egg. Season with salt and pepper and mix until well blended.

2 Spread the pork and shrimp mixture thickly over the slices of bread, so it reaches right up to the edges. Cut off the crusts and slice the bread into 4 squares or triangles.

3 Sprinkle the topping liberally with sesame seeds.

4 Heat a large wok over a medium heat. Add the oil and when hot, cook a few pieces of the bread, topping side down first so it sets the egg, for 2 minutes, or until golden brown. Turn the pieces over to cook on the other side, about 1 minute.

5 Drain the pork and shrimp toasts and drain on paper towels. Cook the remaining pieces. Arrange the toasts on a serving plate and garnish with fresh cilantro sprigs and strips of red bell pepper. Serve.

bruschetta with tomatoes

serves four

10½ oz/300 g cherry tomatoes

4 sun-dried tomatoes

4 tbsp extra virgin olive oil

16 fresh basil leaves, shredded

8 slices of ciabatta bread

2 garlic cloves, peeled

salt and pepper

VARIATION

Plum tomatoes are also good in this recipe. Halve them, then cut them into wedges. Mix them with the sun-dried tomatoes in step 3.

COOK'S TIP

Ciabatta is an Italian rustic bread, which is slightly holey and quite chewy. It is good in this recipe, as it absorbs the full flavor of the garlic and extra virgin olive oil.

1 Using a sharp knife, cut the cherry tomatoes in half.

2 Using a sharp knife, slice the sun-dried tomatoes into strips.

3 Put the cherry tomatoes and sun-dried tomatoes into a small bowl. Add the oil and shredded basil leaves and toss to mix well. Season to taste with salt and pepper.

4 Lightly toast the ciabatta slices under a preheated medium-hot broiler. Cut the garlic cloves in half.

5 Rub the garlic, cut-side down, over both sides of the toasted ciabatta slices.

6 Put the ciabatta slices onto a serving plate or individual plates and top with the tomato mixture. Serve.

pepper salad

serves four

1 onion

2 red bell peppers

2 yellow bell peppers

3 tbsp olive oil

2 large zucchini, sliced

2 garlic cloves, sliced

1 tbsp balsamic vinegar

1¾ oz/50 g canned anchovy
    fillets, chopped

¼ cup pitted ripe black
    olives, halved

1 tbsp chopped fresh basil

salt and pepper

TOMATO TOASTS

small French bread stick

1 garlic clove, minced

1 tomato, peeled and chopped

2 tbsp olive oil

1 Cut the onion into wedges. Core and seed the bell peppers, then cut into thick slices.

2 Heat the oil in a large heavy-bottomed skillet. Add the onion, bell peppers, zucchini, and garlic, and cook gently for about 20 minutes, stirring occasionally.

3 Add the vinegar, anchovies, and olives. Season to taste with salt and pepper. Mix and let cool.

4 To make the tomato toasts, cut the French bread diagonally into ½-inch/1-cm slices.

5 Mix the garlic, tomato, and oil together. Season to taste and spread thinly over each slice of bread.

6 Put the bread onto a cookie sheet, drizzle with the oil and cook in a preheated oven at 425°F/220°C, for 5–10 minutes, or until crisp. Spoon the salad onto 4 serving plates, garnish with a basil sprig, and serve with the tomato toasts.

onions à la grecque

serves four

1 lb/450 g shallots

3 tbsp olive oil

3 tbsp honey

1 garlic clove, chopped

2 tbsp white wine vinegar

3 tbsp dry white wine

1 tbsp tomato paste

2 celery stalks, sliced

2 tomatoes, seeded and chopped

salt and pepper

chopped celery leaves, to garnish

1 Peel the shallots. Heat the oil in a large heavy-bottomed pan over a high heat. Add the shallots and cook, stirring, for 3–5 minutes, or until they start to brown.

2 Add the honey and garlic, and cook for an additional 30 seconds, then add the vinegar and dry white wine, stirring well.

3 Stir in the tomato paste, celery, and tomatoes and bring to a boil over a high heat. Cook for about 5–6 minutes. Season to taste with salt and pepper and let cool slightly.

4 Spoon into a large serving dish, garnish with chopped celery leaves and serve warm or cold.

VARIATION
Use button mushrooms instead of the shallots and fennel instead of the celery for another great appetizer.

shrimp parcels

serves four

1 tbsp corn oil

1 red bell pepper, seeded and
   sliced thinly

¾ cup bean sprouts

finely grated peel and juice of 1 lime

1 fresh red chili, seeded and very
   finely chopped

1 tsp freshly grated fresh gingerroot

8 oz/225 g shelled shrimp

1 tbsp fish sauce

½ tsp arrowroot

2 tbsp chopped fresh cilantro

8 sheets phyllo pastry

2 tbsp butter

2 tsp sesame oil

3 tbsp vegetable oil

chili dipping sauce, to serve

COOK'S TIP

If using cooked shrimp, cook for
1 minute only, otherwise the
shrimp will toughen.

1 Heat a large wok over a high heat. Add the oil and when hot, add the red bell pepper and bean sprouts. Cook for 2 minutes, or until the vegetables have softened.

2 Remove the wok from the heat and toss in the lime peel and juice, red chile, ginger, and shrimp, stirring well.

3 Mix the fish sauce with the arrowroot and stir the mixture into the wok juices. Return the wok to the heat and cook, stirring, for 2 minutes, or until the juices thicken. Toss in the cilantro and mix well.

4 Lay the sheets of phyllo pastry out on a board. Melt the butter and sesame oil over a low heat and brush each pastry sheet with the mixture.

5 Spoon a little of the shrimp filling onto the top of each sheet, fold over each end, and carefully roll up to enclose the filling.

6 Heat a large wok over a medium heat. Add the oil and when hot, add the parcels, in batches. Cook for 2–3 minutes, or until crisp and golden. Put onto a serving plate and serve immediately with a chili dipping sauce.

mussels in white wine

serves four

12 cups fresh mussels

¼ cup butter

1 large onion, chopped very finely

2–3 garlic cloves, minced

1½ cups dry white wine

⅔ cup water

2 tbsp lemon juice

good pinch of finely grated
    lemon peel

1 bouquet garni

1 tbsp all-purpose flour

4 tbsp light or thick cream

2–3 tbsp chopped fresh parsley

salt and pepper

crusty bread, to serve

1 Pull off all the "beards" from the mussels and scrub them under cold running water for 5 minutes to remove any mud, sand, and barnacles. Discard any mussels that refuse to close when tapped with a knife.

2 Melt half the butter in a large pan over a low heat. Add the onion and garlic, and cook gently until softened but not colored.

3 Add the wine, water, lemon juice and peel, and bouquet garni. Season to taste. Bring to a boil, then cover and simmer for 4–5 minutes.

4 Add the mussels to the pan, cover tightly and simmer for 5 minutes, shaking the pan frequently, until all the mussels have opened. Discard any mussels that have not opened. Remove the bouquet garni and discard.

5 Remove the empty half shell from each mussel. Blend the remaining butter with the flour and whisk into the liquid, a little at a time. Simmer for 2–3 minutes, or until thickened.

6 Add the cream and half the parsley and heat gently, then adjust the seasoning. Ladle the mussels and liquid into 4 large, warmed soup bowls, sprinkle with the remaining parsley and serve with plenty of warm crusty bread.

baked fennel

serves four

2 fennel bulbs

2 celery stalks, cut into 3-inch/
    7.5-cm pieces

6 sun-dried tomatoes, halved

scant 1 cup strained tomatoes

2 tsp dried oregano

⅔ cup freshly grated
    Parmesan cheese

1 Using a sharp knife, trim the fennel and discard any of the tough outer leaves and feathery fronds. Cut the bulb into fourths.

2 Bring a pan of water to a boil over a medium heat. Add the fennel and celery and cook until just tender. Remove and drain.

3 Put the fennel pieces, celery, and sun-dried tomatoes into a large ovenproof dish.

4 Mix the tomatoes and oregano together and pour the mixture over the fennel.

5 Sprinkle the top with the Parmesan cheese and cook in a preheated oven at 375°F/190°C, for 20 minutes, or until hot. Serve.

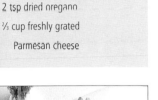

spicy chicken salad

serves four

2 skinless, boneless chicken breast
  portions, about 4½ oz/125 g
  each

2 tbsp butter

1 fresh red chile, seeded
  and chopped

1 tbsp honey

½ tsp ground cumin

2 tbsp chopped fresh cilantro

3½ cups diced potatoes

1¾ oz/50 g green beans, halved

1 red bell pepper, seeded and cut
  into thin strips

2 tomatoes, seeded and diced

DRESSING

2 tbsp olive oil

pinch of chili powder

1 tbsp garlic wine vinegar

pinch of superfine sugar

1 tbsp chopped fresh cilantro

1 Cut the chicken into thin strips. Melt the butter in a heavy pan and add the chicken strips, fresh red chile, honey, and cumin. Cook for 10 minutes, turning until cooked through.

2 Transfer the mixture to a bowl and let cool, then stir in the chopped cilantro.

3 Meanwhile, cook the diced potatoes in a pan of boiling water for 10 minutes, until they are tender. Drain and let cool.

VARIATION

If you like, use lean turkey meat instead of the chicken for a slightly stronger taste. Use the white meat for the best appearance and flavor.

4 Blanch the green beans in a pan of boiling water for 3 minutes. Drain well and leave to cool. Combine the green beans and potatoes in a mixing bowl.

5 Add the bell pepper strips and tomatoes to the potato mixture. Stir in the chicken mixture.

6 In a small bowl, whisk the dressing ingredients together and pour the dressing over the salad, tossing well. Transfer the spicy chicken salad to a serving bowl or large platter and serve immediately.

beet salad & dill dressing

serves four

2⅔ cups diced waxy potatoes

4 small cooked beets, sliced

½ small cucumber, sliced thinly

2 large dill pickles, sliced

1 red onion, halved and sliced

fresh dill sprigs, to garnish

DRESSING

1 garlic clove, crushed

2 tbsp olive oil

2 tbsp red wine vinegar

2 tbsp chopped fresh dill

salt and pepper

1 Cook the potatoes in a pan of boiling water for 15 minutes, or until tender. Drain and leave to cool.

2 When cool, combine the potato and beets in a large bowl and set aside until required.

3 Line a large salad platter with the slices of cucumber, dill pickles, and red onion.

4 Carefully spoon the potato and beet mixture into the center of the platter.

5 In a small bowl, whisk all the dressing ingredients together, then pour over the salad.

6 Serve the potato and beet salad immediately, garnished with fresh dill sprigs.

cured meats, olives & tomatoes

serves four

4 plum tomatoes

1 tbsp balsamic vinegar

salt and pepper

6 canned anchovy fillets, drained
    and rinsed

¾ cup pitted green olives

2 tbsp capers, drained and rinsed

6 oz/175 g mixed, cured
    meats, sliced

8 fresh basil leaves

1 tbsp extra virgin olive oil

crusty bread, to serve

1 Using a sharp knife, cut the tomatoes into even-size slices. Sprinkle the tomato slices with the balsamic vinegar and season to taste with a little salt and pepper. Set aside.

2 Chop the anchovy fillets into pieces measuring about the same length as the olives.

3 Push a piece of anchovy and a caper into each olive.

4 Arrange the sliced meat onto 4 large serving plates, together with the tomatoes, filled olives, and basil leaves.

5 Lightly drizzle the oil over the sliced meat, tomatoes, and olives.

6 Serve the sliced meats, olives, and tomatoes with lots of fresh crusty bread.

stir-fried beancurd with chili sauce

serves four

1 lb 2 oz/500 g marinated or plain
   firm beancurd (drained weight)

2 tbsp rice vinegar

2 tbsp sugar

1 tsp salt

3 tbsp smooth peanut butter

½ tsp chili flakes

3 tbsp barbecue sauce

4 cups corn oil

2 tbsp sesame oil

BATTER

4 tbsp all-purpose flour

2 eggs, beaten

4 tbsp milk

½ tsp baking powder

½ tsp chili powder

1 Cut the beancurd into 1-inch/
2.5-cm chunks, then set aside.

2 Mix the rice vinegar, sugar, and salt together in a pan. Bring to a boil over a low heat, then simmer for 2 minutes.

3 Remove the sauce from the heat and add the peanut butter, chili flakes, and barbecue sauce, stirring well until blended thoroughly.

4 To make the batter, sift the flour into a bowl, make a well in the center, and add the eggs. Draw in the flour, adding the milk slowly. Stir in the baking powder and chili powder.

5 Heat the corn oil and sesame oil together in a deep-fryer or large pan until a light haze appears on top.

6 Dip the beancurd chunks into the batter and deep-fry until golden brown, working in batches, if necessary. Drain on paper towels.

7 Transfer the beancurd chunks to a warmed serving dish and serve immediately with the peanut sauce.

scallop crêpes

3½ oz/100 g fine green beans

1 fresh red chile

1 lb/450 g scallops, without roe

1 egg

3 scallions, sliced

generous ⅓ cup rice flour

1 tbsp Thai fish sauce

oil

salt

sweet chili dip, to serve

1 Using a sharp knife, trim the green beans and slice them very thinly.

2 Seed and very finely chop the red chile.

3 Bring a small pan of lightly salted water to a boil. Add the green beans to the pan and cook for 3–4 minutes, or until just softened.

4 Coarsely chop the scallops and place them in a large bowl. Add the cooked beans to the scallops.

5 Mix the egg, scallions, rice flour, fish sauce, and chile until thoroughly mixed. Add to the scallops and mix well.

6 Heat about 1 inch/2.5 cm of oil in a large preheated wok. Add a ladleful of the mixture to the wok and cook for 5 minutes, until golden and set.

7 Remove the crêpe from the wok and drain on paper towels. Keep warm while cooking the remaining crêpe mixture. Serve the crêpes hot with a sweet chili dip.

deep-fried seafood

1 Carefully rinse the squid, shrimp, and whitebait under cold running water, completely removing any dirt or grit.

2 Using a sharp knife, slice the squid into thin rings, leaving the tentacles whole.

3 Heat the oil in a large pan to 350°–375°F/180°–190°C, or until a cube of bread browns in 30 seconds.

4 Put the flour into a large bowl and season with the salt, pepper, and dried basil.

5 Roll the squid, shrimp, and whitebait in the seasoned flour until coated thoroughly all over. Carefully shake off any excess flour.

6 Cook the seafood, in batches, in the hot oil for 2–3 minutes, or until crispy and golden all over. Remove the seafood with a slotted spoon and let drain thoroughly on paper towels.

7 Transfer the deep-fried seafood to 4 large serving plates and serve with Garlic Mayonnaise (see Cook's Tip).

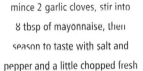

COOK'S TIP

To make the Garlic Mayonnaise, mince 2 garlic cloves, stir into 8 tbsp of mayonnaise, then season to taste with salt and pepper and a little chopped fresh parsley. Cover with plastic wrap and chill in the refrigerator.

chinese omelet

serves four

8 eggs

8 oz/225 g cooked
   chicken, shredded

12 raw jumbo shrimp, shelled
   and deveined

2 tbsp snipped fresh chives

2 tsp light soy sauce

dash of chili sauce

2 tbsp vegetable oil

VARIATION

You could add extra flavor
to the omelet by stirring in
3 tbsp of finely chopped fresh
cilantro or 1 tsp
of sesame seeds with the
fresh chives in step 2.

---

1 Lightly beat the eggs in a large
bowl. Add the shredded chicken
and jumbo shrimps, and mix well.

2 Stir in the snipped chives, light
soy sauce, and chili sauce, mixing
well to blend all the ingredients.

3 Heat the oil in a large, heavy-
bottomed skillet over a medium
heat. Pour in the egg mixture, tilting
the pan to coat the bottom evenly
and completely.

4 Cook over a medium heat, gently
stirring the omelet with a fork,
until the surface is just set and the
underside is golden brown.

5 When the omelet is set, slide it
out of the pan with the aid of a
spatula, then cut into squares or slices
and serve immediately.

sesame ginger chicken

serves four

1 lb 2 oz/500 g boneless
   chicken breasts
dipping sauce, to serve
MARINADE
1 garlic clove, minced
1 shallot, chopped very finely
2 tbsp sesame oil
1 tbsp fish sauce or light soy sauce
finely grated peel of 1 lime or
   ½ lemon
2 tbsp lime juice or lemon juice
1 tsp sesame seeds
2 tsp finely grated fresh gingerroot
2 tsp chopped fresh mint
salt and pepper

1 To make the marinade, put the garlic, shallot, sesame oil, fish sauce or soy sauce, lime or lemon peel and juice, sesame seeds, ginger, and chopped mint into a large non-metallic bowl. Season with a little salt and pepper and stir well until all the ingredients are mixed thoroughly.

2 Using a sharp knife, remove the skin from the chicken breasts and discard. Cut the flesh into chunks.

3 Add the chicken to the marinade, stirring to coat the chicken completely in the mixture. Cover with plastic wrap and chill in the refrigerator for at least 2 hours, so all the flavors are absorbed.

4 Thread the chicken onto presoaked wooden satay sticks. Put them on the rack of a broiler pan and baste with the marinade.

5 Cook the kabobs under a preheated medium-hot broiler for about 8–10 minutes. Turn the kabobs frequently, basting with the remaining marinade.

6 Put the chicken kabobs onto a large serving plate and serve immediately with a dipping sauce.

chicken or beef satay

serves six

4 skinned, boneless chicken breasts
  or 1 lb 10 oz/750 g rump
  steak, trimmed

MARINADE

1 small onion, chopped finely

1 garlic clove, minced

1-inch/2.5-cm piece fresh
  gingerroot, grated

2 tbsp dark soy sauce

2 tsp chili powder

1 tsp ground coriander

2 tsp dark brown sugar

1 tbsp lemon or lime juice

1 tbsp vegetable oil

SAUCE

1¼ cups coconut milk

⅓ cup crunchy peanut butter

1 tbsp fish sauce

1 tsp lemon or lime juice

salt and pepper

1 Using a sharp knife, trim any fat from the chicken or beef and discard. Cut the meat into thin strips, about 3-inches/7-cm long.

2 To make the marinade, put all the ingredients in a shallow dish and mix well. Add the chicken or beef strips and turn in the marinade until well coated. Cover with plastic wrap and let marinate in the refrigerator for 2 hours, or preferably overnight .

3 Remove the meat from the marinade and thread the pieces, concertina style, onto presoaked bamboo or thin wooden skewers.

4 Put the chicken and beef satays under a preheated medium-hot broiler and cook for 8–10 minutes, turning and brushing occasionally with the marinade, until cooked through.

5 To make the sauce. Mix the coconut milk, peanut butter, fish sauce and lemon or lime juice in a pan. Bring to a boil and cook for 3 minutes. Season to taste with salt and pepper.

6 Pour the sauce into a serving bowl and serve with the satays.

Fish & Seafood

The wealth of species and flavors of fish and seafood that the world's oceans and rivers provide is immense. Each country combines its local catch with the region's favorite herb and spices to create a variety of dishes. All of the recipes featured here are easy to prepare and delicious to eat. Moreover, not only are fish and seafood quick to cook, but they are packed full of nutritional goodness. Naturally low in fat, yet rich in minerals and proteins, fish and seafood are important to help balance any diet. The variety of fish and fish prices helps us to choose dishes to suit both mood and pocket.

tuna & vegetable stir-fry

serves four

3 small carrots

1 onion

1½ cups baby corn cobs

2 tbsp corn oil

2¼ cups snow peas

1 lb/450 g fresh tuna

2 tbsp Thai fish sauce

1 tbsp palm sugar

finely grated peel and juice of
　1 orange

2 tbsp sherry

1 tsp cornstarch

cooked rice or noodles, to serve

VARIATION

Try using swordfish steaks
instead of the tuna. Swordfish
steaks are now widely
available and are similar
in texture to tuna.

---

1 Using a sharp knife, cut the carrots into thin sticks, slice the onion, and halve the baby corn cobs.

2 Heat the corn oil in a large preheated wok or skillet.

3 Add the onion, carrots, snow peas, and baby corn cobs to the wok or skillet and stir-fry over medium heat for 5 minutes.

4 Using a sharp knife, thinly slice the fresh tuna. (This is easier if it has been chilled in the freezer.)

5 Add the tuna slices to the wok or skillet and stir-fry for about 2–3 minutes, or until the tuna turns opaque.

6 Mix the fish sauce, palm sugar, orange peel and juice, sherry, and cornstarch together.

7 Pour the mixture over the tuna and vegetables and cook for 2 minutes, or until the juices thicken. Serve the stir-fry with rice or noodles.

sweet & sour tuna salad

1 Heat the oil in a large, heavy-bottomed skillet over a low heat. Add the onion and garlic and cook, stirring occasionally, for 5 minutes, or until softened, but not browned.

2 Add the zucchini slices and cook, stirring occasionally, for an additional 3 minutes.

3 Cut the tomatoes in half, then into thin wedges.

4 Add the tomatoes to the skillet with the beans, olives, capers, sugar, mustard, and vinegar.

5 Simmer for 2 minutes, stirring gently, then let cool slightly.

6 Flake the tuna and stir it into the bean mixture with the parsley. Transfer to 4 serving plates, garnish with the extra chopped parsley, and serve warm with crusty bread.

tuna, bean & anchovy salad

serves four

1 lb 2 oz/500 g tomatoes

7 oz/200 g canned tuna, drained

2 tbsp chopped fresh parsley

½ cucumber

1 small red onion

8 oz/225 g cooked green beans

1 small red bell pepper, seeded

1 small crisp lettuce

6 tbsp Italian-style dressing

3 hard-cooked eggs

2 oz/55 g canned anchovy
    fillets, drained

12 pitted ripe black olives

1 Cut the tomatoes into wedges, flake the tuna and put both into a large bowl with the chopped parsley.

2 Cut the cucumber into slices. Slice the onion. Add the cucumber and onion to the bowl.

3 Cut the green beans in half, chop the bell pepper, and add both to the bowl with the lettuce leaves. Pour over the dressing and toss to mix, then spoon into a salad bowl. Shell the eggs and cut into fourths and add to the salad with the anchovies. Sprinkle over the olives and serve.

mussel salad

2 red bell peppers, halved
and seeded

12 oz/350 g cooked, shelled
mussels, thawed if frozen

1 head radicchio

¾ cup arugula

8 cooked green-lipped mussels in
their shells

strips of lemon peel, to garnish

crusty bread, to serve

DRESSING

1 tbsp olive oil

1 tbsp lemon juice

1 tsp finely grated lemon peel

2 tsp honey

1 tsp French mustard

1 tbsp snipped fresh chives

salt and pepper

1 Put the bell peppers, skin-side up, on a broiler rack and cook under a preheated broiler for 8–10 minutes, or until the skin is charred and blistered and the flesh is soft. Remove from the broiler with tongs, put into a bowl, and cover with plastic wrap. Set aside for 10 minutes, or until cool enough to handle, then peel off the skins.

2 Slice the bell pepper flesh into thin strips and put into a bowl. Gently stir in the shelled mussels.

3 To make the dressing, whisk the oil, lemon juice and peel, honey, mustard, and chives together until well blended. Season to taste with salt and pepper. Add the bell pepper and mussel mixture and toss until coated.

4 Remove the central core of the radicchio and shred the leaves. Put into a serving bowl with the arugula and toss together.

5 Pile the mussel mixture into the center of the leaves and arrange the green-lipped mussels in their shells around the edge. Garnish with lemon peel and serve with crusty bread.

neapolitan seafood salad

serves four

1 lb/450 g prepared squid, cut
   into strips

1 lb 10 oz/750 g cooked mussels

1 lb/450 g cooked cockles in brine

⅝ cup white wine

1¼ cups olive oil

2 cups dried campanelle or other
   small pasta shapes

juice of 1 lemon

1 bunch fresh chives, snipped

1 bunch fresh parsley,
   chopped finely

4 large tomatoes

mixed salad greens

salt and pepper

1 fresh basil sprig, to garnish

1 Put the seafood into a large bowl, pour over the wine and half the oil, then set aside for 6 hours.

2 Put the seafood mixture into a pan and simmer over a low heat for 10 minutes. Let cool.

3 Bring a large pan of lightly salted water to a boil over a medium heat. Add the pasta and 1 tablespoon of the remaining oil and cook until done. Drain and refresh in cold water.

4 Strain off about half the cooking liquid from the seafood and discard the rest. Mix in the lemon juice, chives, parsley, and the remaining oil. Season with salt and pepper. Drain the pasta and add to the seafood.

5 Cut the tomatoes into fourths. Shred the salad greens and arrange them at the bottom of a salad bowl. Spoon in the salad and garnish with the tomatoes and a basil sprig.

seafood stir-fry

serves four

3½ oz/100 g small, thin asparagus
    spears, trimmed

1 tbsp corn oil

2.5-cm/1-inch piece fresh
    gingerroot, cut into thin strips

1 medium leek, shredded

2 medium carrots, julienned

3½ oz/100 g baby corn, cut into
    fourths lengthwise

2 tbsp light soy sauce

1 tbsp oyster sauce

1 tsp honey

1 lb/450 g cooked, assorted
    shellfish, thawed if frozen

freshly cooked egg noodles,
    to serve

TO GARNISH

4 large cooked shrimp

1 small bunch fresh chives, snipped

3 Add the soy sauce, oyster sauce, and honey to the wok. Stir in the shellfish and cook for 2–3 minutes, or until the vegetables are just tender and the shellfish are thoroughly heated through. Add the blanched asparagus and cook for an additional 2 minutes.

4 To serve, pile the cooked noodles onto 4 warmed serving plates and spoon over the seafood and vegetables. Garnish with a large shrimp and the chives, then serve.

1 Bring a small pan of water to a boil over a medium heat. Add the asparagus and blanch for 1–2 minutes. Drain, set aside and keep warm.

2 Heat a large wok over a medium heat. Add the oil and when hot, add the ginger, leek, carrot, and corn. Cook for about 3 minutes.

353

poached salmon with penne

1 Put the salmon into a large, non-stick skillet. Add the butter, wine, sea salt, peppercorns, dill, tarragon, and lemon. Cover, bring to a boil over a low heat, and cook for 10 minutes.

2 Using a spatula, carefully remove the salmon. Strain and set aside the cooking liquid. Remove the salmon skin and center bones and discard. Put the salmon into a warmed dish, cover and keep warm.

3 Meanwhile, bring a pan of lightly salted water to a boil over a medium heat. Add the pasta and 1 teaspoon of the oil and cook for about 12 minutes, or until done. Drain and sprinkle over the remaining oil. Put into a warmed serving dish, top with the salmon and keep warm.

4 To make the sauce, melt the butter over a low heat. Stir in the flour for 2 minutes, then stir in the milk and 7 tablespoons of the cooking liquid. Add the lemon juice and peel and cook, stirring, for 10 minutes.

5 Add the arugula to the sauce, stir gently and season to taste with salt and pepper.

6 Pour the sauce over the salmon, garnish with slices of lemon and serve immediately.

trout with smoked bacon

serves four

1 tbsp butter for greasing

4 x 9½ oz/275 g trout, gutted
   and cleaned

12 canned anchovy fillets in oil,
   drained and chopped

2 apples, peeled, cored, and sliced

4 fresh mint sprigs

juice of 1 lemon

12 slices rindless, smoked fatty bacon

1 lb/450 g dried tagliatelle

1 tsp olive oil

salt and pepper

TO GARNISH

2 apples, cored and sliced

4 fresh mint sprigs

1 Grease a large cookie sheet with the butter.

2 Open up the cavities of each trout and rinse with warm salt water.

3 Season each cavity with salt and pepper. Divide the anchovies, sliced apples, and mint sprigs between each of the cavities, then sprinkle the lemon juice into each cavity.

4 Carefully cover the whole of each trout, except the head and tail, with 3 slices of smoked bacon in a spiral shape.

5 Arrange the trout on the cookie sheet with the loose ends of bacon tucked underneath. Season with pepper to taste and cook in a preheated oven at 400°F/ 200°C, for 20 minutes, turning the trout over after 10 minutes.

6 Meanwhile, bring a large pan of lightly salted water to a boil over a medium heat. Add the pasta and oil and cook for about 12 minutes, or until done. Drain the pasta and keep warm.

7 Remove the trout from the oven. Transfer the pasta to 4 warmed serving plates and arrange the trout on top. Garnish with sliced apples and mint sprigs, and serve immediately.

fillets of red snapper & pasta

serves four

2 lb 4 oz/1 kg red snapper fillets

1¼ cups dry white wine

4 shallots, chopped finely

1 garlic clove, minced

3 tbsp finely chopped mixed
    fresh herbs

finely grated peel and juice of
    1 lemon

pinch of freshly grated nutmeg

3 canned anchovy fillets,
    chopped coarsely

2 tbsp heavy cream

1 tsp cornstarch

1 lb/450 g dried vermicelli

1 tsp olive oil

salt and pepper

TO GARNISH

1 fresh mint sprig

slices of lemon

strips of lemon peel

1 Put the red snapper fillets into a large casserole dish. Pour over the wine and add the shallots, garlic, herbs, lemon peel and juice, nutmeg, and anchovies. Season to taste with salt and pepper. Cover and cook in a preheated oven at 350°F/180°C, for about 35 minutes.

2 Transfer the snapper to a warmed dish. Set aside and keep warm.

3 Pour the cooking liquid into a pan and bring to a boil over a low heat. Simmer gently for 25 minutes, until reduced by half. Mix the cream and cornstarch together and stir into the sauce to thicken.

4 Bring a pan of lightly salted water to a boil over a medium heat. Add the pasta and oil and cook for 8–10 minutes, or until done. Drain the pasta thoroughly and transfer to a warmed serving dish.

5 Arrange the red snapper fillets on top of the pasta and pour the sauce over them. Garnish with a mint sprig, slices of lemon, and strips of lemon peel. Serve immediately.

357

rice with crab & mussels

serves four

1½ cups long-grain rice

6 oz/175 g white crab meat, fresh, canned or frozen (thawed if frozen), or 8 crab sticks, thawed if frozen

2 tbsp sesame or corn oil

1-inch/2.5-cm piece fresh gingerroot, grated

4 scallions, thinly sliced diagonally

4½ oz/125 g snow peas, cut into 2–3 pieces

½ tsp turmeric

1 tsp ground cumin

14 oz/400 g canned mussels, well drained, or 12 oz/350 g frozen mussels, thawed

15 oz/350 g canned bean sprouts, well drained

salt and pepper

1 Bring a large pan of lightly salted water to a boil over a medium heat. Add the rice and cook for about 15 minutes. Drain and keep warm.

2 Extract the crab meat, if using fresh crab. Flake the crab meat or cut the crab sticks into 3–4 pieces.

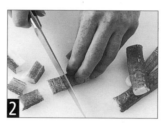

3 Heat a large wok over a high heat. Add the oil and when hot, add the ginger and scallions and cook for 1–2 minutes. Add the snow peas and continue to cook for an additional 1 minute. Sprinkle over the turmeric, cumin, then season to taste with salt and pepper. Mix thoroughly.

4 Add the crab meat and mussels to the wok and cook, stirring, for 1 minute. Stir in the cooked rice and bean sprouts, and cook for 2 minutes, or until hot and well mixed.

5 Adjust the seasoning to taste, if necessary. Transfer to a large serving dish and serve immediately.

flounder fillets with grapes

serves four

1 lb 2 oz/500 g flounder fillets, skinned

4 scallions, white and green parts,
    sliced diagonally

½ cup dry white wine

1 tbsp cornstarch

2 tbsp skim milk

2 tbsp chopped fresh dill

4 tbsp heavy cream

4½ oz/125 g seedless green grapes

1 tsp lemon juice

salt and pepper

fresh dill sprigs, to garnish

TO SERVE

freshly cooked basmati rice

zucchini ribbons

COOK'S TIP

Dill has a fairly strong anise
flavor that goes well with fish.
The feathery leaves are attractive
when used as a garnish.

---

1 Using a sharp knife, cut the fish fillets into strips, about 1½-inches/4-cm long and put into a skillet with the scallions and wine. season to taste with salt and pepper.

2 Bring to a boil over a medium heat, cover, and simmer for about 4 minutes. Carefully transfer the fish to a warmed serving dish. Cover and keep warm while you make the sauce.

3 Mix the cornstarch and milk together, then add to the skillet with the dill and cream. Bring to a boil over a high heat, and boil, stirring, for 2 minutes until thickened.

4 Add the grapes and lemon juice and heat through gently for 1–2 minutes, then pour over the fish. Garnish with dill sprigs and serve with cooked rice and zucchini ribbons.

pasta & anchovy sauce

serves four

6 tbsp olive oil

2 garlic cloves, minced

2 oz/55 g canned anchovy
  fillets, drained

1 lb/450 g dried spaghetti

¼ cup Pesto Sauce (see page 479)

2 tbsp finely chopped fresh oregano

1 cup freshly grated Parmesan
  cheese, plus extra for serving

salt and pepper

2 fresh oregano sprigs, to garnish

1 Set aside 1 tablespoon of the oil and heat the remainder in a small pan over a medium heat. Add the garlic and cook for 3 minutes.

2 Reduce the heat, stir in the anchovies and cook, stirring occasionally, until the anchovies have disintegrated.

3 Bring a pan of lightly salted water to a boil over a medium heat. Add the pasta and remaining oil and cook for 8–10 minutes, or until done.

4 Add the Pesto Sauce (see page 227) and chopped fresh oregano to the anchovy mixture, then season with pepper to taste.

5 Using a slotted spoon, drain the pasta and transfer to a warmed serving dish. Pour the Pesto Sauce over the pasta, then sprinkle over the grated Parmesan cheese.

6 Garnish with oregano sprigs and serve immediately with extra Parmesan cheese.

seafood medley

serves four

12 raw jumbo shrimp

12 raw shrimp

1 lb/450 g fillet of sea bream

4 tbsp butter

12 scallops, shelled

4½ oz/125 g freshwater shrimp

juice and finely grated peel of
  1 lemon

pinch of saffron powder or threads

4 cups vegetable bouillon

⅔ cup rose petal vinegar
  (see Cook' Tip)

4 cups dried farfalle

1 tsp olive oil

⅔ cup white wine

1 tbsp pink peppercorns

4 oz/115 g baby carrots

⅔ cup heavy cream

salt and pepper

COOK'S TIP

To make rose petal vinegar,
infuse the petals of 8 pesticide-
free roses in ⅔ cup white wine
vinegar for 48 hours. Prepare
well in advance to
reduce the preparation time.

1 Shell and devein the jumbo
shrimp and shrimp. Using a sharp
knife, thinly slice the sea bream. Melt
the butter in a large skillet over a
medium heat. Add the sea bream,
scallops, jumbo shrimp, and shrimp
and cook for 1–2 minutes.

2 Season with pepper to taste. Add
the lemon juice and grated peel.
Very carefully add a pinch of saffron
powder or a few strands of saffron to
the cooking juices (not to the seafood).

3 Remove the seafood from the
pan, set aside, and keep warm.

4 Return the pan to the heat and
add the bouillon. Bring to a boil
over a medium heat and reduce by one
third. Add the vinegar and cook for
4 minutes, or until reduced.

5 Bring a pan of lightly salted water
to a boil over a medium heat.
Add the pasta and oil and cook for
8–10 minutes, or until done. Drain the
pasta thoroughly, transfer to a serving
plate and top with the seafood.

6 Add the wine, peppercorns, and
carrots to the pan and reduce the
sauce for 6 minutes. Add the cream
and simmer for 2 minutes.

7 Pour the sauce over the seafood
and pasta and serve immediately.

spaghetti & seafood sauce

serves four

8 oz/225 g dried spaghetti, broken
  into 6-inch/15-cm lengths

1 tbsp olive oil

1¼ cups chicken bouillon

1 tsp lemon juice

1 small cauliflower, cut
  into flowerets

2 carrots, sliced thinly

4 oz/115 g snow peas

4 tbsp butter

1 onion, sliced

8 oz/225 g zucchini, sliced

1 garlic clove, chopped

12 oz/350 g frozen, cooked, shelled
  shrimp, thawed

2 tbsp chopped fresh parsley

¼ cup freshly grated
  Parmesan cheese

½ tsp paprika

salt and pepper

1 Bring a pan of lightly salted water to a boil over a medium heat. Add the pasta and cook until done. Drain the pasta thoroughly and return to the pan. Toss with the oil, cover, and keep warm.

2 Bring the chicken bouillon and lemon juice to a boil. Add the cauliflower and carrot and cook for 3–4 minutes. Remove from the pan and set aside. Add the snow peas to the pan and cook for 1–2 minutes. Set aside with the other vegetables.

3 Melt half the butter in a skillet over a medium heat. Add the onion and zucchini and cook for about 3 minutes. Add the garlic and shrimp and cook until heated through.

4 Stir in the reserved vegetables and heat through. Season to taste with salt and pepper and stir in the remaining butter.

5 Transfer the pasta to a warmed serving dish. Pour over the sauce and add the chopped parsley. Toss well with 2 forks until the pasta is coated. Sprinkle over the Parmesan cheese and paprika, then serve immediately.

mussel & scallop spaghetti

serves four

8 oz/225 g dried
   whole-wheat spaghetti
2 slices rindless, lean back
   bacon, chopped
2 shallots, chopped finely
2 celery stalk, chopped finely
⅔ cup dry white wine
⅔ cup fish bouillon
1 lb 2 oz/500 g fresh
   mussels, prepared
8 oz/225 g shelled queen or China
   bay scallops
1 tbsp chopped fresh parsley
salt and pepper

1 Bring a large pan of lightly salted water to a boil over a medium heat. Add the pasta and cook for about 10 minutes, or until done.

2 Meanwhile, dry-fry the bacon in a large non-stick skillet for about 2–3 minutes. Stir in the shallots, celery, and wine. Simmer gently for 5 minutes, or until softened.

3 Add the bouillon, mussels, and scallops, cover and cook for an additional 6–7 minutes. Discard any mussels that remain unopened.

4 Drain the pasta and add to the skillet. Add the parsley, season to taste with salt and pepper, and toss together. Cook for 1–2 minutes. Pile onto warmed serving plates, spooning over the juices. Serve.

noodles with shrimp

serves four

8 oz/225 g thin egg noodles

2 tbsp groundnut oil

1 garlic clove, minced

½ tsp ground star anise

1 bunch scallions, cut into
2-inch/5-cm pieces

24 raw jumbo shrimp, shelled, with
tails intact

2 tbsp light soy sauce

2 tsp lime juice

slices of lime, to garnish

COOK'S TIP

If fresh egg noodles are
available, these require very little
cooking. Simply put into boiling
water for about 3 minutes, then
drain and toss in oil. Noodles can
be boiled and eaten plain, or
cooked with meat and
vegetables for a light meal.

1 Bring a pan of water to a boil over a medium heat. Add the noodles and blanch for 2–3 minutes.

2 Drain the noodles thoroughly, rinse under cold running water and drain again. Keep warm and set aside until required.

3 Heat a large wok over a high heat. Add the groundnut oil and when almost smoking, add the garlic and ground star anise, and cook for 30 seconds.

4 Add the scallions and jumbo shrimp to the wok, and cook for 2–3 minutes.

5 Stir in the light soy sauce, lime juice, and noodles, and mix well.

6 Cook the mixture in the wok for about 1 minute until thoroughly heated through and all the ingredients are incorporated.

7 Spoon the noodle and shrimp mixture into 4 warmed serving dishes and garnish with slices lime. Serve immediately.

cellophane noodles & shrimp

serves four

6 oz/175 g cellophane noodles

1 tbsp vegetable oil

1 garlic clove, minced

2 tsp grated fresh gingerroot

24 raw jumbo shrimp, shelled
  and deveined

1 red bell pepper, seeded and
  sliced thinly

1 green bell pepper, seeded and
  sliced thinly

1 onion, chopped

2 tbsp light soy sauce

juice of 1 orange

2 tsp wine vinegar

pinch of brown sugar

⅔ cup fish bouillon

1 tbsp cornstarch

2 tsp water

slices of orange, to garnish

1 Bring a pan of water to a boil over a medium heat. Add the noodles and blanch for 1 minute. Drain well, rinse, and drain again.

2 Heat a large wok and over a high heat. Add the oil and when hot, add the garlic and ginger, and cook for 30 seconds.

3 Add the shrimp and cook for 2 minutes. Remove with a slotted spoon and keep warm.

4 Add the bell peppers and onion, and cook for 2 minutes. Stir in the soy sauce, orange juice, vinegar, sugar, and bouillon. Return the shrimp to the wok and cook for 8–10 minutes.

5 Blend the cornstarch with the water and stir into the wok. Bring to a boil over a medium heat. Add the noodles and cook for 1–2 minutes. Transfer to 4 warmed bowls, garnish with orange slices and serve.

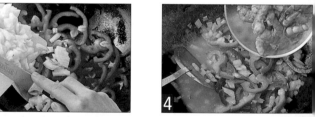

sweet & sour noodles

serves four

3 tbsp fish sauce

2 tbsp distilled white vinegar

2 tbsp palm or superfine sugar

2 tbsp tomato paste

2 tbsp corn oil

3 cloves garlic, minced

12 oz/350 g rice noodles, soaked in
   boiling water for 5 minutes

8 scallions, sliced

2 carrots, grated

1½ cups bean sprouts

2 eggs, beaten

8 oz/225 g shelled king shrimp

½ cup chopped peanuts

1 tsp chili flakes, to garnish

4 Add the scallions, carrots, and bean sprouts to the wok and cook for 2–3 minutes.

5 Move the stir-fry mixture to one side of the wok, add the beaten eggs to the empty part of the wok and cook until the egg sets. Add the noodles, shrimp, and peanuts to the wok and mix well. Transfer to 4 large, warmed serving dishes and garnish with chili flakes. Serve immediately.

COOK'S TIP

Chili flakes may be found in the spice section of large food stores.

1 Mix the fish sauce, vinegar, sugar, and tomato paste together.

2 Heat a large wok over a high heat. Add the oil and when hot, add the garlic. Cook for 30 seconds.

3 Drain the noodles thoroughly and add them to the wok together with the fish sauce and tomato paste mixture. Mix well.

seafood chow mein

serves four

3 oz/85 g squid, cleaned

3–4 fresh scallops

3 oz/85 g raw shrimp, shelled

½ egg white, beaten lightly

1 tbsp cornstarch paste
  (see page 263)

9½ oz/275 g egg noodles

5–6 tbsp vegetable oil

2 tbsp light soy sauce

2 oz/55 g snow peas

½ tsp salt

½ tsp sugar

1 tsp Chinese rice wine

2 scallions, shredded finely

few drops of sesame oil

1 Open up the squid and score the inside in a criss-cross pattern, then cut into pieces about the size of a postage stamp. Soak the squid in a bowl of boiling water until all the pieces curl up. Rinse in cold water and drain.

2 Cut each scallop into 3–4 slices. Cut the shrimp in half lengthwise, if large. Mix the scallops and shrimp together with the egg white, and cornstarch paste.

3 Bring a large pan of water to a boil over a medium heat. Add the noodles and cook according to the package instructions. Drain and rinse under cold water, then drain again. Toss with about 1 tablespoon of oil.

4 Heat a wok over a high heat. Add 3 tablespoons of oil and when hot, add the noodles and 1 tablespoon of soy sauce. Cook for 2–3 minutes. Transfer to a large serving dish.

5 Heat the remaining oil in the wok and add the snow peas and seafood. Cook for 2 minutes, then add the salt, sugar, Chinese rice wine, remaining soy sauce, and about half the scallions. Blend and add a little water, if necessary. Pour the seafood mixture on top of the noodles and sprinkle with sesame oil. Garnish with the remaining scallions and serve.

chili shrimp noodles

serves four

2 tbsp light soy sauce

1 tbsp lime or lemon juice

1 tbsp fish sauce

4½ oz/125 g firm beancurd, cut into chunks (drained weight)

4½ oz/125 g cellophane noodles

2 tbsp sesame oil

4 shallots, sliced finely

2 garlic cloves, minced

1 small fresh red chili, seeded and chopped finely

2 celery stalks, sliced finely

2 carrots, sliced finely

⅔ cup cooked small shrimp, shelled

1 cup bean sprouts

TO GARNISH

celery leaves

fresh chiles

1 Mix the light soy sauce, lime or lemon juice, and fish sauce together in a small bowl. Add the beancurd cubes and toss until coated in the mixture. Cover and set aside for 15 minutes.

2 Put the noodles into a large bowl and pour over enough warm water to cover. Let soak for 5 minutes, then drain thoroughly.

3 Heat a large wok over a high heat. Add the sesame oil and when hot, add the shallots, garlic, and red chile, and stir-fry for 1 minute.

4 Add the sliced celery and carrots to the wok and cook, stirring, for an additional 2–3 minutes.

5 Tip the drained noodles into the wok and cook, stirring, for about 2 minutes, then add the shrimp, bean sprouts, and beancurd with the soy sauce mixture. Cook over a medium high heat for 2–3 minutes, or until heated through.

6 Transfer the mixture to 4 serving bowls, garnish with celery leaves and chiles and serve.

thai-style shrimp noodles

serves four

9 oz/250 g thin glass noodles

2 tbsp corn oil

1 onion, sliced

2 fresh red chiles, seeded and
chopped very finely

4 lime leaves, shredded thinly

1 tbsp fresh cilantro

2 tbsp palm or superfine sugar

2 tbsp fish sauce

1 lb/450 g raw jumbo
shrimp, shelled

1 Put the noodles into a large bowl, pour over enough boiling water to cover and let stand for 5 minutes. Drain thoroughly and set aside.

2 Heat a large wok over a high heat, then add the oil.

3 When the oil is very hot, add the onion, red chiles, and lime leaves and cook for 1 minute.

4 Add the cilantro, palm or superfine sugar, fish sauce, and shrimp to the wok and cook for an additional 2 minutes, or until the shrimp turn pink.

5 Add the drained noodles to the wok, toss to mix thoroughly, and cook for 1–2 minutes, or until heated through.

6 Transfer the noodles and shrimp to 4 large, warmed serving bowls and serve immediately.

COOK'S TIP

If you cannot buy raw jumbo shrimp, substitute with some cooked shrimp, thawed if frozen, and cook them with the cooked noodles in step 5 for 1 minute only, just to heat them through.

fried rice & shrimp

serves four

1½ cups long-grain rice

2 eggs

4 tsp cold water

salt and pepper

3 tbsp corn oil

4 scallions, thinly sliced diagonally

1 garlic clove, minced

4½ oz/125 g closed cup or white
   mushrooms, sliced thinly

2 tbsp oyster or anchovy sauce

7 oz/200 g canned water chestnuts,
   drained and sliced

9 oz/250 g shelled shrimp, thawed
   if frozen

1 cup arugula, chopped coarsely

1 Bring a large pan of lightly salted water to a boil over a medium heat. Add the rice and cook for about 15 minutes. Drain and keep warm.

2 Beat each egg separately with 2 teaspoons of cold water and season to taste with salt and pepper.

3 Heat a large wok over a high heat. Add 2 teaspoons of the oil and carefully swirl it around until hot. Pour in the first egg, swirl it around and let cook, undisturbed, until set. Transfer to a plate or board and repeat with the second egg. Cut the omelets into 1-inch/2.5-cm squares.

4 Heat the remaining oil in the wok and when really hot, add the scallions and garlic. Cook for 1 minute. Add the mushrooms and continue to cook for an additional 2 minutes.

5 Stir in the oyster or anchovy sauce and season, if necessary. Add the water chestnuts and shrimp, and cook for 2 minutes.

6 Stir in the cooked rice and cooked for 1 minute, then add the arugula and omelet squares and cook for an additional 1-2 minutes, or until piping hot. Serve immediately.

aromatic seafood rice

serves four

1¼ cups basmati rice

2 tbsp ghee or vegetable oil

1 onion, chopped

1 garlic clove, minced

1 tsp cumin seeds

½-1 tsp chilli powder

4 cloves

1 cinnamon stick or a piece of
    cassia bark

2 tsp curry paste

8 oz/225 g shelled shrimp

1 lb 2 oz/500 g white fish fillets
    (such as angler fish, cod, or
    haddock), skinned and boned,
    and cut into bite-size pieces

2½ cups boiling water

⅓ cup frozen peas

⅓ cup frozen corn

1–2 tbsp lime juice

2 tbsp toasted shredded coconut

salt and pepper

TO GARNISH

fresh cilantro sprigs

2 slices of lime

1 Put the rice in a strainer and wash well in cold water until the water runs clear, then drain thoroughly.

2 Heat the ghee or oil in a pan over a low heat. Add the onion, garlic, spices, and curry paste, and cook gently for 1 minute.

3 Stir in the rice and mix well until coated in the spiced oil. Add the shrimp and white fish. Season well with salt and pepper. Stir lightly, then pour in the boiling water.

4 Cover and cook for 10 minutes. Add the peas and corn, cover and continue cooking for an additional 8 minutes. Remove from the heat and let stand for 10 minutes.

5 Uncover the pan, fluff up the rice with a fork and transfer to a warmed serving platter.

6 Sprinkle the dish with the lime juice and toasted coconut, and garnish with cilantro sprigs and the lime slices. Serve immediately.

oyster sauce noodles

serves four

9 oz/250 g egg noodles

1 lb/450 g chicken thighs

2 tbsp groundnut oil

3½ oz/100 g carrots, sliced

3 tbsp oyster sauce

2 eggs

3 tbsp cold water

1 Put the egg noodles into a large bowl or dish. Pour over enough boiling water to cover and let stand for 10 minutes.

2 Meanwhile, remove the skin from the chicken thighs and discard. Cut the chicken flesh into small pieces with a sharp knife.

3 Heat a large wok over a high heat, then add the oil.

4 When the oil is hot, add the chicken and carrot slices, and cook for about 5 minutes.

5 Drain the noodles thoroughly, then add to the wok. Cook for an additional 2–3 minutes, or until the noodles are heated through.

6 Beat the oyster sauce, eggs and 3 tablespoons of cold water together. Drizzle the mixture over the noodles and cook for an additional 2–3 minutes, or until the eggs set. Transfer to 4 warmed serving bowls and serve immediately.

VARIATION

Flavor the eggs with soy sauce or hoisin sauce as an alternative to the oyster sauce, if you prefer.

377

shrimp pasta bake

serves four

2 cups dried tricolor pasta shapes

1 tbsp vegetable oil

2½ cups sliced white mushrooms

1 bunch scallions, trimmed
and chopped

14 oz/400 g canned tuna in brine,
drained and flaked

6 oz/175 g shelled shrimp, thawed
if frozen

2 tbsp cornstarch

1¾ cups skim milk

4 tomatoes, sliced thinly

½ cup fresh bread crumbs

¼ cup freshly grated reduced-fat
cheddar cheese

salt and pepper

1 Bring a large pan of lightly salted water to a boil over a medium heat. Add the pasta and cook for 8–10 minutes, or until done. Drain the pasta thoroughly.

2 Meanwhile, heat the oil in a large skillet over a low heat. Add the mushrooms and all but a handful of the scallions and cook, stirring frequently, for about 4–5 minutes, or until softened.

3 Put the cooked pasta into a bowl and mix in the mushroom and scallion mixture, tuna, and shrimp.

4 Blend the cornstarch with a little milk to make a smooth paste. Pour the remaining milk into a pan and stir in the paste. Heat, stirring constantly, until the sauce starts to thicken. Season well with salt and pepper. Add the sauce to the pasta mixture and mix thoroughly. Transfer to an ovenproof gratin dish and put on a cookie sheet.

5 Arrange the tomato slices over the pasta and sprinkle with the bread crumbs and cheese. Cook in a preheated oven at 375°F/190°C, for 25–30 minutes, or until golden brown. Garnished with the scallions and serve.

scallop kabobs

serves four

grated peel and juice of 2 limes

2 tbsp finely chopped lemon grass
   or 1 tbsp lemon juice

2 garlic cloves, minced

1 fresh green chile, seeded
   and chopped

16 scallops, with corals

2 limes, each cut into 8 segments

2 tbsp corn oil

1 tbsp lemon juice

salt and pepper

TO SERVE

1 cup arugula

3 cups mixed salad greens

1 Soak 8 wooden skewers in warm water for at least 10 minutes before you use them to prevent burning on the barbecue.

2 Mix the lime juice and peel, lemon grass, garlic and chile together in a pestle and mortar or spice grinder to make a paste.

3 Thread 2 scallops onto each of the presoaked skewers. Cover the ends with foil to prevent them burning.

4 Alternate the scallops with the lime segments.

5 Put the oil, lemon juice, salt, and pepper into a bowl and whisk together to make the dressing.

6 Coat the scallops with the spice paste and put over medium-hot coals on a barbecue.

7 Cook for 10 minutes, turning once and basting occasionally.

8 Toss the arugula, mixed salad greens, and dressing together well. transfer to a serving bowl.

9 Serve the scallops piping hot, 2 skewers on each plate immediately with the salad.

asian shellfish kabobs

serves twelve

350 g/12 oz raw jumbo shrimp,
  shelled, leaving tails intact
12 oz/350 g scallops, cleaned,
  trimmed and halved (cut into
  fourths if large)
1 bunch scallions, sliced into
  1-inch/2.5-cm pieces
1 medium red bell pepper,
  seeded and cubed
3½ oz/100 g baby corn cobs,
  trimmed and sliced into
  ½-inch/1-cm pieces
3 tbsp dark soy sauce
½ tsp hot chilli powder
½ tsp ground ginger
1 tbsp corn oil
DIP
4 tbsp dark soy sauce
4 tbsp dry sherry
2 tsp honey
1-inch/2.5-cm piece fresh
  gingerroot, grated
1 scallion, trimmed and sliced
  very finely

1 Soak 12 wooden skewers in warm water for at least 10 minutes before you use them to prevent burning. Divide the shrimp, scallops, scallions, bell pepper, and baby corn into 12 portions and thread onto the skewers. Cover the ends with foil so they do not burn and put into a shallow dish.

2 Mix the soy sauce, chili powder, and ground ginger together, and coat the kabobs. Cover and chill in the refrigerator for about 2 hours.

3 Arrange the kabobs on a broiler rack, brush with the oil and cook under a preheated hot broiler for 2–3 minutes on each side until the shrimp turn pink, the scallops become opaque, and the vegetables soften.

4 Mix all the dip ingredients together in a small bowl.

5 Remove the foil and transfer the kabobs to a warmed serving platter and serve with the dip.

lemon angler fish kabobs

serves four

1 lb/450 g angler fish

2 zucchini

1 lemon

12 cherry tomatoes

8 bay leaves

SAUCE

3 tbsp olive oil

2 tbsp lemon juice

1 tsp chopped fresh thyme

½ tsp lemon pepper

salt

TO SERVE

salad greens

crusty bread

VARIATION

Use flounder fillets instead of the angler fish, if you prefer. Allow 2 fillets per person, and skin and cut each fillet lengthwise into 2 pieces. Roll up each piece and thread them onto the skewers.

1 Using a sharp knife, cut the angler fish into 2-inch/ 5-cm chunks.

2 Cut the zucchini into thick slices and the lemon into wedges.

3 Thread the angler fish, zucchini, lemon, tomatoes, and the bay leaves alternately onto 4 wooden or metal skewers.

4 To make the basting sauce, mix the oil, lemon juice, thyme, lemon pepper, and salt to taste together in a small bowl.

5 Brush the skewers liberally with the basting sauce and put on a barbecue grill. Cook over medium-hot coals for 15 minutes, basting with the sauce, until the fish is cooked through. Transfer to plates and serve with salad greens and bread.

Meat

A whole variety of ways in which meat can be
cooked is included in this chapter to create a
sumptuous selection of dishes. Barbecues, stir-

fries, roasts, and casseroles are combined to offer a wealth of textures and

flavors. Classic and traditional recipes feature alongside more exotic dishes

taken from all around the world, incorporating exciting new ingredients

alongside family favorites such as pork and lamb chops. The dishes in this

chapter range from easy, economic midweek suppers to sophisticated and

elegant main courses for special occasions.

creamed strips of short loin

serves four

6 tbsp butter

1 lb/450 g short loin steak, trimmed, and cut into thin strips

6 oz/175 g white mushrooms, sliced

1 tsp mustard

pinch of freshly grated gingerroot

2 tbsp dry sherry

⅔ cup heavy cream

salt and pepper

4 slices hot toast, cut into triangles, to serve

PASTA

1 lb/450 g dried rigatoni

2 fresh basil sprigs

½ cup butter

COOK'S TIP

Dried pasta will keep for up to 6 months. Keep it in the package and reseal it once you have opened it, or transfer it to an airtight jar.

1 Melt the butter in a large skillet over a low heat. Add the steak and gently cook, stirring frequently, for 6 minutes. Using a slotted spoon, transfer the steak to an ovenproof dish and keep warm.

2 Add the sliced mushrooms to the skillet and cook for 2–3 minutes in the juices remaining in the skillet. Add the mustard, ginger, salt, and pepper. Cook for 2 minutes, then add the sherry and cream. Cook for an additional 3 minutes, then pour the cream sauce over the steak.

3 Cook the steak and cream sauce mixture in a preheated oven at 375°F/190°C, for 10 minutes.

4 Meanwhile, bring a large pan of lightly salted water to a boil over a medium heat. Add the pasta and 1 of the basil sprigs, and boil rapidly for 10 minutes, or until done. Drain the pasta and transfer to a warmed serving dish. Toss the pasta with the butter and garnish with the other basil sprig.

5 Serve the steak with the pasta and triangles of hot toast.

fresh spaghetti & meatballs

serves four

2½ cups brown bread crumbs

⅝ cup milk

2 tbsp butter

¼ cup whole-wheat flour

⅞ cup beef bouillon

14 oz/400 g canned
 chopped tomatoes

2 tbsp tomato paste

1 tsp sugar

1 tbsp finely chopped fresh tarragon

1 large onion, chopped

4 cups ground steak

1 tsp paprika

4 tbsp olive oil

1 lb/450 g fresh spaghetti

salt and pepper

fresh tarragon sprigs, to garnish

1 Soak the bread crumbs in the milk for 30 minutes.

2 Melt half the butter in a pan over a low heat. Add the flour and cook, stirring, for 2 minutes. Stir in the bouillon and cook for 5 minutes. Add the tomatoes, tomato paste, sugar, and tarragon. Season with salt and pepper and cook for 25 minutes.

3 Mix the onion, steak, and paprika into the bread crumbs and season to taste. Shape into 14 meatballs.

4 Heat the oil and remaining butter in a skillet over a medium heat. Add the meatballs and cook until browned. Put into a deep casserole and pour over the tomato sauce. Cover and cook in a preheated oven at 350°F/180°C, for 25 minutes.

5 Bring a pan of lightly salted water to a boil over a medium heat. Add the pasta and cook until done.

6 Remove the meatballs from the oven and cool slightly. Pile the pasta onto 4 plates, add the meatballs and garnish with tarragon. Serve.

meatballs in italian red wine sauce

serves four

⅔ cup milk

2 cups white bread crumbs

2 tbsp butter

8 tbsp olive oil

3 cups sliced oyster mushrooms

¼ cup whole-wheat flour

⅞ cup beef bouillon

⅔ cup red wine

4 tomatoes, peeled and chopped

1 tbsp tomato paste

1 tsp brown sugar

1 tbsp finely chopped fresh basil

12 shallots, chopped

4 cups ground steak

1 tsp paprika

1 lb/450 g dried egg tagliarini

salt and pepper

fresh basil sprigs, to garnish

1 Soak the bread crumbs in the milk for 30 minutes. Heat half the butter and 4 tablespoons of the oil in a skillet. Add the mushrooms and cook for 4 minutes. Stir in the flour and cook for 2 minutes. Add the bouillon and wine, and cook for 15 minutes. Add the tomatoes, tomato paste, sugar, and basil. Season and cook for 30 minutes.

2 Mix the shallots, steak, and paprika with the breadcrumbs. Season. Shape into 14 meatballs. Heat 4 tablespoons of the remaining oil and butter in a skillet. Fry the meatballs until browned, then put in a casserole with the sauce. Cook in a preheated oven, at 350°F/180°C, for 30 minutes.

3 Bring a pan of salted water to a boil. Add the pasta and cook until done. Drain and transfer to a dish. Spoon the meatballs on top. Garnish with a basil sprig and serve.

389

citrus pork chops

serves four

½ fennel bulb

1 tbsp juniper berries, minced lightly

about 2 tbsp olive oil

finely grated peel of 1 orange

4 pork chops, each about
5½ oz/150 g

juice of 1 orange

crisp salad, to serve

COOK'S TIP

Juniper berries are most commonly associated with gin, but they are often added to meat dishes in Italy for a delicate citrus flavor. They can be bought dried from most health-food shops and some larger supermarkets.

---

1 Finely chop the fennel bulb with a sharp knife. Discard the tough outer leaves and feathery fronds.

2 Grind the juniper berries in a mortar and pestle. Mix the juniper berries with the fennel flesh, oil, and orange peel.

3 Using a sharp knife, score a few cuts all over each pork chop.

4 Put the pork chops in a roasting pan or ovenproof dish, the spoon the fennel and juniper mixture over the pork chops.

5 Carefully pour the orange juice over the top of each pork chop. Cover and let marinate in the refrigerator for about 2 hours.

6 Cook the pork chops, under a preheated hot broiler, for about 10–15 minutes, depending on the thickness of the meat, turning, until the meat is tender and cooked through.

7 Transfer the pork chops to 4 large, warmed serving plates and serve immediately with a crisp salad.

pork chops with sage

serves four

2 tbsp flour

1 tbsp chopped fresh sage or 1 tsp
   dried sage

4 boneless, lean pork chops,
   trimmed of excess fat

2 tbsp olive oil

1 tbsp butter

2 red onions, sliced into rings

1 tbsp lemon juice

2 tsp superfine sugar

4 plum tomatoes, cut into fourths

salt and pepper

salad greens, to serve

1 Mix the flour, sage, and salt and pepper to taste on a plate. Lightly dust the pork chops on both sides with the seasoned flour.

2 Heat the oil and butter in a skillet over a medium heat. Add the pork chops and cook for 6–7 minutes on each side, or until cooked through. Drain the pork chops and set aside the pan juices. Keep warm.

3 Toss the onion in the lemon juice and cook with the sugar and tomatoes for 5 minutes, or until tender. Transfer the pork chops to 4 warmed serving plates and pour over the pan juices. Serve with the tomato and onion mixture and salad greens.

pasta & pork in cream sauce

serves four

1 lb/450 g pork tenderloin,
  sliced thinly
4 tbsp olive oil
8 oz/225 g white mushrooms, sliced
⅞ cup Italian Red Wine Sauce
  (see page 389)
1 tbsp lemon juice
pinch of saffron
3 cups dried orecchioni
4 tbsp heavy cream
12 quail eggs
salt

1 Pound the slices of pork between 2 sheets of plastic wrap until wafer thin, then cut into strips.

2 Heat the oil in a large skillet over a medium heat. Add the pork and cook, stirring. for 5 minutes. Add the mushrooms and cook, stirring, for an additional 2 minutes.

3 Pour over the Italian Red Wine Sauce (see page 135), reduce the heat and simmer gently for 20 minutes.

4 Meanwhile, bring a large pan of lightly salted water to a boil over a medium heat. Add the lemon juice, saffron, and pasta and cook for about 8–10 minutes, or until done. Drain the pasta thoroughly and keep warm.

5 Stir the cream into the skillet with the pork and heat for 4 minutes.

6 Bring a pan of water to a boil over a medium heat and cook the eggs for 3 minutes. Cool thoroughly in cold water and remove the shells.

7 Transfer the pasta to a large, warmed serving plate, top with the pork and the sauce, and garnish with the eggs. Serve immediately.

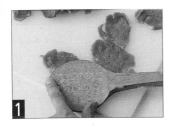

pork with lemon & garlic

serves four

1 lb/450 g pork tenderloin

2½ tbsp chopped almonds

2 tbsp olive oil

3½ oz/100 g prosciutto,
    chopped finely

2 garlic cloves, chopped

1 tbsp fresh oregano, chopped

finely grated peel of 2 lemons

4 shallots, chopped finely

¾ cup ham or chicken bouillon

1 tsp sugar

freshly cooked snow peas, to serve

1 Using a sharp knife, cut the pork into 4 equal pieces. Put the pork between 2 sheets of oiled waxed paper and pound each piece with a meat mallet or the end of a rolling pin to flatten it.

2 Cut a horizontal slit in each piece of pork to make a pocket.

3 Put the almonds onto a cookie sheet and lightly toast under a medium-hot broiler for 2–3 minutes, or until golden.

4 Mix the almonds with 1 tablespoon of the oil, prosciutto, garlic, oregano, and the finely grated peel from 1 lemon. Spoon the mixture into the pork pockets.

5 Heat the remaining oil in a large skillet over a medium heat. Add the shallots and cook for 2 minutes.

6 Add the pork pockets and cook until browned all over.

7 Add the bouillon and bring to a boil over a medium heat. Cook for 45 minutes, or until the meat is tender. Remove the meat and keep warm.

8 Using a zester, pare the remaining lemon. Add the peel and sugar to the skillet, then boil for 3–4 minutes, or until reduced and syrupy. Transfer the pork to 4 warmed serving plates and serve with snow peas.

lamb with black bean sauce & bell peppers

serves four

1 lb/450 g boneless leg of lamb

1 egg white, beaten lightly

4 tbsp cornstarch

1 tsp Chinese five-spice powder

3 tbsp corn oil

1 red onion

1 red bell pepper, seeded and sliced

1 green bell pepper, seeded
    and sliced

1 yellow or orange bell pepper,
    seeded and sliced

5 tbsp black bean sauce

cooked rice or noodles, to serve

1 Using a sharp knife, slice the lamb into very thin strips.

2 Mix the egg white, cornstarch, and Chinese five-spice powder. Toss the lamb strips in the mixture until evenly coated.

3 Heat the corn oil in a preheated wok and stir-fry the lamb over high heat for 5 minutes, or until it crispens around the edges.

4 Slice the red onion. Add the onion and bell pepper slices to the wok and stir-fry for 5–6 minutes, or until the vegetables just start to soften.

5 Stir the black bean sauce into the mixture and heat through.

6 Transfer the lamb and sauce to warmed individual serving plates and serve immediately with freshly cooked rice or noodles.

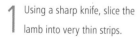

roman pan-fried lamb

serves four

1 tbsp oil

1 tbsp butter

1 lb 5 oz/600 g lamb (shoulder or
   leg), cut in 1-inch/2.5-cm chunks

4 garlic cloves, peeled

3 fresh thyme sprigs, stalks removed

6 canned anchovy fillets

⅔ cup red wine

⅓ cup lamb or vegetable bouillon

1 tsp sugar

4 tbsp pitted ripe black
   olives, halved

2 tbsp chopped fresh parsley,
   to garnish

COOK'S TIP

Rome is the capital of both the
region of Lazio and Italy and has
thus become a focal point for
specialties from all over Italy.
Food from this region tends to
be simple and quick to prepare,
all with plenty of herbs and
seasonings, giving really
robust flavors.

1 Heat the oil and butter in a large
skillet over a medium heat. Add
the lamb and cook for 4–5 minutes,
stirring, until the meat is browned.

2 Using a mortar and pestle, grind
the garlic, thyme, and anchovies
together to make a smooth paste.

3 Add the wine and lamb or
vegetable bouillon to the skillet.
Stir in the garlic and anchovy paste
together with the sugar.

4 Bring the mixture to a boil over a
medium heat. Reduce the heat,
cover and simmer for 30–40 minutes,
or until the lamb is tender. For the last
10 minutes of the cooking time,
remove the lid to reduce the sauce.

5 Stir the olives into the sauce and
mix well.

6 Transfer the lamb and the sauce
to a large, warmed serving bowl
and garnish with freshly chopped
parsley. Serve immediately.

397

barbecued butterfly lamb

serves four

boned leg of lamb, about
4 lb/1.8 kg
8 tbsp balsamic vinegar
grated peel and juice of 1 lemon
⅔ cup corn oil
4 tbsp chopped fresh mint
2 cloves garlic, minced
2 tbsp light brown sugar
salt and pepper
TO SERVE
freshly cooked vegetables
salad greens

1 Open out the boned leg of lamb, so its shape resembles a butterfly. Thread 2–3 skewers through the meat to make it easier to turn on the barbecue grill.

2 Mix the balsamic vinegar, lemon peel and juice, oil, mint, garlic, sugar, and seasoning to taste together in a non-metallic dish large enough to hold the lamb.

3 Put the lamb into the dish and turn until the meat is coated on both sides with the marinade. Let marinate in the refrigerator for at least 6 hours or preferably overnight, turning occasionally.

4 Remove the lamb from the marinade and set aside the liquid for basting.

5 Put the barbecue grill rack about 6 inches/15 cm above the coals on a hot barbecue and grill the lamb for about 30 minutes on each side, turning once and basting frequently with the marinade.

6 Transfer the lamb to a chopping board and remove the skewers. Cut the lamb into slices across the grain and serve with freshly cooked vegetables and salad greens.

scallions & lamb stir-fry with oyster sauce

serves four

1 lb/450 g lamb leg steaks

1 tsp ground Szechuan peppercorns

1 tbsp peanut oil

2 garlic cloves, minced

8 scallions, sliced

2 tbsp dark soy sauce

6 oz/175 g Napa cabbage

6 tbsp oyster sauce

shrimp crackers, to serve (optional)

COOK'S TIP

Oyster sauce is made from oysters, which are cooked in brine and soy sauce. Sold in bottles, it will keep in the refrigerator for months.

1 Using a sharp knife, remove any excess fat from the lamb. Slice the lamb thinly.

2 Sprinkle the ground Szechuan peppercorns over the meat and toss together until well mixed.

3 Heat the peanut oil in a preheated wok or large skillet.

4 Add the slices of lamb to the wok or skillet and cook for about 5 minutes.

5 Crush the garlic cloves with a pestle and mortar and slice the scallions. Add the garlic and scallions to the wok, together with the dark soy sauce, and stir-fry for 2 minutes.

6 Coarsely shred the Napa cabbage leaves and add them to the wok or skillet together with the oyster sauce. Stir-fry for an additional 2 minutes, or until the cabbage has wilted and the juices are bubbling.

7 Transfer the lamb stir-fry to warmed individual serving bowls and serve immediately with shrimp crackers (if using).

399

neapolitan veal chops

serves four

¾ cup butter

4 veal chops, 9 oz/250 g
 each, trimmed

1 large onion, sliced

2 apples, peeled, cored, and sliced

6 oz/175 g white mushrooms

1 tbsp chopped fresh tarragon

8 black peppercorns

1 tbsp sesame seeds

14 oz/400 g dried marille

scant ½ cup extra virgin olive oil

2 large beefsteak tomatoes, halved

leaves of 1 fresh basil sprig

¾ cup mascarpone cheese

salt and pepper

1 Melt ¼ cup of the butter in a skillet over a low heat. Add he veal and cook for 5 minutes on each side. Transfer to a dish and keep warm.

2 Add the onion and apples to the skillet and cook, stirring frequently, until lightly browned. Transfer to a serving dish, put the veal on top and keep warm.

3 Melt the remaining butter in the skillet over a low heat. Add the mushrooms, tarragon, and peppercorns, and cook, stirring occasionally, for 3 minutes. Sprinkle over the sesame seeds.

4 Bring a pan of lightly salted water to a boil over a medium heat. Add the pasta and 1 teaspoon of the oil and cook for 8–10 minutes, or until done. Drain thoroughly and transfer to an ovenproof dish.

5 Broil or cook the tomatoes and basil leaves for 2–3 minutes.

6 Top the pasta with the mascarpone cheese and sprinkle over the remaining oil. Put the onions, apples, and veal chops on top of the pasta, then spoon over the mushrooms, peppercorns, and pan juices onto the chops, put the tomatoes and basil leaves around the edge, and cook in a preheated oven at 300°F/150°C, for about 5 minutes.

7 Season to taste with salt and pepper. Transfer to 4 warmed serving plates and serve.

vitello tonnato

serves four

1 lb 10 oz/750 g boned leg of
    veal, rolled

2 bay leaves

10 black peppercorns

2–3 cloves

½ tsp salt

2 carrots, sliced

1 onion, sliced

2 celery stalks, sliced

about 3 cups bouillon or water

⅔ cup dry white wine, optional

3 oz/85 g canned tuna, well drained

1½ oz/50 g canned anchovy
    fillets, drained

⅔ cup olive oil

2 tsp canned capers, drained

2 egg yolks

1 tbsp lemon juice

salt and pepper

1 Put the veal in a pan with the bay leaves, peppercorns, cloves, salt, and vegetables. Add enough bouillon and the wine (if using) to barely cover the veal. Bring to a boil over a medium heat, remove any scum from the surface, then cover and simmer gently for about 1 hour, or until tender. Let cool in the water, then drain well.

2 To make the tuna sauce. Mash the tuna with 4 anchovy fillets, 1 tablespoon of oil, and the capers. Add the egg yolks and transfer to a food processor or blender, and process until smooth.

3 Stir in the lemon juice, then gradually whisk in the rest of the oil a few drops at a time until the sauce is smooth and has the consistency of thick cream. Season to taste with salt and pepper.

4 Slice the veal thinly and arrange on a platter. Spoon over the sauce and chill in the refrigerator overnight.

5 Uncover the veal. Arrange the remaining anchovy fillets and the capers in a pattern on top and serve.

veal in a rose petal sauce

serves four

1 lb/450 g dried fettuccine

6 tbsp olive oil

1 tsp chopped fresh oregano

1 tsp chopped fresh marjoram

¾ cup butter

1 lb/450 g veal fillet, sliced thinly

⅔ cup rose petal vinegar

(see page 362)

⅔ cup fish bouillon

¼ cup grapefruit juice

¼ cup heavy cream

salt

TO GARNISH

12 pink grapefruit segments

12 pink peppercorns

rose petals, washed

fresh herb leaves

1 Bring a large pan of lightly salted water to a boil over a medium heat. Add the pasta and cook for 8–10 minutes, or until done. Drain thoroughly and transfer to a large, warmed serving dish. Sprinkle over 2 tablespoons of the oil, the oregano, and marjoram.

2 Heat 4 tablespoons of the butter with the remaining oil in a large skillet over a low heat. Add the veal and cook for 6 minutes. Remove the veal from the skillet and put on top of the pasta.

3 Add the vinegar and fish bouillon to the skillet and bring to a boil over a medium heat. Boil vigorously until reduced by two thirds. Reduce the heat to low, add the grapefruit juice and cream and simmer for 4 minutes. Dice the remaining butter and add to the skillet, a piece at a time, whisking constantly until it is incorporated.

4 Pour the sauce around the veal, garnish with pink grapefruit segments, pink peppercorns, rose petals, and fresh herb leaves. Serve immediately.

liver with wine sauce

serves four

4 slices calf's liver or 8 slices lamb's
   liver, about 1 lb 2 oz/500 g

flour, for coating

1 tbsp olive oil

2 tbsp butter

4½ oz/125 g lean bacon strips,
   derinded and cut into
   narrow strips

1 garlic clove, minced

1 onion, chopped

1 celery stalk, sliced thinly

⅔ cup red wine

⅔ cup beef bouillon

good pinch of ground allspice

1 tsp Worcestershire sauce

1 tsp chopped fresh sage or
   ½ tsp dried sage

3–4 tomatoes, peeled, cut into
   fourths, and seeded

salt and pepper

fresh sage leaves, to garnish

saute potatoes, to serve

1 Wipe the liver with paper towels, season o taste with salt and pepper, then coat lightly in flour, shaking off any excess.

2 Heat the oil and butter in a skillet over a medium heat. Add the liver and cook until well sealed on both sides and just cooked through. Remove the liver from the skillet, cover and keep warm, but do not let it dry out.

3 Add the bacon to the fat left in the skillet, with the garlic, onion, and celery. Reduce the heat to low and cook gently until soft.

4 Add the red wine, beef bouillon, allspice, Worcestershire sauce, and sage. Season to taste with salt and pepper. Bring to a boil and simmer for 3–4 minutes.

5 Cut each tomato fourth in half. Add to the sauce and continue to cook for 2–3 minutes.

6 Serve the liver on a little of the sauce, with the remainder spooned over. Garnish with fresh sage leaves and serve with saute potatoes.

veal italienne

serves four

5 tbsp butter

1 tbsp olive oil

1½ lb/675 g potatoes, cubed

4 veal escalopes or chops, about
6 oz/175 g each

1 onion, cut into 8 wedges

2 garlic cloves, minced

2 tbsp all-purpose flour

2 tbsp tomato paste

⅔ cup red wine

1¼ cups chicken bouillon

8 ripe tomatoes, peeled, seeded,
and diced

2 tbsp pitted ripe black olives, halved

2 tbsp chopped fresh basil

salt and pepper

fresh basil leaves, to garnish

COOK'S TIP

For a quicker cooking time and
really tender meat, pound the
meat with a meat mallet to
flatten it slightly before cooking.

1 Heat the butter and oil in a large skillet over a medium heat. Add the potato cubes and cook for 5–7 minutes, stirring frequently, until they start to brown.

2 Remove the potatoes from the skillet and set aside.

3 Put the veal in the skillet and cook for 2–3 minutes on each side until sealed. Remove from the pan and set aside.

4 Stir the onion and garlic into the skillet and cook for 2–3 minutes.

5 Add the flour and tomato paste and cook for 1 minute, stirring. Gradually blend in the red wine and chicken bouillon, stirring constantly, to make a smooth sauce.

6 Return the potatoes and veal to the skillet. Stir in the tomatoes, olives, and chopped basil. Season to taste with salt and pepper.

7 Transfer to a casserole dish and cook in a preheated oven at 350°F/180°C, for 1 hour, or until the potatoes and veal are cooked through. transfer to 4 warmed serving plates and garnish with basil leaves. Serve.

Chicken & Poultry

For the poultry-lover there are pasta dishes, casseroles, and bakes in this chapter, incorporating a variety of healthy and colorful ingredients. For those who enjoy Italian cuisine there are rich sauces as well as old favorites, such as more traditional casseroles. All these recipes are mouthwatering and quick and easy to prepare. These recipes are also extremely wholesome, offering a comprehensive range of tastes. Those on a low-fat diet should choose lean cuts of meat and look out for lowfat mince to enjoy the dishes featured here.

rich chicken casserole

serves four

8 chicken thighs

2 tbsp olive oil

1 medium red onion, sliced

2 garlic cloves, minced

1 large red bell pepper, sliced thickly

thinly pared peel and juice of
   1 small orange

½ cup chicken bouillon

14 oz/400 g canned
   chopped tomatoes

½ cup sun-dried tomatoes,
   sliced thinly

1 tbsp chopped fresh thyme

½ cup pitted ripe black olives

salt and pepper

TO GARNISH

orange peel

fresh thyme sprigs

crusty fresh bread, to serve

COOK'S TIP

Sun-dried tomatoes have a dense
texture and concentrated taste,
and add intense flavor to
slow-cooking casseroles.

---

1 In a large heavy-bottomed skillet, cook the chicken without fat over a fairly high heat, turning occasionally until golden brown. Using a slotted spoon, drain off any excess fat from the chicken and transfer to a flameproof casserole dish.

2 Heat the oil in the skillet over a medium heat. Add the onion, garlic, and bell pepper, and cook for 3–4 minutes. Transfer the vegetables to the casserole dish.

3 Add the orange peel and juice, chicken bouillon, chopped tomatoes, and sun-dried tomatoes to the casserole and stir well.

4 Bring to a boil, then cover the casserole with a lid and simmer very gently over a low heat for about 1 hour, stirring occasionally. Add the chopped thyme and black olives, then season to taste with salt and pepper.

5 Spoon the chicken casserole onto 4 warmed serving plates, garnish with orange peel and thyme, and serve with crusty bread.

garlic & herb chicken

serves four

4 chicken breasts, skin removed

⅓ cup full-fat soft cheese, flavored
with herbs and garlic

8 slices prosciutto

⅔ cup red wine

⅔ cup chicken bouillon

1 tbsp brown sugar

salad greens, to serve

1 Using a sharp knife, make a horizontal slit along the length of each chicken breast to form a pocket.

2 Put the cheese into a bowl and beat with a wooden spoon to soften it. Spoon the cheese into the pocket of the chicken breasts.

3 Wrap 2 slices of prosciutto around each chicken breast and secure in with a length of string.

4 Pour the wine and chicken bouillon into a large skillet and bring to a boil over a medium heat. When the mixture is just starting to boil, add the sugar and stir to dissolve.

5 Add the chicken breasts to the mixture in the skillet. Simmer for 12–15 minutes, or until the chicken is tender and the juices run clear when the point of a sharp knife is inserted into the thickest part of the meat.

6 Remove the chicken from the skillet, set aside and keep warm.

7 Heat the sauce and boil until reduced and thickened. Remove the string from the chicken and cut into slices. Pour the sauce over the chicken and serve with salad greens.

VARIATION

Try adding 2 finely chopped sun-dried tomatoes to the soft cheese in step 2, if you wish.

chicken pepperonata

serves four

8 skinless chicken thighs

2 tbsp whole-wheat flour

2 tbsp olive oil

1 small onion, sliced thinly

1 garlic clove, minced

1 each large red, yellow, and green
bell peppers, sliced thinly

14 oz/400 g canned
chopped tomatoes

1 tbsp chopped fresh oregano

salt and pepper

fresh oregano leaves, to garnish

COOK'S TIP

If you do not have fresh oregano,
use canned tomatoes with herbs
already added.

1 Remove the skin from the chicken
thighs and toss in the flour.

2 Heat the oil in a pan over a high
heat. Add the chicken and cook
until browned. Remove from the pan.
Add the onion and cook until soft. Add
the garlic, peppers, tomatoes, and
oregano, then bring to a boil.

3 Arrange the chicken over the
vegetables. Season well with salt
and pepper, then cover and simmer for
20–25 minutes, or until the chicken is
tender and the juices run clear when
the point of a sharp knife is inserted
into the thickest part of the meat.

4 Season to taste, then transfer the
chicken to a large dish and
garnish with oregano. Serve.

chicken with orange sauce

serves four

2 tbsp canola oil

2 tbsp olive oil

4 x 8 oz/225 g chicken breasts

⅔ cup brandy

2 tbsp all-purpose flour

⅔ cup freshly squeezed
  orange juice

1 oz/25 g zucchini, cut into
  thin batons

1 oz/25 g red bell pepper, cut into
  thin batons

1 oz/25 g leek, shredded finely

14 oz/400 g dried
  whole-wheat spaghetti

3 large oranges, peeled and cut
  into segments

peel of 1 orange, cut into very
  fine strips

2 tbsp chopped fresh tarragon

⅔ cup ricotta cheese

salt and pepper

1 Heat the canola oil and 1 tablespoon of the olive oil in a large skillet over a fairly high heat. Add the chicken and cook until golden brown. Add the brandy and cook for about 3 minutes. Sprinkle in the flour and cook, stirring constantly, for about 2 minutes.

2 Reduce the heat and add the orange juice, zucchini, red bell pepper, and leek. Season to taste with salt and pepper. Simmer for 5 minutes until the sauce has thickened.

3 Meanwhile, bring a pan of lightly salted water to a boil over a medium heat. Add the pasta and cook for 10 minutes, or until done. Drain the pasta thoroughly and transfer to a warmed serving dish. Drizzle over the remaining oil.

4 Add half the orange segments, half the orange peel, the chopped tarragon, and ricotta cheese to the sauce in the skillet and cook for about 3 minutes.

5 Put the chicken on top of the pasta, pour over a little sauce, garnish with the remaining orange segments, peel, and tarragon. Serve immediately with any extra sauce.

rolled chicken slices with mortadella

serves four

1 chicken, weighing about
   5 lb/2.25 kg

8 slices mortadella or salami

2 cups fresh white or brown
   bread crumbs

1 cup freshly grated
   Parmesan cheese

2 garlic cloves, minced

6 tbsp chopped fresh basil
   or parsley

1 egg, beaten

pepper

fresh spring vegetables, to serve

VARIATION

Replace the mortadella with
strips of lean bacon,
if you prefer.

1 Bone the chicken, keeping the skin intact. Dislocate each leg by breaking it at the thigh joint. Cut down each side of the backbone, taking care not to pierce the breast skin.

2 Pull the backbone clear of the flesh and discard. Remove the ribs, carefully severing any attached flesh with a sharp knife.

3 Scrape the flesh from each leg and cut away the bone at the joint with a knife or shears.

4 Use the bones for bouillon. Lay out the boned chicken on a board, skin-side down. Arrange the mortadella slices over the chicken, overlapping slightly.

5 Put the bread crumbs, Parmesan cheese, garlic, and basil into a bowl. Season with pepper and mix, then stir in the beaten egg. Pile the mixture down the center of the boned chicken, then roll the meat around it and tie securely with fine cotton string.

6 Put into a roasting pan and brush with oil. Roast in a preheated oven at 400°F/200°C, for 1½ hours, or until the chicken is tender and the juices run clear when the point of a sharp knife is inserted into the thickest part of the meat.

7 Serve hot or cold, in slices, with fresh spring vegetables.

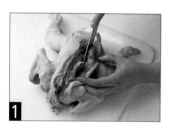

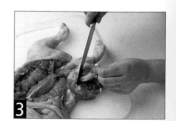

mustard-baked chicken

serves four

8 chicken portions, 4 oz/115 g each

4 tbsp butter, melted

4 tbsp mild mustard (see Cook's Tip)

2 tbsp lemon juice

1 tbsp brown sugar

1 tsp paprika

3 tbsp poppy seeds

3½ cups dried pasta shells

1 tsp olive oil

salt and pepper

COOK'S TIP

Dijon is the type of mustard most often used in cooking, as it has a clean and only mildly spicy flavor. German mustard has a sweet-sour taste, with Bavarian mustard being slightly sweeter. American mustard is mild and sweet.

1 Arrange the chicken portions in a single layer in a large oven-proof dish.

2 Mix the butter, mustard, lemon juice, sugar, and paprika together in a bowl and season to taste with salt and pepper. Brush the mixture over the upper surfaces of the chicken portions and cook in a preheated oven at 400°F/200°C, for 15 minutes.

3 Remove the dish from the oven and carefully turn over the chicken portions. Coat the upper surfaces of the chicken with the remaining mustard mixture, sprinkle the chicken portions with poppy seeds. Return to the oven for an additional 15 minutes.

4 Meanwhile, bring a large pan of lightly salted water to a boil over a medium heat. Add the pasta shells and oil and cook for 8–10 minutes, or until done.

5 Drain the pasta thoroughly and transfer to 4 warmed serving plates. Top the pasta with 1 or 2 of the chicken portions, pour over the mustard sauce and serve immediately.

chicken with green olives

serves four

3 tbsp olive oil

2 tbsp butter

4 part boned chicken breasts

1 large onion, chopped finely

2 garlic cloves, minced

2 red, yellow, or green bell peppers,
   seeded and cut into large pieces

9 oz/250 g white mushrooms, sliced
   or cut into fourths

6 oz/175 g tomatoes, peeled
   and halved

⅔ cup dry white wine

1½ cups pitted green olives

4–6 tbsp heavy cream

14 oz/400 g dried pasta

salt and pepper

chopped fresh Italian parsley,
   to garnish

1 Heat 2 tablespoons of the oil and the butter in a skillet over a medium heat. Add the chicken breasts and cook until golden brown all over. Remove the chicken from the skillet.

2 Add the onion and garlic to the skillet and cook until starting to soften. Add the bell peppers and mushrooms, and cook for 2–3 minutes.

3 Add the tomatoes and season to taste with salt and pepper. Transfer the vegetables to a casserole dish and arrange the chicken on top.

4 Add the wine to the skillet and bring to a boil over a medium heat. Pour the wine over the chicken. Cover and cook in a preheated oven at 350°F/180°C, for 50 minutes.

5 Add the olives to the casserole and stir well. Pour in the cream, cover, and return to the oven for an additional 10–20 minutes.

6 Meanwhile, bring a large pan of lightly salted water to a boil over a medium heat. Add the pasta and the remaining oil and cook for about 8–10 minutes, or until done. Drain the pasta thoroughly and keep warm.

7 Remove the chicken from the oven and garnish with the chopped parsley. Transfer the pasta to a warmed serving plate and serve the chicken straight from the casserole. Alternatively, transfer the pasta to a warmed serving dish, put the chicken on top, spoon over the sauce, and garnish with the parsley. Serve.

chicken marengo

serves four

8 chicken portions

1 tbsp olive oil

10½ oz/300 g strained tomatoes

¾ cup white wine

2 tsp dried mixed herbs

3 tbsp butter, melted

2 garlic cloves, minced

8 slices white bread

3½ oz/100 g mixed mushrooms
(such as white, oyster, and cèpes)

⅓ cup ripe black olives, chopped

1 tsp sugar

fresh basil leaves, to garnish

COOK'S TIP

If you have time, marinate the chicken portions in the wine and herbs and chill in the refrigerator for 2 hours. This will make the chicken more tender and accentuate the wine flavor of the sauce.

1 Remove the bone from each of the chicken portions, using a sharp knife.

2 Heat the oil in a large skillet over a medium heat. Add the chicken portions and cook for 4–5 minutes, turning occasionally, or until browned.

3 Add the tomato paste, wine, and mixed herbs to the skillet. Bring to a boil over a medium heat, then cook for 30 minutes, or until the chicken is tender and the juices run clear when the point of a sharp knife is inserted into the thickest part of the meat.

4 Mix the melted butter and garlic together in a small bowl. Lightly toast the slices of bread and brush with the garlic butter. Keep warm.

5 Heat the remaining oil in a separate skillet over a low heat. Add the mushrooms and cook for 2–3 minutes, or until just brown.

6 Add the olives and sugar to the chicken mixture and cook until warmed through.

7 Transfer the chicken and sauce to 4 warmed serving plates. Garnish with basil leaves and serve with the bruschetta, and cooked mushrooms.

chicken cacciatora

serves four

1 roasting chicken, about
    3 lb 5 oz/1.5 kg, cut into
    6–8 serving pieces

1 cup all-purpose flour

3 tbsp olive oil

⅔ cup dry white wine

1 green bell pepper, seeded
    and sliced

1 red bell pepper, seeded and sliced

1 carrot, chopped finely

1 celery stalk, chopped finely

1 garlic clove, minced

7 oz/200 g canned
    chopped tomatoes

salt and pepper

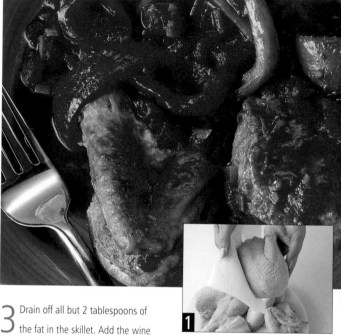

1 Rinse the chicken pieces and pat dry with paper towels. Mix the flour and salt and pepper to taste on a plate, then lightly dust the chicken with seasoned flour.

2 Heat the oil in a large skillet over a medium heat. Add the chicken and cook until browned. Remove from the skillet and set aside.

3 Drain off all but 2 tablespoons of the fat in the skillet. Add the wine and stir for a few minutes. Add the bell peppers, carrots, celery, and garlic. Season to taste with salt and pepper and simmer for about 15 minutes.

4 Add the chopped tomatoes to the skillet. Cover and simmer for 30 minutes, stirring often, until the chicken is completely cooked through.

5 Transfer the chicken and sauce to 4 warmed plates and serve.

broiled chicken

serves four

8 part-boned chicken thighs

1 tbsp olive oil for brushing

1⅔ cups strained tomatoes

½ cup green or red pesto sauce
(store bought)

12 slices French bread

1 cup freshly grated
Parmesan cheese

½ cup pine nuts or slivered almonds

assorted salad greens, to serve

COOK'S TIP

Although leaving the skin on the chicken means that it will have a higher fat content, many people like the rich taste and crispy skin, especially when it is blackened by the grill. The skin also keeps in the cooking juices.

1 Arrange the chicken thighs in a single layer in a wide flameproof dish and brush lightly with oil. Cook under a preheated hot broiler for about 15 minutes, turning occasionally, until golden brown.

2 Insert the point of a sharp knife into the thickest part of the meat to ensure that there is no trace of pink in the juices.

3 Pour off any excess fat. Warm the strained tomatoes and half the pesto sauce in a small pan and pour over the chicken. Broil for a few more minutes, turning until coated.

4 Spread the remaining pesto onto the bread and arrange over the chicken and sprinkle with Parmesan cheese. Sprinkle the pine nuts over the cheese. Broil until browned and bubbling. Serve with salad greens.

italian chicken spirals

serves four

4 skinless, boneless chicken breasts

1 cup fresh basil leaves

2 tbsp hazelnuts

1 garlic clove, minced

2 cups whole-wheat pasta spirals

2 sun-dried tomatoes or
   fresh tomatoes

1 tbsp lemon juice

1 tbsp olive oil

1 tbsp capers

½ cup ripe black olives

salt and pepper

VARIATION

Sun-dried tomatoes have a
wonderful, rich flavor; but if
you can't find them, use
fresh tomatoes instead.

1 Beat a chicken breast between
2 sheets of plastic wrap with a
rolling pin to flatten evenly. Repeat
with the remaining chicken breasts.

2 Put the basil and hazelnuts into a
food processor and process until
finely chopped. Mix with the garlic and
season to taste with salt and pepper.

3 Spread the basil mixture over the
chicken and roll up from a short
end to enclose. Wrap in foil and seal.

4 Bring a pan of lightly salted water
to a boil over a medium heat.
Add the pasta and cook until done.

5 Put the chicken parcels into a
steamer basket or strainer set
over the pan. Cover and steam for
10 minutes. Dice the tomatoes.

6 Drain the pasta and return to the
pan with the lemon juice, oil,
tomatoes, capers, and olives. Heat.

7 Insert the point of a sharp knife
into the chicken to make sure the
juices run clear, then slice. Transfer the
pasta to a large serving dish and put
the chicken on top, then serve.

chicken spirals

serves four

4 skinless, boneless chicken breasts
1 garlic clove, minced
2 tbsp tomato paste
4 slices smoked lean bacon
large handful of fresh basil leaves
2 tbsp vegetable oil for brushing
salt and pepper
salad greens, to serve

1 Spread out a chicken breast between 2 sheets of plastic wrap and beat firmly with a rolling pin or meat mallet to flatten the chicken to an even thickness. Repeat with the remaining chicken portions.

2 Mix the garlic and tomato paste together and spread the mixture over the chicken. Lay a bacon slice over each, then sprinkle with the basil. Season to taste with salt and pepper.

3 Roll up each piece of chicken firmly, then cut into thick slices. Thread the slices onto 4 skewers, making sure the skewer holds the chicken in a spiral shape.

4 Brush lightly with oil and cook on a hot barbecue or under a preheated hot broiler for 10 minutes, turning once. Serve immediately with salad greens.

pesto-baked partridge

serves four

8 partridge pieces, 115 g/4 oz each

4 tbsp butter, melted

4 tbsp Dijon mustard

2 tbsp lime juice

1 tbsp brown sugar

6 tbsp Pesto Sauce (see page 479)

1 lb/450 g dried rigatoni

1 tsp olive oil

1 cup freshly grated
  Parmesan cheese

salt and pepper

VARIATION

You could also prepare
young pheasant in the
same way.

1 Arrange the partridge pieces,
smooth-side down, in a single
layer in a large ovenproof dish.

2 Mix the butter, Dijon mustard,
lime juice, and brown sugar
together in a small bowl. Season to
taste with salt and pepper, then brush
this mixture over the partridge pieces
and cook in a preheated oven at
400°F/200°C, for 15 minutes.

3 Remove the dish from the oven
and coat the partridge with
3 tablespoons of the Pesto Sauce (see
page 227). Return to the oven and
cook for an additional 12 minutes.

4 Remove the dish from the oven
and turn the partridge over. Coat
with the remaining mustard mixture
and return to the oven for 10 minutes.

5 Meanwhile, bring a large pan of
lightly salted water to a boil over
a medium heat. Add the pasta and oil
and cook for 8–10 minutes, or until
done. Drain and transfer to a serving
dish. Toss the pasta with the remaining
Pesto Sauce and Parmesan cheese.
Serve the partridge with the pasta,
pouring over the cooking juices.

slices of duck with pasta

serves four

4 x 9 oz/250 g boneless
   duck breasts

2 tbsp butter

⅓ cup finely chopped carrots

4 tbsp finely chopped shallots

1 tbsp lemon juice

⅔ cup meat bouillon

4 tbsp honey

⅔ cup fresh or thawed
   frozen raspberries

¼ cup all-purpose flour

1 tbsp Worcestershire sauce

14 oz/400 g dried linguine

salt and pepper

TO GARNISH

fresh raspberries

fresh Italian parsley sprigs

1 Trim and score the duck breasts with a sharp knife and season to taste with salt and pepper. Melt the butter in a skillet over a medium heat. Add the duck breasts, and cook until lightly colored.

2 Add the carrots, shallots, lemon juice, and half the bouillon and simmer over a low heat for 1 minute. Stir in half the honey and half the raspberries. Sprinkle over half the flour and cook, stirring constantly, for 3 minutes. Season with pepper to taste and add the Worcestershire sauce.

3 Stir in the remaining bouillon and cook for 1 minute. Stir in the remaining honey and remaining raspberries and sprinkle over the remaining flour. Cook for an additional 3 minutes.

4 Remove the duck breasts from the skillet, but leave the sauce to continue simmering over a very low heat.

5 Meanwhile, bring a large pan of lightly salted water to a boil over a medium heat. Add the pasta and cook for 8–10 minutes, or until done. Drain and transfer to 4 large, warmed serving plates.

6 Slice the duck breast lengthwise into ¼-inch/5-mm thick pieces. Pour a little sauce over the pasta and arrange the sliced duck in a fan shape on top of it. Garnish with raspberries and parsley sprigs, then serve.

Pasta & Rice

Pasta and rice are quick and easy to cook and,

when combined with a variety of ingredients,

can produce an enormous variety of dishes.

To cook pasta, bring a pan of lightly salted water to a boil over a medium

heat. Add the pasta and 1 teaspoon of olive oil. Do not cover, but bring the

water to a rolling boil. When the pasta is tender, but firm to the bite, drain

thoroughly and toss with butter, olive oil, or a sauce of your choice. As a rough

guide, fresh unfilled pasta will take three minutes, filled fresh pasta will take

10 minutes to cook. Dried pasta will take approximately 10–15 minutes. To

cook a good quality rice like basmati, soak it for about 20–30 minutes to

prevent the grains from sticking to each other. Add it to gently boiling, lightly

salted water, stir once and cook until tender, but firm to the bite. This will take

up to 20 minutes.

sicilian spaghetti cake

serves four

⅝ cup olive oil, plus extra
   for brushing

2 eggplant

3 cups ground beef

1 onion, chopped

2 garlic cloves, minced

2 tbsp tomato paste

14 oz/400 g canned
   chopped tomatoes

1 tsp Worcestershire sauce

1 tsp chopped fresh marjoram or
   oregano or ½ tsp dried marjoram
   or oregano

½ cup pitted ripe black olives, sliced

1 green, red, or yellow bell pepper,
   cored, seeded, and chopped

6 oz/175 g dried spaghetti

1 cup freshly grated
   Parmesan cheese

salt and pepper

1 Brush an 8 inch loose-based round cake pan with oil. Line the base with baking parchment and brush with oil.

2 Slice the eggplant. Heat a little oil in a pan over a medium heat. Add the eggplant and cook, in batches, until browned on both sides. Add more oil, as necessary. Drain on paper towels.

3 Put the beef, onion, and garlic in a pan and cook over a medium heat, stirring, until browned. Add the tomato paste, tomatoes, Worcestershire sauce, marjoram or oregano, and salt and pepper. Simmer, stirring, for 10 minutes. Add the olives and bell pepper, and cook for 10 minutes.

4 Bring a pan of salted water to a boil over a medium heat. Add the pasta and cook until just done. Drain the pasta and transfer to a large bowl. Add the meat mixture and cheese and toss with 2 forks.

5 Arrange the eggplant slices over the bottom and up the sides of the pan. Add the pasta and cover with the rest of the eggplant slices. Cook in a preheated oven at 400°F/200°C, for 40 minutes. Let stand for 5 minutes, then invert onto a large serving dish. Discard the baking parchment and serve immediately.

pasticcio

serves six

2 cups fusilli, or other short
    pasta shapes

1 tsp olive oil

4 tbsp heavy cream

salt

fresh rosemary sprigs, to garnish

MEAT SAUCE

2 tbsp olive oil, plus extra
    for brushing

1 onion, sliced thinly

1 red bell pepper, seeded
    and chopped

2 garlic cloves, chopped

1 lb 6 oz/625 g lean ground beef

14 oz/400 g canned
    chopped tomatoes

⅓ cup dry white wine

7 tbsp chopped fresh parsley

1¾ oz/50 g canned anchovy fillets,
    drained and chopped

salt and pepper

TOPPING

1¼ cups plain yogurt

3 eggs

pinch of freshly grated nutmeg

⅔ cup freshly grated
    Parmesan cheese

1 To make the sauce, heat the oil in a large skillet over a medium heat. Add the onion and bell pepper and cook for 3 minutes. Stir in the garlic and cook for 1 minute. Add the beef and cook, stirring, until browned.

2 Add the tomatoes and wine, stir well, and bring to a boil over a medium heat. Simmer for 20 minutes, or until the sauce is fairly thick. Stir in the parsley and anchovies. Season to taste with salt and pepper.

3 Bring a large pan of lightly salted water to a boil over a medium heat. Add the pasta and oil and cook for 8–10 minutes, or until just done. Drain, then transfer to a bowl. Stir in the cream and set aside.

4 To make the topping, beat the yogurt with the eggs and nutmeg until well mixed and season to taste.

5 Brush a large shallow casserole with oil. Spoon in half the pasta mixture and cover with half the meat sauce. Repeat these layers, then spread the topping over the final layer. Sprinkle the Parmesan cheese on top.

6 Cook in a preheated oven at 375°F/190°C, for 25 minutes, or until the topping is golden brown and bubbling. Garnish with rosemary sprigs and serve immediately.

spaghetti bolognese

serves four

1 tbsp olive oil

1 onion, chopped finely

2 garlic cloves, chopped

1 carrot, scraped and chopped

1 celery stalk, chopped

1¾ oz/50 g pancetta or lean
    bacon, diced

1½ cups lean minced beef

400 g/14 oz canned tomatoes

2 tsp dried oregano

scant ½ cup red wine

2 tbsp tomato paste

1 lb 7 oz/650 g fresh spaghetti or
    12 oz/350 g dried spaghetti

salt and pepper

VARIATION

Try adding 25 g/1 oz dried
porcini, soaked for 10 minutes
in 2 tablespoons of warm water,
to the bolognese sauce in
step 4, if you wish.

---

1 Heat the oil in a large skillet over a medium heat. Add the onions and cook for 3 minutes.

2 Add the garlic, carrot, celery, and pancetta or bacon and cook over a fairly high heat for 3–4 minutes, or until just starting to brown.

3 Add the beef and cook over a high heat for 3 minutes, or until the meat has browned.

4 Stir in the tomatoes, oregano, and red wine . Bring to a boil over a medium heat. Reduce the heat and simmer for about 45 minutes.

5 Stir in the tomato paste and season with salt and pepper.

6 Bring a large pan of lightly salted water to a boil over a medium heat. Add the pasta and cook for about 8–10 minutes, or until just done. Drain the pasta thoroughly.

7 Transfer the pasta to a large serving plate and pour over the bolognese sauce. Toss with 2 forks to mix and serve immediately.

tagliatelle & chicken sauce

serves four

Tomato Sauce (see page 439)

8 oz/225 g fresh or dried
   green tagliatelle

salt

fresh basil leaves, to garnish

CHICKEN SAUCE

4 tbsp sweet butter

14 oz/400 g skinless, boneless
   chicken breast portions,
   sliced thinly

¾ cup blanched almonds

1¼ cups heavy cream

salt and pepper

1 Make the Tomato Sauce (see page 187), set aside, and keep warm.

2 To make the chicken sauce, melt the butter in a large, heavy-bottomed skillet over a medium heat. Add the chicken strips and almonds and cook, stirring frequently, for about 5–6 minutes, or until the chicken is cooked through.

3 Meanwhile, pour the cream into a small pan, set over a low heat, and bring to a boil. Boil for 10 minutes until reduced by almost half. Pour the cream over the chicken and almonds, stir well, and season to taste with salt and pepper. Remove the pan from the heat, set aside, and keep warm.

4 Bring a large pan of lightly salted water to a boil over a medium heat. Add the pasta and cook until just done. Fresh tagliatelle will take about 2–3 minutes and dried pasta will take 8–10 minutes. Drain, return to the pan, cover, and keep warm.

5 When ready to serve, turn the pasta into a warmed serving dish and spoon the tomato sauce over it. Spoon the chicken and cream into the center, sprinkle with fresh basil leaves, and serve immediately.

tagliatelle & meatballs

serves four

1 lb 2 oz/500 g ground lean beef

1 cup soft white bread crumbs

1 garlic clove, minced

2 tbsp chopped fresh parsley

1 tsp dried oregano

pinch of freshly grated nutmeg

¼ tsp ground coriander

⅔ cup freshly grated
   Parmesan cheese

2–3 tbsp milk

all-purpose flour, for dusting

3 tbsp olive oil

14 oz/400 g dried tagliatelle

2 tbsp butter, diced

salt and pepper

SAUCE

3 tbsp olive oil

2 large onions, sliced

2 celery stalks, sliced thinly

2 garlic cloves, chopped

14 oz/400 g canned
   chopped tomatoes

4½ oz/125 g sun-dried tomatoes in
   oil, drained and chopped

2 tbsp tomato paste

1 tbsp molasses sugar

⅔ cup white wine or water

1 To make the tomato sauce, heat the oil in a skillet over a medium heat. Add the onions and celery, and cook until translucent. Add the garlic and cook for 1 minute. Stir in the tomatoes, tomato paste, sugar, and wine, and season to taste. Bring to a boil and cook for 10 minutes.

2 Break up the meat in a bowl with a wooden spoon until it becomes a sticky paste. Stir in the bread crumbs, garlic, herbs, and spices. Stir in the cheese and enough milk to make a firm paste. Flour your hands, take spoonfuls of the mixture, and shape into 12 balls. Heat the oil in a skillet over a high heat. Add the meatballs and cook for 5–6 minutes, or until browned.

3 Pour the tomato sauce over the meatballs. Reduce the heat, cover, and simmer for 30 minutes, turning once or twice.

4 Bring a large pan of lightly salted water to a boil over a medium heat. Add the pasta and cook for 8–10 minutes, or until just done. Drain the pasta thoroughly, then transfer to a warmed serving dish, dot with the butter, and toss with 2 forks. Spoon the meatballs and sauce over the pasta and serve immediately.

spaghetti with ricotta cheese sauce

serves four

12 oz/350 g dried spaghetti

3 tbsp butter

2 tbsp chopped fresh Italian parsley

1 tbsp pine nuts

salt and pepper

1 fresh Italian parsley sprig,
   to garnish

SAUCE

1 cup freshly ground almonds

½ cup ricotta cheese

pinch of freshly grated nutmeg

pinch of ground cinnamon

⅔ cup sour cream

2 tbsp olive oil

½ cup hot chicken bouillon

1 Bring a pan of lightly salted water to a boil over a medium heat. Add the pasta and cook for about 8–10 minutes, or until just done.

2 Drain the pasta, return to the pan, and toss with the butter and parsley. Set aside and keep warm.

3 To make the sauce, mix the ground almonds, ricotta cheese, nutmeg, cinnamon, and sour cream in a small pan and stir over a low heat to a thick paste. Gradually stir in the oil. When the oil has been incorporated, gradually stir in the hot chicken bouillon, until smooth. Season with pepper to taste.

4 Transfer the pasta to a warmed serving dish, pour the sauce over, and toss together well (see Cook's Tip). Sprinkle over the pine nuts, garnish with the an Italian parsley sprig parsley, and serve immediately.

COOK'S TIP

It is best to use 2 large forks to toss the cooked spaghetti or other long pasta, to make sure that the pasta is thoroughly coated with the sauce. You can also purchase specially designed spaghetti forks, which are available from some cookware departments and large kitchen stores.

penne & butternut squash

serves four

2 tbsp olive oil

1 garlic clove, minced

1 cup fresh white bread crumbs

1 lb 2 oz/500 g butternut squash,
   peeled and seeded

8 tbsp water

1 lb 2 oz/500 g fresh penne, or
   other pasta shapes

1 tbsp butter

1 onion, sliced

4 oz/115 g ham, cut into strips

scant 1 cup light cream

½ cup freshly grated cheddar cheese

2 tbsp chopped fresh parsley

salt and pepper

1 Mix the oil, garlic, and bread crumbs together and spread out on a large plate. Cook in the microwave on HIGH for 4–5 minutes, stirring every minute, until crisp and starting to brown. Remove from the microwave and set aside.

2 Dice the squash. Put into a large bowl with half the water. Cover and cook on HIGH for 8–9 minutes, stirring occasionally. Let stand for 2 minutes.

3 Put the pasta into a large bowl, add a little salt, and pour over boiling water to cover by 1 inch/ 2.5 cm. Cover and cook on HIGH for 5 minutes, stirring once, until the pasta is just done. Let stand, covered, for 1 minute before draining.

4 Put the butter and onion into a large bowl. Cover and cook on HIGH for 3 minutes.

5 Coarsely mash the squash, using a fork. Add to the onion with the pasta, ham, cream, cheese, parsley, and remaining water. Season to taste and mix well. Cover and cook on HIGH for 4 minutes until heated through.

6 Transfer the pasta to a large, warmed serving plate, sprinkle with the crisp garlic crumbs and serve.

spaghetti olio e aglio

serves four

½ cup olive oil

3 garlic cloves, minced

1 lb.450 g fresh spaghetti

3 tbsp coarsely chopped
  fresh parsley

salt and pepper

COOK'S TIP

Oils produced by different countries—mainly Italy, Spain, and Greece—have their own characteristic flavors. Some produce an oil that has a hot, peppery taste while others have a "green" flavor.

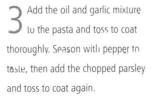

1 Reserve 1 teaspoon of the oil and heat the remainder in a pan over a low heat. Add the garlic and a pinch of salt, and cook, stirring constantly, until golden brown, then remove the pan from the heat. Do not let the garlic burn as this will taint the flavor of the oil. (If it does burn, you will have to start all over again!)

2 Meanwhile, bring a large pan of lightly salted water to a boil over a medium heat. Add the pasta and remaining oil, and cook for about 2–3 minutes, or until just done. Drain the thoroughly and return to the pan.

3 Add the oil and garlic mixture to the pasta and toss to coat thoroughly. Season with pepper to taste, then add the chopped parsley and toss to coat again.

4 Transfer the pasta to a warmed serving dish and serve.

pasta with green vegetables

serves four

2 cups dried gemelli or other
    pasta shapes

1 broccoli head, cut into flowerets

2 zucchini, sliced

8 oz/225 g asparagus spears

4 oz/115 g snow peas

1 cup frozen peas

2 tbsp butter

3 tbsp vegetable bouillon

4 tbsp heavy cream

freshly grated nutmeg

2 tbsp chopped fresh parsley

2 tbsp freshly grated
    Parmesan cheese

salt and pepper

1 Bring a large pan of lightly salted water to a boil over a medium heat. Add the pasta and cook for 8–10 minutes, or until just done. Drain the pasta thoroughly, return to the pan, cover, and keep warm.

2 Put the broccoli, zucchini, asparagus spears, and snow peas into a steamer basket set over a pan of boiling salted water until they are just starting to soften. Remove from the heat and refresh in cold water. Drain and set aside.

3 Bring a small pan of lightly salted water to a boil over a medium heat. Add the frozen peas and cook for 3 minutes. Drain the peas, refresh in cold water, and then drain again. Set aside with the other vegetables.

4 Put the butter and vegetable bouillon in a pan over a medium heat. Add the vegetables, setting aside a few of the asparagus spears, and toss carefully with a wooden spoon until they have heated through, taking care not to break them up.

5 Stir in the cream and heat through without bringing to a boil. Season to taste with salt, pepper, and nutmeg.

6 Transfer the pasta to a large, warmed serving dish and stir in the chopped parsley. Spoon over the vegetable sauce and sprinkle over the Parmesan cheese. Arrange the reserved asparagus spears in a decorative pattern on top and serve.

pasta with cheese & broccoli

1 Bring a large pan of lightly salted water to a boil over a medium heat. Add the pasta and cook for 8–10 minutes, or until just done.

2 Meanwhile, cook the broccoli in a small amount of lightly salted, boiling water. Avoid overcooking, so it retains much of its color and texture.

3 Heat the mascarpone and blue cheeses together gently in a pan over a low heat until they are melted. Stir in the oregano and season to taste with salt and pepper.

4 Drain the pasta thoroughly. Return it to the pan. Add the butter, and, using 2 forks, toss the pasta to coat it thoroughly. Drain the broccoli and add to the pasta with the sauce, tossing gently to mix.

5 Transfer the pasta to 4 large, warmed serving plates. Garnish with oregano sprigs and serve with Parmesan cheese.

pasta & vegetable sauce

serves four

3 tbsp olive oil

1 onion, sliced

2 garlic cloves, chopped

3 red bell peppers, seeded and
   cut into strips

3 zucchini, sliced

14 oz/400 g canned
   chopped tomatoes

3 tbsp sun-dried tomato paste

2 tbsp chopped fresh basil

2 cups fresh fusilli

1 cup freshly grated Swiss cheese

salt and pepper

4 fresh basil sprigs, to garnish

1 Heat the oil in a large pan or casserole dish. Add the onion and garlic and cook, stirring occasionally, until softened. Add the bell peppers and zucchini, and cook, stirring occasionally, for 5 minutes.

2 Add the tomatoes, sun-dried tomato paste, and basil, and season to taste with salt and pepper. Cover and cook for 5 minutes.

3 Meanwhile, bring a large pan of salted water to a boil over a medium heat. Add the pasta and cook for 3 minutes, or until just tender. Drain the pasta thoroughly and add to the vegetable mixture. Toss gently to mix .

4 Transfer the pasta to a shallow flameproof dish and sprinkle with the grated cheese.

5 Cook under a preheated hot broiler for 5 minutes, until the cheese is golden brown and bubbling. Transfer to 4 serving plates and garnish with basil sprigs. Serve immediately.

447

tagliatelle & garlic sauce

serves four

2 tbsp walnut oil

1 bunch scallions, sliced

2 garlic cloves, sliced thinly

8 oz/225 g mushrooms, sliced

1 lb 2 oz/500 g fresh green and
white tagliatelle

1 cup frozen chopped leaf spinach,
thawed and drained

½ cup full-fat soft cheese flavored
with garlic and herbs

4 tbsp light cream

½ cup chopped, unsalted
pistachio nuts

2 tbsp shredded fresh basil

salt and pepper

4 fresh basil sprigs, to garnish

Italian bread, to serve

1 Heat the walnut oil in a skillet over a low heat. Add the scallions and garlic and cook for 1 minute, or until just softened. Add the mushrooms, stir well, cover, and cook gently for about 5 minutes, or until softened.

2 Meanwhile, bring a large pan of lightly salted water to a boil over a medium heat. Add the pasta and cook for 3–5 minutes, or until just done. Drain the pasta thoroughly and return to the pan.

3 Add the spinach to the mushrooms and heat through for 1–2 minutes. Add the cheese and let melt slightly. Stir in the cream and heat without letting it boil.

4 Pour the vegetable mixture over the pasta, season to taste with salt and pepper, and mix well. Heat gently, stirring, for 2–3 minutes.

5 Transfer the pasta to a large, warmed serving plates and sprinkle over the pistachio nuts and shredded basil. Garnish with fresh basil sprigs and serve with Italian bread.

spicy tomato tagliatelle

serves four

3 tbsp butter

1 onion, chopped finely

1 garlic clove, minced

2 small fresh red chiles, seeded
and diced

1 lb/450 g fresh tomatoes, peeled,
seeded, and diced

¾ cup vegetable bouillon

2 tbsp tomato paste

1 tsp sugar

salt and pepper

1 lb 7 oz/650 g fresh green
and white tagliatelle, or
12 oz/350 g dried tagliatelle

VARIATION
Try topping your pasta
dish with 1¾ oz/50 g pancetta or
unsmoked bacon, diced and
dry fried for 5 minutes,
or until crispy.

1 Melt the butter in a large pan over a low heat. Add the onion and garlic and cook for 3–4 minutes, or until softened.

2 Add the chiles to the pan and continue cooking for about 2 minutes.

3 Add the tomatoes and bouillon, then reduce the heat and simmer for 10 minutes, stirring.

4 Pour the sauce into a food processor and blend for 1 minute, or until smooth. Alternatively, rub the sauce through a strainer.

5 Return the sauce to the pan and add the tomato paste, sugar, and salt and pepper to taste. Gently heat over a low heat, until piping hot.

6 Bring a large pan of lightly salted water to a boil over a medium heat. Add the pasta and cook until just done. Drain the pasta and transfer to 4 warmed serving plates, and serve with the tomato sauce.

tagliatelle with pumpkin

serves four

1 lb 2 oz/500 g pumpkin or
   butternut squash

2 tbsp olive oil

1 onion, chopped finely

2 garlic cloves, minced

4–6 tbsp chopped fresh parsley

good pinch of ground or freshly
   grated nutmeg

about 1 cup chicken or
   vegetable bouillon

4½ oz/125 g prosciutto, cut into
   narrow strips

9 oz/275 g dried tagliatelle

⅓ cup heavy cream

salt and pepper

freshly grated Parmesan cheese,
   to serve

1 Peel the pumpkin or squash and scoop out the seeds and membrane. Cut the flesh into ½-inch/1-cm dice.

2 Heat the oil in a pan over a low heat. Add the onion and garlic and cook until softened. Add half the parsley and cook for 1–2 minutes.

3 Add the pumpkin or squash and cook for 2–3 minutes. Season well with salt, pepper, and nutmeg.

4 Add half the bouillon, bring to a boil over a medium heat, cover and simmer for about 10 minutes, or until the pumpkin is tender, adding more bouillon as necessary. Add the prosciutto and continue to cook for 2 minutes, stirring frequently.

5 Meanwhile, bring a large pan of lightly salted water to a boil over a medium heat. Add the pasta and cook until just done. Drain the pasta thoroughly and transfer to a large, warmed serving dish.

6 Add the cream to the ham mixture and heat. Season to taste and spoon over the pasta. Sprinkle with the remaining parsley and serve with the Parmesan cheese.

451

fettuccine all'alfredo

serves four

2 tbsp butter

⅞ cup heavy cream

1 lb/450 g fresh fettuccine

1 tsp olive oil

1 cup freshly grated Parmesan
cheese, plus extra to serve

pinch of freshly grated nutmeg

salt and pepper

1 fresh Italian parsley sprig,
to garnish

VARIATION

This classic Roman dish is often
served with the addition of strips
of ham and fresh peas. Add
2 cups shelled cooked peas and
6 oz/175 g ham strips with the
Parmesan cheese in step 4.

---

1 Put the butter and ⅝ cup of the cream in a large pan and bring the mixture to a boil over a medium heat. Reduce the heat, then simmer gently for about 1½ minutes, or until thickened slightly.

2 Meanwhile, bring a large pan of lightly salted water to a boil over a medium heat. Add the pasta and oil and cook for 2–3 minutes, or until just done. Drain the pasta thoroughly, then pour over the cream sauce.

3 Toss the pasta in the sauce over a low heat until coated thoroughly.

4 Add the remaining cream, the Parmesan cheese, and nutmeg to the pasta mixture and season to taste with salt and pepper. Toss thoroughly while gently heating through.

5 Transfer the pasta mixture to a large, warmed serving plate and garnish with a fresh parsley sprig. Serve immediately, with extra Parmesan cheese if you wish.

fettuccine & walnut sauce

serves four to six

2 thick slices whole-wheat bread,
   crusts removed

1¼ cups milk

2½ cups shelled walnuts

2 garlic cloves, minced

1 cup pitted ripe black olives

⅔ cup freshly grated
   Parmesan cheese

8 tbsp extra virgin olive oil

⅝ cup heavy cream

1 lb/450 g fresh fettuccine

2–3 tbsp chopped fresh parsley

salt and pepper

1 Put the bread into a large shallow dish. Pour over the milk and set aside to soak until all the liquid has been absorbed.

2 Spread the walnuts out onto a large cookie sheet and toast in a preheated oven at 375°F/190°C, for about 5 minutes, or until golden. Let cool.

3 Put the soaked bread, walnuts, garlic, olives, Parmesan cheese, and 6 tablespoons of the oil into a food processor and process to make a paste. Season to taste with salt and pepper, then stir in the cream.

4 Bring a large pan of lightly salted water to a boil over a medium heat. Add the pasta and 1 teaspoon of the remaining oil, and cook for about 2–3 minutes, or until just done. Drain the pasta thoroughly and toss with the remaining oil.

5 Transfer the pasta to large serving plates and spoon the olive, garlic, and walnut sauce on top. Sprinkle over the parsley and serve immediately.

pasta & chili tomatoes

serves four

10 oz/280 g dried pappardelle

3 tbsp groundnut oil

2 garlic cloves, minced

2 shallots, sliced

8 oz/225 g green beans, sliced

3½ oz/100 g cherry tomatoes, halved

1 tsp chili flakes

4 tbsp crunchy peanut butter

⅔ cup coconut milk

1 tbsp tomato paste

VARIATION

Add slices of chicken or beef to the recipe and stir-fry with the beans and pasta in step 3 for a more substantial main meal.

1 Bring a large pan of lightly salted water to a boil over a medium heat. Add the pasta and cook for about 8–10 minutes, or until just done. Drain thoroughly and set aside.

2 Meanwhile, heat a large wok over a medium heat. Add the oil and when hot, add the garlic and shallots. Cook for 1 minute.

3 Add the green beans and drained pasta to the wok and cook, stirring, for 5 minutes. Add the cherry tomatoes and mix well.

4 Mix the chili flakes, peanut butter, coconut milk, and tomato paste. Pour the chili mixture into the wok, toss well and heat through.

5 Transfer the pasta to 4 large, warmed serving dishes and serve immediately.

chili and bell pepper pasta

serves four

2 red bell peppers, halved
    and seeded

1 small fresh red chile

4 tomatoes, halved

2 garlic cloves

½ cup ground almonds

7 tbsp olive oil

1 lb 7 oz/650 g fresh pasta or
    12 oz/350 g dried pasta

fresh oregano leaves, to garnish

VARIATION

Add 2 tablespoons of red wine
vinegar to the sauce and use as
a dressing for a cold pasta salad,
if you wish.

---

1 Put the peppers, skin-side up, onto a cookie sheet with the chile and tomatoes, skin-side down. Cook under a preheated hot broiler for 15 minutes or until charred. After 10 minutes turn the tomatoes over. Put the peppers and chiles into a plastic bag and set aside for 10 minutes.

2 Peel the skins from the bell peppers and chile and slice the flesh into strips. Peel the garlic, and peel, and seed the tomato halves.

3 Put the ground almonds onto a cookie sheet and put under the broiler for 2–3 minutes until golden.

4 Put the bell peppers, chile, garlic, and tomatoes into a processor and process until smooth. With the motor still running, slowly add the oil through the feeder tube to form a thick sauce. Alternatively, put the mixture into a bowl and mash with a fork. Beat in the oil, drop by drop.

5 Stir the toasted ground almonds into the mixture. Warm the sauce in a pan until it is heated through.

6 Bring a large pan of lightly salted water to a boil over a medium heat. Add the pasta and cook for until just done. Drain the pasta thoroughly and transfer to a large, warmed serving dish. Pour over the sauce and toss to mix. Garnish with fresh oregano leaves and serve.

456

vegetables & beancurd

serves four

8 oz/225 g asparagus spears

4 oz/115 g snow peas

8 oz/225 g green beans

1 leek

8 oz/225 g shelled small fava beans

2½ cups dried fusilli

2 tbsp olive oil

2 tbsp butter

1 garlic clove, minced

8 oz/225 g beancurd, cut into
   1-inch/2.5-cm cubes
   (drained weight)

½ cup pitted green olives in
   brine, drained

salt and pepper

freshly grated Parmesan cheese,
   to serve

1 Cut the asparagus into 2-inch/ 5-cm lengths. Thinly slice the snow peas diagonally and slice the green beans into 1-inch/2.5-cm pieces. Thinly slice the leek.

2 Bring a large pan of water to a boil over a medium heat. Add the asparagus, green beans, and fava beans. Bring back to a boil and cook for 4 minutes. Drain well, rinse in cold water, and drain again. Set aside.

3 Bring a large pan of lightly salted water to a boil over a medium heat. Add the pasta and cook for 8–10 minutes, or until done. Drain and toss in 1 tablespoon of the oil. Season to taste with salt and pepper.

4 Meanwhile, heat the remaining oil and the butter in a wok and add the leek, garlic, and beancurd. Cook gently for 1–2 minutes, or until the vegetables have just softened.

5 Stir in the snow peas and cook for 1 additional minute.

6 Add the blanched vegetables and olives to the wok and heat through for 1 minute. Carefully stir in the pasta and adjust the seasoning, if necessary. Cook for 1 minute and pile into a warmed serving dish. Serve sprinkled with Parmesan cheese.

pasta with nuts & cheese

serves four

1 cup pine nuts

3 cups dried pasta shapes

2 zucchini, sliced

1¼ cups broccoli flowerets

1 cup full-fat soft cheese

⅔ cup milk

1 tbsp chopped fresh basil

4½ oz/125 g white
   mushrooms, sliced

3 oz/85 g blue cheese, crumbled

salt and pepper

1 fresh basil sprig, to garnish

salad greens, to serve

1 Sprinkle the pine nuts on a cookie sheet. Put under a preheated hot broiler and cook, turning occasionally, until lightly browned. Set aside.

2 bring a large pan of lightly salted water to a boil over a medium heat. Add the pasta and cook for 8–10 minutes, or until just done.

3 Meanwhile, cook the zucchini and broccoli in a small amount of boiling, lightly salted water for about 5 minutes, or until just tender.

4 Put the soft cheese into a pan and heat gently, stirring. Add the milk and stir to mix. Add the basil and mushrooms and cook for 2–3 minutes. Stir in the blue cheese and season to taste with salt and pepper.

5 Drain the pasta and vegetables and mix together Pour over the sauce and add the pine nuts. Toss gently and garnish with a basil sprig. Serve with salad greens.

italian tomato sauce & pasta

serves two

1 tbsp olive oil

1 small onion, chopped finely

1–2 cloves garlic, minced

12 oz/350 g tomatoes, peeled
    and chopped

2 tsp tomato paste

2 tbsp water

2¾–3 cups dried pasta shapes

¾ cup lean bacon, derinded
    and diced

½ cup mushrooms, sliced

1 tbsp chopped fresh parsley or
    1 tsp chopped fresh cilantro

2 tbsp sour cream, optional

salt and pepper

COOK'S TIP

Sour cream contains
18–20% fat, so if you are
following a lowfat diet you can
leave it out of this recipe or
substitute a lowfat alternative.

1 Heat the oil in a pan over a low heat. Add the onion and garlic, and cook gently until soft.

2 Add the tomatoes, tomato paste, and water. Season to taste with salt and pepper and bring to a boil over a low heat. Cover and simmer gently for 10 minutes.

3 Bring a large pan of lightly salted water to a boil over a medium heat. Add the pasta and cook until just done. Drain thoroughly and transfer to 2 warmed serving dishes.

4 Heat the bacon gently in a skillet over a low heat until the fat runs, then add the mushrooms and cook for 3–4 minutes. Drain off any excess oil.

5 Add the bacon and mushrooms to the tomato mixture, together with the parsley or cilantro and the sour cream. Heat through gently and serve immediately with the pasta.

macaroni & corn crêpes

serves four

2 corn cobs

4 tbsp butter

115 g/4 oz red bell peppers, seeded
and diced finely

1¼ cups dried short-cut macaroni

½ cup heavy cream

2 tbsp all-purpose flour

4 egg yolks

4 tbsp olive oil

salt and pepper

TO SERVE

oyster mushrooms

cooked leeks

1 Bring a pan of water to a boil over a medium heat. Add the corn cobs and cook for 8 minutes. Drain thoroughly and refresh under cold running water for 3 minutes. Carefully cut away the kernels onto paper towels and let dry.

2 Melt 2 tablespoons of the butter in a large skillet over a low heat. Add the bell peppers and cook for about 4 minutes. Drain and pat dry on paper towels.

3 Bring a large pan of lightly salted water to a boil over a medium heat. Add the macaroni and cook for about 12 minutes, or until done. Drain the macaroni thoroughly and let cool in cold water until required.

4 Beat the cream with the flour, a pinch of salt, and the egg yolks in a bowl until smooth. Add the corn and bell peppers. Drain the macaroni, then toss into the corn and cream mixture. Season with pepper to taste.

5 Heat the remaining butter with the oil in a skillet. Drop spoonfuls of the mixture into the skillet and press down to form flat crêpes. Cook until golden, and all the mixture is used up. Serve with mushrooms and leeks.

three-cheese macaroni

serves four

2 cups Bechamel sauce

2 cups dried macaroni

1 egg, beaten

1¼ cups freshly grated sharp
cheddar cheese

1 tbsp whole-grain mustard

2 tbsp chopped fresh chives

4 tomatoes, sliced

1¼ cups freshly grated brick cheese

½ cup freshly grated blue cheese

2 tbsp sunflower seeds

salt and pepper

snipped fresh chives, to garnish

1 Make the Bechamel sauce, transfer it into a bowl, and cover with plastic wrap to prevent a skin forming on the surface of the sauce. Set aside.

2 Bring a pan of lightly salted water to a boil over a medium heat. Add the macaroni and cook for 8–10 minutes, or until just done. Drain and put into a greased ovenproof dish.

3 Stir the beaten egg, cheddar cheese, mustard, and chives into the Bechamel sauce and season to taste with salt and pepper.

4 Spoon the sauce over the macaroni, making sure it is well covered. Arrange the sliced tomatoes in a layer over the top.

5 Sprinkle the brick and blue cheeses and the sunflower seeds evenly over the pasta bake. Put the dish on a cookie sheet and cook in a preheated oven at 190°C/375°F, for 25–30 minutes, or until the topping is bubbling and golden.

6 Garnish the pasta bake with snipped chives and serve immediately on 4 warmed plates.

spaghetti & salmon sauce

serves four

1 lb 2 oz/500 g dried
   buckwheat spaghetti
1 tbsp olive oil
½ cup feta cheese, crumbled
   (drained weight)
1 tbsp fresh cilantro or parsley,
   to garnish
SAUCE
1¼ cups heavy cream
⅔ cup whiskey or brandy
4½ oz/125 g smoked salmon
large pinch of cayenne pepper
2 tbsp chopped fresh cilantro
   or parsley
salt and pepper

1 Bring a large pan of lightly salted water to a boil over a medium heat. Add the pasta and 1 teaspoon of the oil, and cook for 8–10 minutes, or until done. Drain the pasta thoroughly, then return the pasta to the pan, sprinkle over the remaining oil, cover and shake well. Set aside and keep warm until required.

2 To make the sauce, heat the cream and whiskey or brandy in separate small pans, to simmering point. Do not let them boil.

3 Mix the cream with the whiskey or brandy together in a bowl.

4 Cut the smoked salmon into thin strips and add to the cream mixture. Season to taste with a little pepper and cayenne pepper, then stir in the chopped cilantro or parsley.

5 Transfer the pasta to a large, warmed serving dish, pour on the sauce and toss thoroughly with 2 large forks. Sprinkle the crumbled cheese over the pasta and garnish with the chopped cilantro or parsley. Serve immediately.

vermicelli & clam sauce

serves four

14 oz/400 g dried vermicelli,
spaghetti or other long pasta

1 tbsp olive oil

2 tbsp butter

2 onions, chopped

2 garlic cloves, chopped

400 g/14 oz bottled clams in brine

½ cup white wine

4 tbsp chopped fresh parsley

½ tsp dried oregano

pinch of freshly grated nutmeg

salt and pepper

2 tbsp fresh Parmesan
cheese shavings

1 fresh basil sprig, to garnish

1 Bring a large pan of lightly salted water to a boil over a medium heat. Add the pasta and and cook until just done. Drain, then return to the pan and add the butter. Cover the pan and shake well. Keep warm.

2 Heat the oil in a pan over a medium heat. Add the onions and cook until translucent. Stir in the garlic and cook for 1 minute.

3 Strain the liquid from the bottled clams into bowl. Add half of it to the pan with the white wine and discard the remaining liquid. Stir, then bring to simmering point and simmer for 3 minutes.

4 Add the clams, parsley, and oregano to the pan and season to taste with pepper and nutmeg. Reduce the heat and cook until the sauce is heated through.

5 Transfer the pasta to a warmed serving dish and pour over the sauce. Sprinkle with the Parmesan cheese, garnish with the basil and serve immediately.

pasta & mussel sauce

serves six

3½ cups pasta shells

1 tsp olive oil

SAUCE

6 pints/3.5 litres mussels, scrubbed

1 cup dry white wine

2 large onions, chopped

½ cup sweet butter

6 large garlic cloves, chopped finely

5 tbsp chopped fresh parsley

1¼ cups heavy cream

salt and pepper

1 To make the sauce, pull off the "beards" from the mussels and rinse well in several changes of water. Discard any mussels that refuse to close when tapped. Put the mussels into a large pan with the wine and half the onions. Cover, shake and cook over a medium heat for about 2–3 minutes, or until the mussels open.

2 Remove the pan from the heat, lift out the mussels with a slotted spoon and set aside the liquid. Let cool. Discard any mussels that have not opened.

3 Melt the butter in a pan over a medium heat. Add the remaining onion and cook for 3–4 minutes, or until translucent. Stir in the garlic and cook for 1 minute. Gradually pour on the reserved cooking liquid, stirring to blend thoroughly. Stir in the parsley and cream. Season to taste with salt and pepper and bring to simmering point. Taste and adjust the seasoning, if necessary.

4 Bring a pan of lightly salted water to a boil over a medium heat. Add the pasta and oil and cook until done. Drain and return to the pan.

5 Remove the mussels from their shells and set aside a few shells. Stir the mussels into the cream sauce. Tip the pasta into a dish, pour on the sauce and mix. Garnish with a few of the reserved mussel shells and serve.

pasta vongole

serves four

1 lb 7 oz/650 g fresh clams or

   10 oz280 g canned

   clams, drained

2 tbsp olive oil

2 cloves garlic, chopped finely

14 oz/400 g mixed seafood, such

   as shrimp, squid, and mussels,

   thawed if frozen

⅔ cup white wine

⅔ cup fish bouillon

2 tbsp chopped tarragon

salt and pepper

1 lb 7 oz/650 g fresh pasta or

   12 oz/350 g dried pasta

VARIATION

Red clam sauce can be made by adding 8 tbsp of tomato paste to the sauce along with the bouillon in step 4. Follow the same cooking method.

---

1 If you are using fresh clams, scrub them clean and discard any that are already open.

2 Heat the oil in a large skillet over a medium heat. Add the garlic and the clams and cook for 2 minutes, shaking the pan to ensure that all of the clams are coated in the oil.

3 Add the remaining seafood mixture to the skillet and cook for an additional 2 minutes.

4 Pour the wine and bouillon over the mixed seafood and garlic. Bring to a boil over a medium heat. Cover, then reduce the heat and simmer for 8–10 minutes, or until the shells open. Discard any clams or mussels that refuse to open.

5 Bring a large pan of lightly salted water to a boil over a medium heat. Add the pasta and cook until just done. Drain thoroughly.

6 Stir the chopped tarragon into the sauce and season to taste with salt and pepper.

7 Transfer the pasta to a plate and pour over the sauce. Serve.

macaroni & squid casserole

serves six

2 cups dried short-cut macaroni, or
other short pasta shapes

1 tsp olive oil

2 tbsp chopped fresh parsley

salt and pepper

SAUCE

12 oz/350 g cleaned squid, cut into
½-inch/4-cm strips

6 tbsp olive oil

2 onions, sliced

1 cup fish bouillon

⅔ cup red wine

12 oz/350 g tomatoes, peeled and
sliced thinly

2 tbsp tomato paste

1 tsp dried oregano

2 bay leaves

1 Bring a large pan of lightly salted water to a boil over a medium heat. Add the pasta and oil, and cook for 3 minutes. Drain well, return to the pan, cover and keep warm.

2 To make the sauce, heat the oil in a skillet over a medium heat. Add the onion and cook until translucent. Add the squid and bouillon and cook for 5 minutes. Pour over the wine and add the tomatoes, tomato paste, oregano, and bay leaves. Bring to a boil, season to taste with salt and pepper, and cook for 5 minutes.

3 Add the pasta, stir well, cover, and simmer for 10 minutes, or until the macaroni and squid are almost tender. By this time the sauce should be thick and syrupy. If it is too liquid, uncover the pan and continue cooking for a few minutes. Taste and adjust the seasoning. if necessary.

4 Remove the bay leaves and stir in most of the chopped parsley, and set aside a little to garnish. Transfer to a warmed serving dish. Sprinkle on the remaining parsley and serve.

pasta with sicilian sauce

serves four

1 lb/450 g tomatoes, halved

¼ cup pine nuts

¼ cup golden raisins

1¼ oz/50 g canned anchovy fillets,
   drained and halved lengthwise

2 tbsp concentrated tomato paste

1 lb 7 oz/650 g fresh penne or
   12 oz/350 g dried penne

COOK'S TIP

If you are making fresh pasta,
remember that pasta dough
prefers warm conditions and
responds well to handling. Do
not let chill and do not use a
marble counter for kneading.

1 Cook the tomatoes under a
preheated broiler for about
10 minutes. Let cool. Once cool
enough to handle, peel off the skin and
dice the flesh.

2 Place the pine nuts on a cookie
sheet and lightly toast under the
broiler for 2–3 minutes, or until
golden.

3 Soak the golden raisins in a bowl
of warm water for 20 minutes.
Drain the golden raisins thoroughly.

4 Put the tomatoes, pine nuts, and
golden raisins in a pan and heat.

5 Add the anchovies and tomato
paste and cook until hot.

6 Bring a large pan of lightly salted
water to a boil over a medium
heat. Add the pasta and cook until
done. Drain thoroughly.

7 Transfer the pasta to a large
serving plate and serve with the
hot Sicilian sauce.

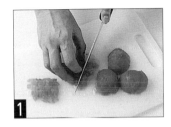

471

milanese risotto

serves four

2 good pinches of saffron threads

6 tbsp butter

1 large onion, chopped finely

1–2 garlic cloves, minced

3 cups risotto rice

⅔ cup dry white wine

5 cups boiling vegetable bouillon

¾ cup freshly grated
   Parmesan cheese

salt and pepper

1 Put the saffron into a small bowl, cover with 3–4 tablespoons of boiling water, and let soak while you prepare the risotto.

2 Melt 4 tablespoons of the butter in a pan over a low heat. Add the onion and garlic and cook until soft but not colored. Add the rice and cook for 2–3 minutes, or until the grains are coated in butter and starting to color.

3 Add the wine to the rice and simmer gently, stirring from time to time, until it is all absorbed.

4 Add the boiling bouillon a little at a time, about ⅝ cup, cooking until the liquid is fully absorbed before adding more, and stirring frequently.

5 When all the bouillon has been absorbed (this should take about 20 minutes), the rice should be tender but not soft and soggy. Add the saffron liquid, Parmesan cheese, and remaining butter. Season to taste with salt and pepper. Simmer for 2 minutes until piping hot and thoroughly mixed.

6 Cover the pan tightly and let stand for 5 minutes off the heat. Give a good stir and serve.

sun-dried risotto

serves six

about 12 sun-dried tomatoes, not
   in oil

2 tbsp olive oil

1 large onion, chopped finely

4–6 garlic cloves, chopped finely

2 cups risotto rice

6¼ cups chicken or vegetable
   bouillon, simmering

1 cup frozen peas, thawed

2 tbsp chopped fresh Italian parsley

1 cup freshly grated aged
   romano cheese

1 tbsp extra virgin olive oil

1 Put the sun-dried tomatoes into a bowl and pour over enough boiling water to cover. Let stand for about 30 minutes, or until the tomatoes are soft and supple. Drain and dry on paper towels, then shred thinly and set aside.

2 Heat the oil in a large pan over a medium heat. Add the onion and cook for 2 minutes. Add the garlic and cook for 15 seconds, then add the rice and cook for 2 minutes, or until the rice is translucent and coated with oil.

3 Add a ladleful of the hot bouillon: it will bubble and steam rapidly. Cook, stirring continuously, until all the liquid has been absorbed.

4 Continue stirring in the bouillon, about half a ladleful at a time, letting each addition be absorbed by the rice before adding the next.

5 After 15 minutes, stir in the sun-dried tomatoes. Cook, adding the bouillon, until the rice is tender, but firm to the bite. Add the peas with the last addition of the bouillon.

6 Remove from the heat and stir in the parsley and half the cheese. Cover, let stand for 1 minute, then spoon into serving dishes. Drizzle with the oil and sprinkle the remaining cheese over the top. Serve.

green risotto

serves four

1 onion, chopped

2 tbsp olive oil

1¼ cups risotto rice

1½ cups hot vegetable bouillon

12 oz/350 g mixed green vegetables,
    such as asparagus, thin green
    beans, snow peas, zucchini,
    broccoli flowerets, frozen peas

2 tbsp chopped fresh parsley

½ cup fresh Parmesan cheese,
    shaved thinly

salt and pepper

COOK'S TIP

For extra texture, stir in a few
toasted pine nuts or coarsely
chopped cashew nuts at the end
of the cooking time.

---

1 Put the onion and oil into a large bowl. Cover and cook in the microwave on HIGH for 2 minutes.

2 Add the rice and stir until coated in the oil. Pour in ⅓ cup of the bouillon. Cook for 2 minutes, until the liquid has been absorbed. Pour in another ⅓ cup of the bouillon and cook on HIGH for 2 minutes. Repeat.

3 Chop the vegetables into even-size pieces. Stir into the rice with the remaining bouillon. Cover and cook on HIGH for 8 minutes, stirring, until most of the liquid has been absorbed and the rice is tender.

4 Stir in the chopped parsley and season generously to taste with salt and pepper.

5 Let the risotto stand, covered, for about 5 minutes. The rice should be tender and creamy.

6 Transfer to a large serving dish and sprinkle the Parmesan cheese over the risotto before serving

exotic mushroom risotto

serves six

¼ cup dried porcini or
   morel mushrooms

about 1 lb 2 oz/500 g mixed fresh
   exotic mushrooms, such as
   porcini, girolles, horse
   mushrooms, and chanterelles,
   halved if large

4 tbsp olive oil

3–4 garlic cloves, chopped finely

4 tbsp sweet butter

1 onion, chopped finely

3 cups risotto rice

¼ cup dry white vermouth

5 cups chicken bouillon, simmering

1⅓ cups freshly grated
   Parmesan cheese

4 tbsp chopped fresh Italian parsley

salt and pepper

6 fresh parsley sprigs, to garnish

crusty bread, to serve

1 Put the dried mushrooms into a bowl and add enough boiling water to cover. Let soak for 30 minutes, then carefully lift out and pat dry. Strain the soaking liquid through a strainer lined with paper towels and set aside.

2 Trim the exotic mushrooms and gently brush clean.

3 Heat 3 tablespoons of the oil in a large skillet over a low heat. Add the mixed fresh mushrooms and cook, stirring, for 1–2 minutes. Add the garlic and the soaked mushrooms, and cook, stirring frequently, for 2 minutes. Transfer to a plate.

4 Heat the remaining oil and half the butter in a large pan over a low heat. Add the onion and cook, stirring occasionally, for 2 minutes until softened. Add the rice and cook, stirring frequently, for about 2 minutes until translucent and well coated.

5 Add the vermouth. When almost absorbed, add a ladleful (about 1 cup) of the bouillon. Cook, stirring continuously, until the liquid is absorbed.

6 Continue adding the bouillon, about half a ladleful at a time, letting each addition to be completely absorbed before adding the next. This should take 20–25 minutes. The risotto should have a creamy consistency and the rice should be tender, but firm to the bite.

7 Add half the reserved mushroom soaking liquid to the risotto and stir in the mushrooms. Season to taste with salt and pepper and add more mushroom liquid, if necessary. Remove the pan from the heat and stir in the remaining butter, the Parmesan cheese, and parsley. Transfer the risotto to 6 warmed dishes, garnish with parsley sprigs and serve immediately.

rice & peas

serves four

1 tbsp olive oil

4 tbsp butter

2oz/55 g pancetta or lean
   bacon, chopped

1 small onion, chopped

6 cups hot chicken bouillon

1¾ cups risotto rice

3 tbsp chopped fresh parsley

2 cups frozen or canned baby peas

½ cup freshly grated Parmesan
   cheese

pepper

1 Heat the oil and half the butter in a large pan over a low heat. Add the pancetta or bacon and onion and cook, stirring occasionally, for about 5 minutes, or until the onion is translucent, but not browned.

2 Add the bouillon to the pan and bring to a boil over a medium heat. Stir in the rice and season to taste with pepper. Bring to a boil, reduce the heat, and simmer, stirring occasionally, for about 20–30 minutes, or until the rice is tender, but still firm to the bite.

3 Add the parsley and frozen or canned baby peas and cook for about 8 minutes, or until the peas are heated through. Stir in the remaining butter and the Parmesan cheese.

4 Transfer the risottos to a large warmed serving dish and serve immediately with pepper.

pesto rice with garlic bread

serves four

2¾ oz mixed long-grain and
   wild rice

fresh basil sprigs, to garnish

tomato and orange salad, to serve

PESTO SAUCE

4 tbsp fresh basil sprigs

1¼ cups pine nuts

2 garlic cloves, minced

6 tbsp olive oil

½ cup freshly grated
   Parmesan cheese

GARLIC BREAD

2 small granary or whole-wheat
   French bread sticks

5 tbsp butter , softened

2 garlic cloves, minced

1 tsp dried mixed herbs

salt and pepper

1 Put the rice in a pan and cover with water. Bring to a boil over a medium heat and cook for about 15 20 minutes. Drain and keep warm.

2 To make the pesto sauce, remove the basil leaves from the stalks and finely chop the leaves. Set aside ¼ cup of the pine nuts and finely chop the remainder. Mix with the chopped basil and the rest of the dressing ingredients. Alternatively, put all the ingredients into a food processor or blender and process for a few seconds until smooth. Set aside.

3 To make the garlic bread, slice the bread at 1 inch/2.5 cm intervals, taking care not to slice all the way through. Mix the butter with the garlic, and herbs. Season to taste with salt and pepper. Spread thickly between each slice.

4 Wrap the bread in foil and cook in a preheated oven at 200°C/400°F, for 10–15 minutes.

5 To serve, toast the reserved pine nuts under a preheated medium-hot broiler for 2–3 minutes, or until golden. Toss the pesto sauce into the hot rice and pile into a warmed serving dish. Sprinkle with toasted pine nuts and garnish with a few basil sprigs. Serve with the garlic bread and a tomato and orange salad.

green easter pie

serves four

1 tbsp butter for greasing

3 oz/85 g arugula

2 tbsp olive oil

1 onion, chopped

2 garlic cloves, chopped

1 cup risotto rice

3 cups hot chicken or
    vegetable bouillon

½ cup white wine

⅔ cup freshly grated
    Parmesan cheese

1 cup frozen peas, thawed

2 tomatoes, diced

4 eggs, beaten

3 tbsp chopped fresh marjoram

1 cup fresh bread crumbs

salt and pepper

1 Grease a 9-inch/23-cm deep cake pan and line the bottom.

2 Using a sharp knife, coarsely chop the arugula.

3 Heat the oil in a skillet over a low heat. Add the onion and garlic and cook for 4–5 minutes.

4 Add the rice to the skillet, mix well, then start adding the bouillon a ladleful at a time. Wait until each ladleful of bouillon has been absorbed before adding the next.

5 Continue to cook the mixture, adding the wine, until the rice is tender. This will take at least 15 minutes. Remove the skillet from the heat.

6 Stir in the Parmesan cheese, peas, arugula, tomatoes, eggs, and 2 tablespoons of the marjoram. Season to taste with salt and pepper.

7 Spoon the risotto into the prepared pan and level the surface by pressing down with the back of a wooden spoon.

8 Top with the bread crumbs and the remaining marjoram.

9 Cook in a preheated oven at 350°F/180°C, for 30 minutes, or until set. Cut into slices and serve.

genoese seafood risotto

serves four

5 cups hot fish or chicken bouillon

3 cups risotto rice

3 tbsp butter

2 garlic cloves, chopped

9 oz/250 g mixed seafood, preferably raw, such as shrimp, squid, mussels, and clams

2 tbsp chopped oregano, plus extra for garnishing

½ cup freshly grated romano or Parmesan cheese

COOK'S TIP

The Genoese are excellent cooks, and they make particularly delicious fish dishes, which are delicately flavored with the local olive oil.

1 In a large pan, bring the bouillon to a boil over a medium heat. Add the rice and cook for 12 minutes, stirring, until the rice is tender. Drain and set aside any excess liquid.

2 Heat the butter in a large skillet and add the garlic, stirring.

3 Add the seafood to the skillet and cook for 5 minutes. If the seafood is cooked, cook for about 2–3 minutes.

4 Stir the oregano into the seafood mixture in the skillet.

5 Add the rice to the skillet and cook for 2–3 minutes, stirring, until hot. Add the reserved bouillon if the mixture gets too sticky. Add the romano or Parmesan cheese and mix.

6 Transfer the risotto to 4 large, warmed serving dishes and serve.

chicken risotto milanese

serves four–six

½–1 tsp saffron threads

5⅔ cups chicken
    bouillon, simmering

6 tbsp unsalted butter

2–3 shallots, chopped finely

2 cups risotto rice

2 cups freshly grated
    Parmesan cheese

salt and pepper

1 Put the saffron threads into a small bowl. Pour over enough of the bouillon to cover the threads, then set aside to infuse.

2 Melt 2 tablespoons of the butter in a large pan over a medium heat. Add the shallots and cook for about 2 minutes, or until starting to soften. Add the rice and cook, stirring frequently, for about 2 minutes, or until the rice is starting to turn translucent and is coated with the butter.

3 Add a ladleful (about 1 cup) of the bouillon; it will steam and bubble. Cook, stirring continuously, until the liquid is absorbed.

4 Continue adding the bouillon, about half a ladleful at a time, allowing each addition to be absorbed before adding the next. Don't let the rice cook "dry."

5 After about 15 minutes, stir in the saffron-infused bouillon; the rice will turn a vibrant yellow and the color will become deeper as it cooks. Continue cooking, adding the bouillon in the same way until the rice is tender, but still firm to the bite. The risotto should have a creamy consistency.

6 Stir in the remaining butter and half the Parmesan cheese, then remove from the heat. Cover and let stand for about 1 minute.

7 Spoon the risotto into serving bowls and serve immediately with the remaining Parmesan cheese.

spinach & ricotta gnocchi

serves four

2 lb 4 oz/1 kg spinach

2 cups ricotta cheese

1¼ cups freshly grated
    romano cheese

3 eggs, beaten

¼ tsp freshly grated nutmeg

all-purpose flour, to mix

dash of olive oil

9 tbsp sweet butter

¼ cup pine nuts

⅓ cup raisins

salt and pepper

1 Wash and drain the spinach. Cook in a covered pan without any extra liquid until soft, 8 minutes. Put the spinach into a strainer and press well to remove as much liquid as possible. Put the spinach into a blender and process until smooth. Alternatively, rub the spinach through a strainer.

2 Mix the spinach puree with the ricotta cheese, half the romano cheese, the eggs, and nutmeg. Season to taste with salt and pepper, mixing lightly but thoroughly. Work in enough flour, lightly and quickly, to make the mixture easy to handle.

3 Shape the dough quickly into small lozenge shapes, and dust lightly with a little flour.

4 Add a dash of oil to a large pan of salted water and bring to a boil over a medium heat. Add the gnocchi carefully and boil for about 2 minutes, or until they float to the surface. Using a slotted spoon, transfer the gnocchi to a buttered ovenproof dish. Keep warm.

5 Melt the butter in a small skillet over a low heat. Add the pine nuts and raisins and cook until the nuts start to brown slightly, but do not let the butter burn.

6 Transfer the gnocchi to 4 dishes, pour the mixture over and add the remaining cheese. Serve.

potato & spinach gnocchi

serves four

1⅓ cups diced mealy potatoes

6 oz/175 g spinach

1 egg yolk

1 tsp olive oil

1 cup all-purpose flour

salt and pepper

fresh spinach leaves, to garnish

SAUCE

1 tbsp olive oil

2 shallots, chopped

1 garlic clove, minced

1¼ cups strained tomatoes

2 tsp soft light brown sugar

1 Bring a pan of water to a boil over a medium heat. Add the potatoes and cook for 10 minutes, then drain and mash.

2 Blanch the spinach in a little boiling water for 1–2 minutes. Drain and shred the leaves.

3 Transfer the mashed potato to a lightly floured cutting board and make a well in the center. Add the egg yolk, oil, spinach, and a little of the flour. Quickly mix the ingredients into the potato, adding more flour, until you have a firm dough. Divide the mixture into very small dumplings.

4 Bring a large pan of lightly salted water to a boil over a medium heat, Add the gnocchi, in batches, and cook for about 5 minutes, or until they rise to the surface.

5 To make the sauce. Put the oil, shallots, garlic, strained tomatoes, and sugar into a pan and cook over a low heat for 10–15 minutes. or until the sauce has thickened.

6 Drain the gnocchi with a slotted spoon and transfer to 4 warmed serving dishes. Spoon the sauce over the gnocchi and garnish with the fresh spinach leaves. Serve.

baked semolina gnocchi

1 Put the bouillon into a large pan and bring to a boil over a medium heat. Add the semolina in a steady trickle, stirring continuously. Keep stirring for 3–4 minutes until the mixture is thick enough to hold a spoon upright. Let cool slightly.

2 Add the thyme leaves, egg, and half the cheese to the semolina mixture, and season to taste with salt and pepper.

3 Spread the semolina mixture onto a board to a thickness of about ½ inch/12 mm, and let stand until it has cooled and set.

4 When the semolina is cold, cut it into 1-inch 2.5-cm squares, and set aside any offcuts.

5 Grease an ovenproof dish, putting the reserved offcuts in the bottom. Arrange the semolina squares on top and sprinkle with the remaining cheese.

6 Melt the butter in a pan over a low heat. Add the garlic and season with pepper to taste. Pour the butter mixture over the gnocchi. Cook in a preheated oven at 220°C/425°F, for 15–20 minutes, or until the gnocchi are puffed up and golden. Serve.

polenta kabobs

serves four

1 cup instant polenta

scant 3¾ cups water

2 tbsp fresh thyme, stalks removed

8 slices prosciutto (about 2¾ oz)

1 tbsp olive oil

salt and pepper

salad greens, to serve

COOK'S TIP

Try flavoring the polenta with chopped oregano, basil, or marjoram instead of the thyme, if you prefer. You should use 1½ tbsp of chopped fresh herbs to every 1 cup instant polenta.

1 Cook the polenta with the water, stirring occasionally. Alternatively, follow the package instructions.

2 Add the fresh thyme leaves to the polenta mixture and season to taste with salt and pepper.

3 Spread out the polenta, about 1-inch/2.5-cm thick, onto a cutting board. Let cool.

4 Using a sharp knife, cut the cooled polenta into 1-inch/2.5-cm cubes.

5 Cut the prosciutto slices into 2 pieces lengthwise. Wrap the prosciutto around the polenta cubes.

6 Thread the polenta cubes onto presoaked wooden skewers.

7 Brush the kabobs with oil and cook under a preheated hot broiler, turning, for 7–8 minutes. Alternatively, grill the kabobs until golden. Transfer to 4 serving plates and serve with salad greens.

Desserts

For many people the favorite part of any meal is the desserts. The recipes that have been selected here will be a treat for all palates. Whether you are a chocolate-lover or are even on a diet, in this chapter there is a recipe to tempt you. Choose from a light summer delicacy or a hearty hot winter treat, you will find plenty of desserts to indulge in all year round. If you are looking for an afternoon treat, choose the Banana & Lime Cake or Carrot & Ginger Cake, or if a sumptuous dessert takes your fancy, Chocolate Zabaglione will definitely do the trick.

carrot & ginger cake

serves ten

1 tbsp butter for greasing

2 cups all-purpose flour

1 tsp baking powder

1 tsp baking soda

2 tsp ground ginger

½ tsp salt

¾ cup molasses sugar

1⅔ cups grated carrots

2 pieces chopped preserved ginger

1 tbsp grated fresh gingerroot

generous ⅓ cup seedless raisins

2 eggs, beaten

3 tbsp corn oil

juice of 1 orange

FROSTING

1 cup lowfat soft cheese

4 tbsp confectioners' sugar

1 tsp vanilla extract

TO DECORATE

grated carrot

finely chopped preserved ginger

ground ginger

1 Grease and line an 8-inch/20-cm round cake pan with a piece of baking parchment.

2 Sift the flour, baking powder, baking soda, ground ginger, and salt into a bowl. Stir in the sugar, carrots, preserved ginger, fresh ginger root, and raisins. Beat the eggs, oil, and orange juice together, then pour into the bowl. Mix all the ingredients together well.

3 Spoon the mixture into the pan and cook in a preheated oven at 350°F/180°C, for 1–1¼ hours, or until a toothpick inserted into the center of the cake comes out clean.

4 To make the frosting, put the soft cheese in a bowl and beat to soften. Sift in the confectioners' sugar and add the vanilla extract. Mix well.

5 Remove the cake from the pan and smooth the frosting over the top. Decorate with the carrot and ginger. Serve.

banana & lime cake

serves ten

1 tbsp butter for greasing

generous 2 cups all-purpose flour

1 tsp salt

1½ tsp baking powder

scant 1 cup light brown sugar

1 tsp lime peel, grated

1 egg, beaten lightly

1 banana, mashed with
   1 tbsp lime juice

⅔ cup lowfat plain yogurt

⅔ cup golden raisins

TOPPING

generous 1 cup confectioners' sugar

1–2 tsp lime juice

½ tsp finely grated lime peel

TO DECORATE

banana chips

finely grated lime peel

1 Grease a deep round 7-inch/18-cm cake pan with butter and line with baking parchment.

2 Sift the flour, salt, and baking powder into a mixing bowl and stir in the sugar and lime peel.

3 Make a well in the center and add the egg, banana, yogurt, and golden raisins. Mix until incorporated.

4 Spoon into the pan and level the surface. Cook in a preheated oven at 350°F/180°C, for 40–45 minutes, or until a toothpick inserted in the center comes out clean. Let cool in the pan for 10 minutes, then turn out onto a rack.

5 To make the topping, sift the confectioners' sugar into a small bowl and mix with the lime juice to form a soft, but not too runny frosting. Stir in the grated lime peel. Drizzle the lime frosting over the cake, letting it run down the sides.

6 Decorate the cooled cake with a few banana chips and lime peel. Let the cake stand for 15 minutes so the frosting sets, then serve.

pear & ginger cake

serves six

scant 1 cup sweet butter, softened,
    plus extra for greasing
generous ¾ cup superfine sugar
1¼ cups self-rising flour, strained
1 tbsp ground ginger
3 eggs, beaten lightly
1 lb/450 g dessert pears, peeled,
    cored, and sliced thinly
1 tbsp brown sugar
ice cream or cream, to serve

3 Spoon the cake mixture into the prepared pan and level out the surface with a spoon.

4 Arrange the pear slices over the cake mixture. Sprinkle with the brown sugar and dot the top with the remaining butter.

5 Cook in a preheated oven at 350°F/180°C, for 35–40 minutes, or until the cake is golden on top and feels springy to the touch.

6 Serve the pear and ginger cake warm, with ice cream or cream, if you wish.

COOK'S TIP

Store ground ginger in an airtight
jar, preferably made of colored
glass, or store in a clear glass jar
in a cool, dark place.

1 Lightly grease a deep 8-inch/ 20.5-cm cake pan with butter and line with baking parchment.

2 Using a whisk, combine all but 2 tablespoons of the butter with the sugar, flour, ginger, and eggs, and mix to form a smooth consistency.

mascarpone cheesecake

serves eight

4 tbsp sweet butter, plus extra
    for greasing
3 cups ginger cookie crumbs
1 tbsp chopped preserved ginger
2¼ cups mascarpone cheese
finely grated peel and juice of
    2 lemons
½ cup superfine sugar
2 large eggs, separated
fruit coulis (see Cook's Tip), to serve

COOK'S TIP

Fruit coulis can be made by
cooking 14 oz/400 g fruit, such
as blueberries, for 5 minutes
with 2 tbsp of water. Strain the
mixture, then stir in
1 tbsp (or more to taste) of
strained confectioners' sugar. Let
cool before serving.

---

1 Grease and line the bottom of a 10-inch/25-cm spring-form cake pan or loose-bottomed pan.

2 Melt the butter in a pan over a low heat. Stir in the crushed cookies and ginger. Use the mixture to line the pan, pressing the mixture about ¼ inch/5 mm up the sides.

3 Beat the cheese, lemon peel and juice, sugar, and egg yolks together until quite smooth.

4 Whisk the egg whites in a separate spotlessly clean grease-free until stiff peaks form, then fold into the cheese and lemon mixture.

5 Pour the mixture into the pan and cook in a preheated oven at 350°F/180°C, for 35–45 minutes, or until just set. Don't worry if it cracks or sinks—this is quite normal.

6 Let cool in the pan, then serve the cheesecake with fruit coulis (see Cook's Tip).

tuscan dessert

serves four

1 tbsp butter

⅔ cup mixed dried fruit

generous 1 cup ricotta cheese

3 egg yolks

¼ cup superfine sugar

1 tsp cinnamon

finely grated peel of 1 orange, plus
  extra to decorate

crème fraîche, to serve

COOK'S TIP

Crème fraîche has a slightly sour,
nutty taste and is very thick. It is
suitable for cooking, but has the
same fat content as heavy cream.

1 Grease 4 mini ovenproof bowls or
ramekin dishes with the butter.

2 Put the dried fruit into a bowl and
cover with warm water. Let soak
for 10 minutes.

3 Beat the ricotta cheese with the
egg yolks in a bowl. Stir in the
superfine sugar, cinnamon, and orange
peel and mix.

4 Drain the dried fruit in a strainer
set over a bowl. Mix the drained
fruit with the ricotta cheese mixture.

5 Spoon the mixture into the bowls
or ramekin dishes.

6 Cook in a preheated oven at
350°F/180°C, for 15 minutes. The
tops should just be firm to the touch,
but they should not brown.

7 Decorate the desserts with
some grated orange peel. Serve
warmed or chilled with a spoon of
crème fraîche, if you wish.

498

summer desserts

serves six

1 tbsp vegetable oil or butter
  for greasing
6–8 thin slices white bread,
  crusts removed
¾ cup superfine sugar
1¼ cups water
1 cup strawberries
2 cups raspberries
¾ cup black and/or red currants
¾ cup blackberries or loganberries
6 fresh mint sprigs, to decorate
pouring cream, to serve

1 Grease 6 ⅔ cup molds with a little butter or oil.

2 Line the molds with the bread, cutting it so it fits snugly.

3 Put the sugar into a pan with the water and heat gently, stirring frequently until dissolved, then bring to a boil over a medium heat and boil for 2 minutes.

4 Set aside 6 large strawberries for decoration. Add half the raspberries and the rest of the fruits to the syrup, cutting the strawberries in half if large, and simmer gently for a few minutes, until they are just soft, but still retain their shape.

5 Spoon the fruits and some of the liquid into the molds. Cover with more bread. Spoon a little juice around the sides of the molds so the bread is well soaked. Cover with a saucer and a heavy weight, let cool, then chill in the refrigerator, preferably overnight.

6 Process the remaining raspberries in a food processor or blender, or press through a non metallic strainer. Add enough of the liquid from the fruits to give a coating consistency.

7 Transfer to 6 serving plates and spoon the raspberry sauce over. Decorate with mint sprigs and reserved strawberries. Serve with cream.

chocolate zabaglione

serves four

4 egg yolks

4 tbsp superfine sugar

1¾ oz/50 g dark chocolate

½ cup Marsala wine

amaretti cookies, to serve

COOK'S TIP

Make the dessert just before serving as it will separate if you let it stand. If it begins to curdle, remove it from the heat immediately and put it into a bowl of cold water to stop the cooking. Whisk furiously until the mixture comes together.

---

1 In a large glass mixing bowl, using an electric whisk, whisk the egg yolks and superfine sugar together until you have a very pale mixture.

2 Grate the chocolate finely and fold into the egg mixture.

3 Fold the Marsala wine into the chocolate mixture.

4 Put the mixing bowl over a pan of gently simmering water and set the electric whisk on the lowest speed or change to a hand-held balloon whisk. Cook, whisking continuously until the mixture thickens; take care not to overcook or the mixture will curdle.

5 Spoon the hot mixture into 4 warmed glass dishes or large coffee cups. Serve the zabaglione as soon as possible so that it is warm, light, and fluffy accompanied by amaretti cookies.

mocha creams

serves four

8 oz/225 g semisweet chocolate

1 tbsp instant coffee powder

1¼ cups boiling water

1 envelope powdered gelatin

3 tbsp cold water

1 tsp vanilla extract

1 tbsp coffee-flavored liqueur, optional

1¼ cups heavy cream

4 chocolate-coated coffee beans

8 amaretti cookies

VARIATION

To add a delicious almond flavor to the dessert, replace the coffee-flavored liqueur with Amaretto liqueur.

1 Break the chocolate into small pieces and place in a pan with the coffee. Stir in the boiling water and heat gently, stirring until the chocolate melts.

2 Sprinkle the gelatin over the cold water and let it go spongy, then whisk it into the hot chocolate mixture to dissolve it.

3 Stir in the vanilla extract and coffee-flavored liqueur (if using). Let the chocolate mixture stand in a cool place until just starting to thicken. Whisk from time to time.

4 Whisk the cream until it is standing in soft peaks, then set aside a little for decorating the desserts and fold the remainder into the chocolate mixture. Spoon the mixture into tall glass serving dishes and let set.

5 Decorate with the reserved cream and chocolate coffee beans and serve with the amaretti cookies.

quick tiramisù

serves four

1 cup mascarpone or full-fat
  soft cheese
1 egg, separated
2 tbsp natural yogurt
2 tbsp superfine sugar
2 tbsp dark rum
2 tbsp strong black coffee
8 lady-fingers
2 tbsp grated dark chocolate

1 Put the cheese into a large mixing bowl, add the egg yolk, and yogurt, and beat until smooth.

2 Put the egg white into a large, spotlessly clean grease-free bowl and whisk until stiff but not dry. Whisk in the sugar and carefully fold into the cheese mixture.

3 Spoon half of the mixture into 4 large sundae glasses.

4 Mix the rum and coffee together in a shallow dish. Dip the ladyfingers into the rum mixture. Break them in half, or into smaller pieces if necessary, and divide among the sundae glasses.

5 Stir any remaining coffee mixture into the remaining cheese and spoon over the top.

6 Sprinkle with grated chocolate, and serve or chill until required.

honey & nut nests

serves four

8 oz/225 g angel hair pasta

8 tbsp butter

1½ cups shelled pistachio
  nuts, chopped

½ cup sugar

⅓ cup honey

⅝ cup water

2 tsp lemon juice

salt

strained plain yogurt, to serve

COOK'S TIP

Angel hair pasta is also known
as capelli d'Angelo. Long and
very fine, it is usually sold in
small bunches that already
resemble nests.

1 Bring a large pan of lightly salted water to a boil over a medium heat. Add the pasta and cook until done. Drain the pasta thoroughly and return to the pan. Add the butter and, using 2 forks, toss to coat the pasta thoroughly. Let cool.

2 Arrange 4 small flan or poaching rings on a cookie sheet. Divide the pasta into 8 equal quantities and spoon 4 of them into the rings. Press down lightly. Top with half the nuts, then add the remaining pasta.

3 Cook in a preheated oven at 350°F/180°C, for 45 minutes, or until golden brown.

4 Meanwhile, put the sugar, honey, and water in a small pan and bring to a boil over a low heat, stirring continuously until the sugar has dissolved. Simmer for 10 minutes, then add the lemon juice and simmer for an additional 5 minutes.

5 Using a spatula, carefully transfer the angel hair nests to a serving dish. Pour over the honey syrup, then sprinkle over the remaining nuts and let cool completely before serving. Serve with the strained plain yogurt.

A

aïoli 40
almonds
    chicken soup with almonds 24
anchovies
    anchovy butter 162
    crostini alla fiorentina 320
    lamb & anchovies with thyme 119
    pasta & anchovy sauce 361
    pasta with sicilian sauce 471
    tuna, bean & anchovy salad 349
    tuna with anchovy butter 162
angler fish
    gingered angler fish 180
    lemon angler fish kabobs 383
    stuffed angler fish tail 165
apple
    ham steaks with apple rings 132
    smoked trout & apple salad 96
aromatic seafood rice 376
artichoke
    artichoke soup 266
    cream of artichoke soup 14
arugula
    green easter pie 480
asian pork balls in broth 65
asian shellfish kabobs 382
asparagus packages 196
avocado
    authentic guacamole 42
    avocado & mint soup 304
    chicken, avocado & chipotle soup 26

B

bacon
    bean & garlic soup 295
    leek, potato & bacon soup 33
    trout with smoked bacon 356
baked dishes
    baked eggplant gratin 206
    baked fennel 331
    baked ham with sauce 121
    baked sea bass 168
    baked semolina gnocchi 487
balsamic strawberries 220
bamboo with spinach 85
banana
    banana & lime cake 494
    chicken in banana leaves 140
bang-bang chicken 62
barbecued butterfly lamb 398
beancurd *see also* tofu
    lettuce & beancurd soup 271
    stir-fried beancurd with chili sauce 336
    vegetables & beancurd 458
beans
    bacon, bean & garlic soup 295

creamy onion & fava bean soup 288
garbanzo bean soup 274
hummus & garlic toasts 322
mint & cannellini bean dip 308
mixed bean pan-fry 199
mixed bean pâté 314
tuna, bean & anchovy salad 349
beef
    beef & noodle soup 296
    beef broth 38
    beef in barolo 104
    beef with exotic mushrooms 106
    chicken or beef satay 343
    chunky potato & beef soup 292
    creamed strips of short loin 386
    fresh spaghetti & meatballs 388
    meatballs in italian red wine sauce 389
    pasticcio 435
    sicilian spaghetti cake 434
    spaghetti bolognese 436
    tagliatelle & meatballs 439
    tomato & olive kabobs 107
beet
    beet & potato soup 279
    beet salad & dill dressing 334
bell pepper
    bell peppers with chestnuts 198
    chicken pepperonata 413
    chili & bell pepper pasta 456
    lamb with black bean sauce and bell
        peppers 396
    pepper salad 326
    red bell pepper soup 267
bhajis
    brindil bhaji 76
    okra bhaji 71
blackened fish 155
blinis
    wild rice blinis 61
bok choy with crabmeat 74
bouillabaisse 30
bouillon
    fresh chicken bouillon 262
    fresh fish bouillon 263
    fresh lamb bouillon 263
    fresh vegetable bouillon 262
braised fennel 82
braised tofu home-style 192
brindil bhaji 76
broccoli
    broccoli in oyster sauce 211
    easy cauliflower & broccoli 86
    pasta with cheese & broccoli 446
brochettes *see also* kabobs, skewers
    marinated brochettes 190
    meatball brochettes 110
broiled chicken 425

bruschetta with tomatoes 324
butterfly shrimp 156
butternut squash
    penne & butternut squash 442

C

cabbage
    sweet & sour cabbage soup 280
cake
    banana & lime cake 494
    carrot & ginger cake 492
    pear & ginger cake 495
cantonese garden vegetables 204
capri salad 99
carnitas 128
carrot
    carrot & ginger cake 492
    spicy dhal & carrot soup 272
cauliflower
    easy cauliflower & broccoli 86
celery root, leek & potato soup 32
cellophane noodles & shrimp 368
charbroiled vegetables 193
cheese
    baked eggplant gratin 206
    chicken risotto milanese 483
    chocolate cheese pots 252
    fettuccine all'alfredo 454
    garlic & herb chicken 412
    garlic & herb pâté 319
    grapefruit & cheese salad 100
    green easter pie 480
    mascarpone cheesecake 496
    milanese risotto 472
    pasta with cheese & broccoli 446
    pasta with nuts & cheese 459
    quick tiramisù 503
    spaghetti with ricotta cheese
        sauce 440
    spinach & ricotta gnocchi 484
    spinach cheese molds 52
    three-cheese macaroni 463
    turkey stuffed with cheese 151
    tuscan dessert 498
    walnut, egg & cheese pâté 318
chicken
    avocado & chipotle soup 26
    bang-bang chicken 62
    broiled chicken 425
    chicken & corn soup 36
    chicken & ginger stir-fry 139
    chicken & leek soup 291
    chicken & pasta broth 290
    chicken cacciatora 424
    chicken consommé 17
    chicken in banana leaves 140
    chicken in spicy yogurt 145

chicken marengo 422
chicken or beef satay 343
chicken pepperonata 413
chicken risotto milanese 483
chicken soup with almonds 24
chicken spirals 428
chicken with balsamic vinegar 144
chicken with green olives 420
chicken with orange sauce 414
clear chicken & egg soup 298
curried chicken & corn soup 302
fat horses 46
fresh chicken bouillon 262
garlic & herb chicken 412
green salsa chicken breasts 142
italian chicken spirals 426
jerk chicken 146
karahi chicken 136
lemongrass skewers 147
minty lime chicken 138
mustard-baked chicken 418
parsley, chicken & ham pâté 45
rich chicken casserole 410
rolled chicken slices with mortadella 416
sesame ginger chicken 342
spicy chicken salad 332
sweet mango chicken 135
tagliatelle & chicken sauce 438
thai stir-fried chicken 134
chili
    chicken, avocado & chipotle soup 26
    chili & bell pepper pasta 456
    chili & watercress soup 28
    chili shrimp noodles 372
    stir-fried beancurd with chili sauce 336
chinese omelet 340
chocolate
    chocolate biscotti 241
    chocolate cheese pots 252
    chocolate zabaglione 500
    italian chocolate truffles 230
    rich chocolate loaf 222
chop suey
    vegetable chop suey 201
chow mein
    seafood chow mein 370
chunky potato & beef soup 292
citrus duckling skewers 148
citrus pork chops 390
clam
    pasta vongole 468
    vermicelli & clam sauce 466
clear chicken & egg soup 298
coconut candy 224
cod
    indonesian-style spicy cod 183
cool cucumber salad 92

corn
    chicken & corn soup 36
    curried chicken & corn soup 302
    macaroni & corn crêpes 462
court-bouillon 163
crab
    bok choy with crabmeat 74
    crab & ginger soup 18
    fat horses 46
    partan bree 300
    rice with crab & mussels 358
    steamed crab cakes 58
cream of artichoke soup 14
creamed strips of short loin 386
creamy fruit parfait 242
creamy onion & fava bean soup 288
creamy stuffed mushrooms 210
crispy golden seafood 57
crispy pork & peanut baskets 56
crostini alla fiorentina 320
cucumber
    cool cucumber salad 92
    tzatziki 41
    tzatziki & black olive dips 310
cumberland sauce 121
cured meats, olives & tomatoes 335
curried chicken & corn soup 302
curry
    red curry fish cakes 179
    tomato curry 208

D
daikon
    pork with daikon 130
deep-fried seafood 339
dips
    eggplant dip 48
    eggplant dipping platter 311
    heavenly garlic dip 312
    mint & cannellini bean dip 308
    tzatziki 41
    tzatziki & black olive dips 310
dolmades 202
duck
    citrus duckling skewers 148
    duck with berry sauce 150
    slices of duck with pasta 430

E
easy cauliflower & broccoli 86
eggplant
    baked eggplant gratin 206
    eggplant & rice rolls 54
    eggplant bake 194
    eggplant dip 48
    eggplant dipping platter 311
    eggplant rolls 49

eggs
    chocolate zabaglione 500
    clear chicken & egg soup 298
    vegetable stir-fry with eggs 200
    walnut, egg & cheese pâté 318
    zabaglione 228
exotic fruit packages 232
exotic mushroom risotto 476
exotic mushroom soup 34

F
fat horses 46
fennel
    baked fennel 331
    braised fennel 82
fettuccine
    fettuccine all'alfredo 452
    fettuccine & walnut sauce 454
figs
    figs & prosciutto 53
    figs with orange cream 236
fillets of red snapper & pasta 357
fish see also individual fish
    blackened fish 155
    fish soup with won tons 20
    fish with yucatan flavors 174
    fresh fish bouillon 263
    marinated fish 159
    provençal fish soup 37
    red curry fish cakes 179
    smoked fish & potato pâté 316
    smoky fish skewers 164
    szechuan white fish 166
florentines
    mini florentines 225
flounder fillets with grapes 360
frangipane
    mini frangipane tartlets with lime 248
fresh chicken bouillon 262
fresh fish bouillon 263
fresh lamb bouillon 263
fresh mushroom soup 282
fresh spaghetti & meatballs 300
fresh vegetable bouillon 262
fried rice & shrimp 374
frittata
    spinach & herb frittata 215
    spinach frittata 212
fruit see also individual fruits
    creamy fruit parfait 242
    exotic fruit packages 232
    paper-thin fruit pies 237
    summer desserts 499

G
garbanzo bean soup 274

gardener's broth 286
garlic
  bacon, bean & garlic soup 295
  cheese, garlic & herb pâté 319
  garlic & herb chicken 412
  garlic bread 479
  garlic shrimp 176
  garlic toasts 322
  heavenly garlic dip 312
  pork with lemon & garlic 394
  spaghetti olio e aglio 443
  tagliatelle & garlic sauce 448
gazpacho 16
genoese seafood risotto 482
ginger
  carrot & ginger cake 492
  chicken & ginger stir-fry 139
  crab & ginger soup 18
  gingered angler fish 180
  mushroom & ginger soup 270
  parsnip soup with ginger 283
  pear & ginger cake 495
  sesame ginger chicken 342
  spinach & ginger soup 29
  stir-fried ginger mushrooms 75
gnocchi
  baked semolina gnocchi 487
  potato & spinach gnocchi 486
  spinach & ricotta gnocchi 484
grapefruit & cheese salad 100
grapes
  flounder fillets with grapes 360
green easter pie 480
green risotto 475
green salsa chicken breasts 142
gremolata 122
griddled pork with orange sauce 122
ground lamb with peas 111
guacamole
  authentic guacamole 42

H
haddock
  smoked haddock soup 301
halibut
  pan-seared halibut 184
ham
  baked ham with sauce 121
  ham steaks with apple rings 132
  parsley, chicken & ham pâté 45
heavenly garlic dip 312
herrings
  lemon herrings 154
honey & nut nests 504
hot & sour soup 21
hummus 44
  hummus & garlic toasts 322

I
indonesian-style spicy cod 183
italian dishes
  italian chicken spirals 426
  italian chocolate truffles 230
  italian mozzarella salad 93
  italian tomato sauce & pasta 460
  scallops and italian sausage 108

J
jerk chicken 146

K
kabobs see also brochettes, skewers
  asian shellfish kabobs 382
  beef, tomato & olive kabobs 107
  lemon angler fish kabobs 383
  moroccan lamb kabobs 112
  polenta kabobs 488
  pork & sage kabobs 126
  scallop kabobs 380
karahi chicken 136
kiwifruit
  melon & kiwifruit salad 246

L
lamb
  barbecued butterfly lamb 398
  fresh lamb bouillon 263
  ground lamb with peas 111
  lamb & anchovies with thyme 119
  lamb & rice soup 294
  lamb chops with rosemary 117
  lamb with bay & lemon 114
  lamb with black bean sauce & bell
    peppers 396
  lamb with olives 118
  moroccan lamb kabobs 112
  red wine lamb skewers 116
  roman pan-fried lamb 397
  scallions & lamb stir-fry with oyster
    sauce 399
lavender hearts 226
leek
  celery root, leek & potato soup 32
  chicken & leek soup 291
  leek, potato & bacon soup 33
  roast leeks 79
lemon
  lamb with bay & lemon 114
  lemon & lime syllabub 244
  lemon angler fish kabobs 383
  lemon herrings 154
  pork with lemon & garlic 394
lemongrass
  lemongrass skewers 147
  mussels with lemongrass 177

lentil pâté 315
lettuce & beancurd soup 271
lime
  banana & lime cake 494
  lemon & lime syllabub 244
  lime mousse with mango 245
  mackerel with lime & cilantro 158
  mini frangipane tartlets with lime 248
  minty lime chicken 138
liver
  crostini alla fiorentina 320
  liver with wine sauce 404
lobster salad 94

M
macaroni
  macaroni & corn crêpes 462
  macaroni & squid casserole 470
mackerel with lime & cilantro 158
mango
  mango sauce 245
  sweet mango chicken 135
marinated brochettes 190
marinated fish 159
mascarpone
  mascarpone cheesecake 496
  spinach & mascarpone soup 278
meatballs
  meatball brochettes 110
  meatballs in italian red wine
    sauce 389
mediterranean sardines 160
melba toast 286
melon & kiwifruit salad 246
milanese risotto 472
mini florentines 225
mini frangipane tartlets with lime 248
mint
  avocado & mint soup 304
  mint & cannellini bean dip 308
  minty lime chicken 138
mixed bean pan-fry 199
mixed bean pâté 314
mixed leaf salad 89
mocha
  mocha creams 502
  mocha swirl mousse 234
moroccan lamb kabobs 112
mousse
  lime mousse with mango 245
  mocha swirl mousse 234
mozzarella
  italian mozzarella salad 93
  mozzarella & tomato salad 98
mushroom
  beef with exotic mushrooms 106
  creamy stuffed mushrooms 210

exotic mushroom risotto 476
exotic mushroom soup 34
fresh mushroom soup 282
marinated brochettes 190
mushroom & ginger soup 270
mushroom noodle soup 268
mushroom salad 88
stir-fried ginger mushrooms 75
thai-spiced mushrooms 216
mussels
  mussel & scallop spaghetti 365
  mussel salad 350
  mussels in white wine 330
  mussels with lemongrass 177
  pasta & mussel sauce 467
  rice with crab & mussels 358
  thai steamed mussels 178
mustard-baked chicken 418

N

neapolitan dishes
  neapolitan seafood salad 352
  neapolitan veal chops 400
noisettes of salmon 172
noodles
  cellophane noodles & shrimp 368
  chili shrimp noodles 372
  noodles with shrimp 366
  oyster sauce noodles 377
  sweet & sour noodles 369
  thai-style shrimp noodles 373
nuts
  bell peppers with chestnuts 198
  crispy pork & peanut baskets 56
  fettuccine & walnut sauce 454
  honey & nut nests 504
  pasta with nuts & cheese 459
  pork with lemon & garlic 394
  walnut, egg & cheese pâté 318

O

okra bhaji 71
olives
  beef, tomato & olive kabobs 107
  chicken with green olives 420
  cured meats, olives & tomatoes 335
  lamb with olives 118
  tzatziki & black olive dips 310
omelet
  chinese omelet 340
  soufflé omelet 50
onion
  creamy onion & fava bean soup 288
  onions à la grecque 327
  thick onion soup 284
orange
  griddled pork with orange sauce 122

orange blossom cream 236
oven-baked risotto 205
oyster
  broccoli in oyster sauce 211
  oyster sauce noodles 377

P

pan-seared halibut 184
paper-thin fruit pies 231
parsnip soup with ginger 283
partan bree 300
partridge
  pesto-baked partridge 429
pasta
  chicken & pasta broth 290
  chicken with orange sauce 414
  chili & bell pepper pasta 456
  fettuccine all'alfredo 452
  fettuccine & walnut sauce 454
  fillets of red snapper & pasta 357
  fresh spaghetti & meatballs 388
  honey & nut nests 504
  italian tomato sauce & pasta 460
  macaroni & corn crêpes 462
  macaroni & squid casserole 470
  meatballs in italian red wine sauce 389
  mussel & scallop spaghetti 365
  pasta & anchovy sauce 361
  pasta & chili tomatoes 455
  pasta & mussel sauce 467
  pasta & pork in cream sauce 393
  pasta & vegetable sauce 447
  pasta vongole 468
  pasta with cheese & broccoli 446
  pasta with green vegetables 444
  pasta with nuts & cheese 459
  pasta with sicilian sauce 471
  pasticcio 435
  penne & butternut squash 442
  poached salmon with penne 354
  shrimp pasta bake 378
  sicilian spaghetti cake 434
  slices of duck with pasta 430
  spaghetti & salmon sauce 464
  spaghetti bolognese 436
  spaghetti olio e aglio 443
  spaghetti with ricotta cheese sauce 440
  spicy tomato tagliatelle 450
  tagliatelle & chicken sauce 438
  tagliatelle & garlic sauce 448
  tagliatelle & meatballs 439
  tagliatelle with pumpkin 451
  three-cheese macaroni 463
  tomato & pasta soup 275
  veal in a rose petal sauce 403
  vermicelli & clam sauce 466
pasticcio 435

pâté
  cheese, garlic & herb pâté 319
  lentil pâté 315
  mixed bean pâté 314
  parsley, chicken & ham pâté 45
  smoked fish & potato pâté 316
  walnut, egg & cheese pâté 318
peaches in white wine 238
pear
  pear & ginger cake 495
  poached allspice pears 251
peas
  ground lamb with peas 111
  rice & peas 478
penne & butternut squash 442
pepper salad 326
pesto
  pesto-baked partridge 429
  pesto rice with garlic bread 479
  pesto sauce 479
  sardines with pesto 60
  pineapple with tequila & mint 254
pink syllabubs 250
poached allspice pears 251
poached salmon with penne 354
polenta kabobs 488
pork
  asian pork balls in broth 65
  carnitas 128
  citrus pork chops 390
  crispy pork & peanut baskets 56
  fat horses 46
  griddled pork with orange sauce 122
  pasta & pork in cream sauce 393
  pork & sage kabobs 126
  pork chops with sage 392
  pork sesame toasts 323
  pork stir-fry with vegetables 120
  pork with daikon 130
  pork with lemon & garlic 394
  spare ribs 66
  stuffed pork with prosciutto 124
potato
  beet & potato soup 279
  celery root, leek & potato soup 32
  chunky potato & beef soup 292
  leek, potato & bacon soup 33
  potato & spinach gnocchi 486
  smoked fish & potato pâté 316
prosciutto
  figs & prosciutto 53
  stuffed pork with prosciutto 124
provençal fish soup 37
pumpkin
  pumpkin soup 276
  tagliatelle with pumpkin 451

Q

quick tiramisù 503

R

raspberries
  duck with berry sauce 150
  raspberry fool 256
  slices of duck with pasta 430
ratatouille 214
red bell pepper soup 267
red curry fish cakes 179
red snapper
  fillets of red snapper & pasta 357
red wine lamb skewers 116
rice
  aromatic seafood rice 376
  chicken risotto milanese 483
  dolmades 202
  eggplant & rice rolls 54
  exotic mushroom risotto 476
  fried rice & shrimp 374
  genoese seafood risotto 482
  green easter pie 480
  green risotto 475
  lamb & rice soup 294
  milanese risotto 472
  oven-baked risotto 205
  pesto rice with garlic bread 479
  rice & peas 478
  rice with crab & mussels 358
  steamed lotus rice 84
  sun-dried risotto 474
  wild rice blinis 61
rich chicken casserole 410
rich chocolate loaf 222
risotto
  chicken risotto milanese 483
  exotic mushroom risotto 476
  genoese seafood risotto 482
  green risotto 475
  milanese risotto 472
  oven-baked risotto 205
  sun-dried risotto 474
roast leeks 79
roasted vegetables 77
rolled chicken slices with mortadella 416
roman pan-fried lamb 397
rose ice 233

S

salads
  beet salad & dill dressing 334
  capri salad 99
  cool cucumber salad 92
  grapefruit & cheese salad 100
  italian mozzarella salad 93
  lobster salad 94
  melon & kiwifruit salad 246
  mixed leaf salad 89
  mozzarella & tomato salad 98
  mushroom salad 88
  mussel salad 350
  neapolitan seafood salad 352
  pepper salad 326
  sesame seed salad 90
  smoked trout & apple salad 96
  spicy chicken salad 332
  sweet & sour tuna salad 348
  tropical salad 240
  tuna, bean & anchovy salad 349
salmon
  noisettes of salmon 172
  poached salmon with penne 354
  salmon fillet with herbs 170
  spaghetti & salmon sauce 464
  thai-spiced salmon 167
salsa
  green salsa chicken breasts 142
sardines
  mediterranean sardines 160
  sardines with pesto 60
satay
  chicken or beef satay 343
sauces
  cumberland sauce 121
  mango sauce 245
  pesto sauce 479
  raspberry sauce 150
  smoked salmon sauce 464
  tomato sauce 78
scallions & lamb stir-fry with oyster
  sauce 399
scallops
  mussel & scallop spaghetti 365
  scallop crêpes 338
  scallop kabobs 380
sea bass
  baked sea bass 168
seafood
  aromatic seafood rice 376
  asian shellfish kabobs 382
  crispy golden seafood 57
  deep-fried seafood 339
  genoese seafood risotto 482
  neapolitan seafood salad 352
  seafood chow mein 370
  seafood medley 362
  seafood stir-fry 353
  spaghetti & seafood sauce 364
semolina
  baked semolina gnocchi 487
sesame
  pork sesame toasts 323
  sesame ginger chicken 342
  sesame seed chutney 70
  sesame seed salad 90
shrimp
  butterfly shrimp 156
  cellophane noodles & shrimp 368
  chili shrimp noodles 372
  fried rice & shrimp 374
  garlic shrimp 176
  noodles with shrimp 366
  shrimp parcels 328
  shrimp pasta bake 378
  shrimp soup 299
  spicy salt & pepper shrimp 173
  sweet & sour noodles 369
  thai-style shrimp noodles 373
sicilian spaghetti cake 434
skate with black butter 163
skewers *see also* brochettes, kabobs
  citrus duckling skewers 148
  lemongrass skewers 147
  red wine lamb skewers 116
  smoky fish skewers 164
slices of duck with pasta 430
smoked fish
  smoked fish & potato pâté 316
  smoked haddock soup 301
  smoked trout & apple salad 96
  smoky fish skewers 164
  spaghetti & salmon sauce 464
soufflé omelet 50
soup
  artichoke soup 266
  avocado & mint soup 304
  bacon, bean & garlic soup 295
  beef & noodle soup 296
  beef broth 38
  beet & potato soup 279
  bouillabaisse 30
  celery root, leek & potato soup 32
  chicken & corn soup 36
  chicken & pasta broth 290
  chicken, avocado & chipotle soup 26
  chicken consommé 17
  chicken soup with almonds 24
  chili & watercress soup 28
  chunky potato & beef soup 292
  clear chicken & egg soup 298
  crab & ginger soup 18
  cream of artichoke soup 14
  creamy onion & fava bean soup 288
  curried chicken & corn soup 302
  exotic mushroom soup 34
  fish soup with won tons 20
  fresh mushroom soup 282
  garbanzo bean soup 274
  gardener's broth 286
  gazpacho 16

hot & sour soup 21
lamb & rice soup 294
leek, potato & bacon soup 33
lettuce & beancurd soup 271
mushroom & ginger soup 270
mushroom noodle soup 268
parsnip soup with ginger 283
partan bree 300
provençal fish soup 37
pumpkin soup 276
red bell pepper soup 267
shrimp soup 299
smoked haddock soup 301
spicy dhal & carrot soup 272
spinach & ginger soup 29
spinach & mascarpone soup 278
spinach & tofu soup 22
sweet & sour cabbage soup 280
thick onion soup 284
tomato & pasta soup 275
spaghetti
spaghetti & salmon sauce 464
spaghetti & seafood sauce 364
spaghetti bolognese 436
spaghetti ollo e aglio 443
spaghetti with ricotta cheese sauce 440
spare ribs 66
spicy dishes
spicy chicken salad 332
spicy dhal & carrot soup 272
spicy salt & pepper shrimp 173
spicy tomato tagliatelle 450
spinach
bamboo with spinach 85
potato & spinach gnocchi 486
spinach & ginger soup 29
spinach & herb frittata 215
spinach & mascarpone soup 278
spinach & ricotta gnocchi 484
spinach & tofu soup 22
spinach cheese molds 52
spinach frittata 212
squid
macaroni & squid casserole 470
steamed crab cakes 58
steamed lotus rice 84
stir-fried dishes
chicken & ginger stir-fry 139
mixed bean pan-fry 199
pork stir-fry with vegetables 120
scallions & lamb stir-fry with oyster
sauce 399
seafood stir-fry 353
stir-fried beancurd with chili sauce 336
stir-fried ginger mushrooms 75
thai stir-fried chicken 134
tuna & vegetable stir-fry 346

vegetable stir-fry with eggs 200
strawberries
balsamic strawberries 220
stuffed angler fish tail 165
stuffed pork with prosciutto 124
summer desserts 499
sun-dried risotto 474
sweet & sour dishes
sweet & sour cabbage soup 280
sweet & sour noodles 369
sweet & sour tuna salad 348
sweet & sour zucchini 80
sweet mango chicken 135
swordfish steaks 182
sylabub
lemon & lime syllabub 244
pink syllabubs 250
szechuan white fish 166

T
tagliatelle
tagliatelle & chicken sauce 438
tagliatelle & garlic sauce 448
tagliatelle & meatballs 439
tagliatelle with pumpkin 451
thai dishes
thai-spiced mushrooms 216
thai-spiced salmon 167
thai steamed mussels 178
thai stir-fried chicken 134
thai-style shrimp noodles 373
thick onion soup 284
three-cheese macaroni 463
tofu see also beancurd
braised tofu home-style 192
marinated brochettes 190
spinach & tofu soup 22
tomato
beef, tomato & olive kabobs 107
bruschetta with tomatoes 324
cured meats, olives & tomatoes 335
italian tomato sauce & pasta 460
mozzarella & tomato salad 98
pasta & chili tomatoes 455
spicy tomato tagliatelle 450
sun-dried risotto 474
tomato & pasta soup 275
tomato curry 208
tomato sauce 78
tropical salad 240
trout
smoked trout & apple salad 96
trout in red wine 186
trout with smoked bacon 356
tuna
bean & anchovy salad 349
sweet & sour tuna salad 348

tuna & vegetable stir-fry 346
tuna with anchovy butter 162
vitello tonnato 402
turkey
scallops & italian sausage 108
turkey & vegetable loaf 64
turkey stuffed with cheese 151
tuscan dessert 498
tzatziki 41
tzatziki & black olive dips 310

V
veal
neapolitan veal chops 400
veal in a rose petal sauce 403
veal italienne 406
vitello tonnato 402
vegetables see also individual vegetables
cantonese garden vegetables 204
charbroiled vegetables 193
fresh vegetable bouillon 262
green risotto 475
pasta & vegetable sauce 447
pasta with green vegetables 444
pork stir-fry with vegetables 120
roasted vegetables 77
tuna & vegetable stir-fry 346
turkey & vegetable loaf 64
vegetable chop suey 201
vegetable rolls 217
vegetable stir-fry with eggs 200
vegetables à la grecque 72
vegetables & beancurd 458
vermicelli & clam sauce 466
vitello tonnato 402

W
walnut
fettuccine & walnut sauce 454
walnut, egg & cheese pâté 318
watercress
chili & watercress soup 28
wild rice blinis 61
won tons
fish soup with won tons 20

Y
yogurt
chicken in spicy yogurt 145
tzatziki 41
tzatziki & black olive dips 310

Z
zabaglione 228
chocolate zabaglione 500
zucchini
sweet & sour zucchini 80